Fluent in Nihongo: Unlocking the Secrets of Japanese Gramma

Gregory G. Dawson

Introduction

Welcome to this book—a comprehensive resource that will help you navigate the intricacies of the Japanese language. Whether you are a beginner starting your Japanese language journey or an intermediate learner looking to deepen your understanding, this guide will provide you with a solid foundation in Japanese grammar.

First, we will delve into the Japanese writing system. You will learn about the three main scripts: Hiragana, Katakana, and Kanji. We will guide you through their usage and help you recognize and write the characters.

Building on the writing system, we will introduce you to basic grammar concepts. You will learn how to express the state-of-being, understand the role of particles in Japanese sentences, and gain insights into adjectives and verbs. We will cover negative verbs, past tense, and the particles used with verbs. You will also explore the distinction between transitive and intransitive verbs and learn about relative clauses and sentence order.

Continuing with our exploration of Japanese grammar, we will dive deeper into noun-related particles, adverbs, sentence-ending particles, and essential grammar concepts. You will gain an understanding of polite forms and verb stems, as well as address people appropriately based on social dynamics. We will explore compound sentences, the various uses of the te-form, potential form, and expressions using the particles する and なる.

As you progress further, we will cover additional grammar topics such as conditionals, expressing necessity, desires, suggestions, and more. You will learn how to act on relative clauses, define and describe, attempt something, make requests, and master numbers and counting.

For those looking to expand their knowledge, we offer advanced topics that delve into formal expressions, honorific and humble forms, unintended actions, various degrees of certainty, and expressing amounts. We will explore similarity or hearsay, using 「方」 and 「よる」, actions that are easy or hard to do, and more negative verbs. You will also discover how to hypothesize and conclude, express time-specific actions, and convey a lack of change.

Throughout the guide, we provide ample examples, explanations, and practical tips to reinforce your understanding and facilitate your learning journey. You will gain the tools necessary to communicate effectively in Japanese and navigate a wide range of language situations.

Whether you are studying Japanese for personal interest, travel, work, or academic pursuits, this guide will equip you with the essential grammar knowledge needed to communicate accurately and confidently. Japanese grammar may seem complex, but with dedication and practice, you will develop a solid command of the language and embark on a rewarding language-learning experience.

Let's dive into the rich world of Japanese grammar and unlock the door to effective communication in this beautiful language!

Contents

The Writing System

The Scripts

Japanese consists of two scripts (referred to as *kana*) called *Hiragana* and *Katakana*, which are two versions of the same set of sounds in the language. Hiragana and Katakana consist of a little less than 50 "letters", which are actually simplified Chinese characters adopted to form a phonetic script.

Chinese characters, called *Kanji* in Japanese, are also heavily used in the Japanese writing. Most of the words in the Japanese written language are written in Kanji (nouns, verbs, adjectives). There exists over 40,000 Kanji where about 2,000 represent over 95% of characters actually used in written text. There are no spaces in Japanese so Kanji is necessary in distinguishing between separate words within a sentence. Kanji is also useful for discriminating between homophones, which occurs quite often given the limited number of distinct sounds in Japanese.

Hiragana is used mainly for grammatical purposes. We will see this as we learn about particles. Words with extremely difficult or rare Kanji, colloquial expressions, and onomatopoeias are also written in

Hiragana. It's also often used for beginning Japanese students and children in place of Kanji they don't know.

While Katakana represents the same sounds as Hiragana, it is mainly used to represent newer words imported from western countries (since there are no Kanji associated with words based on the roman alphabet). The next three sections will cover Hiragana, Katakana, and Kanji.

Intonation

As you will find out in the next section, every character in Hiragana (and the Katakana equivalent) corresponds to a [vowel] or [consonant + vowel] syllable sound with the single exception of the 「ん」 and 「ン」 characters (more on this later). This system of letter for each syllable sound makes pronunciation absolutely clear with no ambiguities. However, the simplicity of this system does not mean that pronunciation in Japanese is simple. In fact, the rigid structure of the fixed syllable sound in Japanese creates the challenge of learning proper intonation.

Intonation of high and low pitches is a crucial aspect of the spoken language. For example, homophones can have different pitches of low and high tones resulting in a slightly different sound despite sharing the same pronunciation. The biggest obstacle for obtaining proper and natural sounding speech is incorrect intonation. Many students often speak without paying attention to the correct enunciation of pitches making speech sound unnatural (the classic foreigner's accent). It is not practical to memorize or attempt to logically create rules for pitches, especially since it can change depending on the context or the dialect. The only practical approach is to get the general sense of pitches by mimicking native Japanese speakers with careful listening and practice.

Hiragana

Hiragana is the basic Japanese phonetic script. It represents every sound in the Japanese language. Therefore, you can theoretically write everything in Hiragana. However, because Japanese is written with no spaces, this will create nearly indecipherable text.

Here is a table of Hiragana and similar-sounding English consonant-vowel pronunciations. It is read up to down and right to left, which is how most Japanese books are written. In Japanese, writing the strokes in the correct order and direction is important, especially for Kanji. Because handwritten letters look slightly different from typed letters (just like how 'a' looks totally different when typed), you will want to use a resource that uses handwritten style fonts to show you how to write the characters (see below for links). I must also stress the importance of correctly learning how to pronounce each sound. Since every word in Japanese is composed of these sounds, learning an incorrect pronunciation for a letter can severely damage the very foundation on which your pronunciation lies.

Hiragana

n	w	r	y	m	h	n	t	s	k		
ん (n)	わ	ら	や	ま	は	な	た	さ	か	あ	a
	ゐ*	り		み	ひ	に	ち (chi)	し (shi)	き	い	i
		る	ゆ	む	ふ (fu)	ぬ	つ (tsu)	す	く	う	u
	ゑ*	れ		め	へ	ね	て	せ	け	え	e
を (o)	ろ	よ	も	ほ	の	と	そ	こ	お	o

* = no longer used

You can listen to the pronunciation for character by downloading them at http://www.guidetojapanese.org/audio/basic_sounds.zip. There are also other free resources with audio samples.

Hiragana is not too tough to master or teach and as a result, there are a variety of web sites and free programs that are already available on the web. I also suggest recording yourself and comparing the sounds to make sure you're getting it right.

When practicing writing Hiragana by hand, the important thing to remember is that the stroke order and direction of the strokes *matter*. There, I underlined, italicized, bolded, and highlighted it to boot. Trust me, you'll eventually find out why when you read other people's hasty notes that are nothing more than chicken scrawls.

The only thing that will help you is that everybody writes in the same order and so the "flow" of the characters is fairly consistent. I strongly recommend that you pay close attention to stroke order from the beginning starting with Hiragana to avoid falling into bad habits. While there are many tools online that aim to help you learn Hiragana, the best way to learn how to write it is the old fashioned way: a piece of paper and pen/pencil. Below are handy PDFs for Hiragana writing practice.

- Hiragana trace sheets
- japanese-lesson.com
- Hiroshi & Sakura

※ As an aside, an old Japanese poem called 「いろは」 was often used as the base for ordering of Hiragana until recent times. The poem contains every single Hiragana character except for 「ん」 which probably did not exist at the time it was written. You can check out this poem for yourself in this wikipedia article. As the article mentions, this order is still sometimes used in ordering lists so you may want to spend some time checking it out.

Notes

1. Except for 「し」、「ち」、「つ」、and 「ん」、you can get a sense of how each letter is pronounced by matching the consonant on the top row to the vowel. For example, 「き」 would become / ki / and 「ゆ」 would become / yu / and so on.
2. As you can see, not all sounds match the way our consonant system works. As written in the table, 「ち」 is pronounced "chi" and 「つ」 is pronounced "tsu".

---

3. The / r / or / l / sound in Japanese is quite different from any sound in English. It involves more of a roll and a clip by hitting the roof of your mouth with your tongue. Pay careful attention to that whole column.
4. Pay careful attention to the difference between / tsu / and / su /.
5. The 「ん」 character is a special character because it is rarely used by itself and does not have a vowel sound. It is attached to another character to add a / n / sound. For example, 「かん」 becomes 'kan' instead of 'ka', 「まん」 becomes 'man' instead of 'ma', and so on and so forth.
6. <u>You must learn the correct stroke order and direction!</u> Use either of the following pdf practice sheets.
   ◦ <u>Hiragana trace sheets</u>
   ◦ <u>japanese-lesson.com</u>
   ◦ <u>Hiroshi & Sakura</u>

The Muddied Sounds

Once you memorize all the characters in Hiragana, there are still some additional sounds left to be learned. There are five more consonant sounds that are written by either affixing two tiny lines similar to a double quotation mark called *dakuten* （濁点） or a tiny circle called *handakuten* （半濁点）. This essentially creates a "muddy" or less clipped version of the consonant (technically called a voiced consonant or 「濁り」, which literally means to become muddy).

All the voiced consonant sounds are shown in the table below.

Voiced Hiragana

p	b	d	z	g	
ぱ	ば	だ	ざ	が	a
ぴ	び	ぢ (ji)	じ (ji)	ぎ	i
ぷ	ぶ	づ (dzu)	ず	ぐ	u
ぺ	べ	で	ぜ	げ	e
ぽ	ぼ	ど	ぞ	ご	o

Note

- Notice that 「ぢ」 sounds essentially identical to 「じ」 and both are pronounced as / ji /, while 「づ」 is pronounced like / dzu /.

The Small 「や」、「ゆ」、and 「よ」

You can also combine a consonant with a / ya / yu / yo / sound by attaching a small 「や」、「ゆ」、or 「よ」 to the / i / vowel character of each consonant.

All small や、 ゆ、 and よ combinations in Hiragana

p	b	j	g	r	m	h	n	c	s	k	
ぴゃ	びゃ	じゃ	ぎゃ	りゃ	みゃ	ひゃ	にゃ	ちゃ	しゃ	きゃ	**ya**
ぴゅ	びゅ	じゅ	ぎゅ	りゅ	みゅ	ひゅ	にゅ	ちゅ	しゅ	きゅ	**yu**
ぴょ	びょ	じょ	ぎょ	りょ	みょ	ひょ	にょ	ちょ	しょ	きょ	**yo**

Notes

1. The above table is the same as before. Match the top consonants to the vowel sound on the right. Ex: きゃ = kya.
2. Also note that since 「じ」 is pronounced / ji /, all the small 「や」、 「ゆ」、 「よ」 sounds are also based off of that, namely: / jya / jyu / jyo /.
3. The same thing also applies to 「ち」 which becomes / cha / chu / cho / and 「し」 which becomes / sha / shu / sho /. (Though arguably, you can still think of it as / sya / syu / syo /.)

The Small 「つ」

A small 「つ」 is inserted between two characters to carry the consonant sound of the second character to the end of the first. For example, if you inserted a small 「つ」 between 「び」 and 「く」 to make 「びっく」, the / k / consonant sound is carried back to the end of the first character to produce "bikku". Similarly, 「はっぱ」 becomes "happa", 「ろっく」 becomes "rokku" and so on and so forth.

Examples

1. ざっし (za<u>s</u>-shi) - magazine
2. カップ (ka<u>p</u>-pu) - cup

Notes

1. A small 「っ」 is used to carry the consonant sound of the second character to the end of the first. Ex: 「がっき」 = "ga<u>k</u>ki".
2. The addition of another consonant almost always creates the characteristic clipping sound. But make sure you're clipping with the right consonant (the consonant of the second character).

The Long Vowel Sound

Whew! You're almost done. In this last portion, we will go over the long vowel sound which is simply extending the duration of a vowel sound. You can extend the vowel sound of a character by adding either 「あ」、「い」、or 「う」 depending on the vowel in accordance to the following chart.

Extending Vowel Sounds

Vowel Sound	Extended by
/ a /	あ
/ i / e /	い
/ u / o /	う

For example, if you wanted to create an extended vowel sound from 「か」, you would add 「あ」 to create 「かあ」. Other examples would include: 「き → きい」, 「く → くう」, 「け → けい」, 「こ → こう」, 「さ → さあ」 and so on. The reasoning for this is quite simple. Try saying 「か」 and 「あ」 separately. Then say them in succession as fast as you can. You'll notice that soon enough, it sounds like you're dragging out the / ka / for a longer duration than just saying / ka / by itself. When pronouncing long vowel sounds, try to remember that they are really two sounds merged together.

It's important to make sure you hold the vowel sound long enough because you can be saying things like "here" （ここ） instead of "high school" （こうこう） or "middle-aged lady" （おばさん） instead of "grandmother" （おばあさん） if you don't stretch it out correctly!

Examples

1. がくせい (ga-ku-se) - student
2. せんせい (sen-se) - teacher
3. きょう (kyo) - today
4. おはよう (o-ha-yo) - good morning

5. おか<u>あ</u>さん (o-k<u>a</u>-san) - mother

There are rare exceptions where an / e / vowel sound is extended by adding 「え」 or an / o / vowel sound is extended by 「お」. Some examples of this include 「おねえさん」、「おおい」、and 「おおきい」. Pay careful attention to these exceptions but don't worry, there aren't too many of them.

Katakana

As mentioned before, *Katakana* is mainly used for words imported from foreign languages. It can also be used to emphasize certain words similar to the function of *italics*. For a more complete list of usages, refer to the Wikipedia entry on katakana.

Katakana represents the same set of phonetic sounds as Hiragana except all the characters are different. Since foreign words must fit into this limited set of [consonants+vowel] sounds, they undergo many radical changes resulting in instances where English speakers can't understand words that are supposed to be derived from English! As a result, the use of Katakana is extremely difficult for English speakers because they expect English words to sound like... well... English. Instead, it is better to completely forget the original English word, and treat the word as an entirely separate Japanese word, otherwise you can run into the habit of saying English words with English pronunciations (whereupon a Japanese person may or may not understand what you are saying).

Katakana

n	w	r	y	m	h	n	t	s	k		
ン (n)	ワ	ラ	ヤ	マ	ハ	ナ	タ	サ	カ	ア	a
	ヰ*	リ		ミ	ヒ	ニ	チ (chi)	シ (shi)	キ	イ	i
		ル	ユ	ム	フ (fu)	ヌ	ツ (tsu)	ス	ク	ウ	u
	ヱ*	レ		メ	ヘ	ネ	テ	セ	ケ	エ	e
ヲ* (o)		ロ	ヨ	モ	ホ	ノ	ト	ソ	コ	オ	o

* = obsolete or rarely used

Katakana is significantly tougher to master compared to Hiragana because it is only used for certain words and you don't get nearly as much practice as you do with Hiragana. To learn the proper stroke order (and yes, you need to), here are links to practice sheets for Katakana.

- Katakana trace sheets
- japanese-lesson.com
- Hiroshi & Sakura

Also, since Japanese doesn't have any spaces, sometimes the symbol 「・」 is used to show the spaces like 「ロック・アンド・ロール」 for "rock and roll". Using the symbol is completely optional so sometimes nothing will be used at all.

Notes

1. All the sounds are identical to what they were for Hiragana.
2. As we will learn later, 「を」 is only ever used as a particle and all particles are in Hiragana. Therefore, you will almost never need to use 「ヲ」 and it can be safely ignored. (Unless you are reading very old telegrams or something.)
3. The four characters 「シ」、「ン」、「ツ」、and 「ソ」 are fiendishly similar to each other. Basically, the difference is that the first two are more "horizontal" than the second two. The little lines are slanted more horizontally and the long line is drawn in a curve from bottom to top. The second two have almost vertical little lines and the long line doesn't curve as much as it is drawn from top to bottom. It is almost like a slash while the former is more like an arc. These characters are hard to sort out and require some patience and practice.
4. The characters 「ノ」、「メ」、and 「ヌ」 are also something to pay careful attention to, as well as, 「フ」、「ワ」、and 「ウ」. Yes, they all look very similar. No, I can't do anything about it.
5. <u>You must learn the correct stroke order and direction!</u> Use the following pdf practice sheets to practice.
   - <u>Katakana trace sheets</u>
   - <u>japanese-lesson.com</u>
   - <u>Hiroshi & Sakura</u>
6. Sometimes 「・」 is used to denote what would be spaces in English.

The Long Vowel Sound

Long vowels have been radically simplified in Katakana. Instead of having to muck around thinking about vowel sounds, all long vowel sounds are denoted by a simple dash like so: ー.

Examples

1. ツアー (tsu-a) - tour
2. メール (me-ru) - email
3. ケーキ (ke-ki) - cake

Summary

- All long vowel sounds in Katakana are denoted by a dash. For example, "cute" would be written in Katakana like so: 「キュート」.

The Small 「ア、イ、ウ、エ、オ」

Due to the limitations of the sound set in Hiragana, some new combinations have been devised over the years to account for sounds that were not originally in Japanese. Most notable is the lack of the / ti / di / and / tu / du / sounds (because of the / chi / tsu / sounds), and the lack of the / f / consonant sound except for 「ふ」. The / sh / j / ch / consonants are also missing for the / e / vowel sound. The decision to resolve these deficiencies was to add small versions of the five vowel sounds. This has also been done for the / w / consonant sound to replace the obsolete characters. In addition, the convention of using the little double slashes on the 「ウ」 vowel （ヴ） with the small 「ア、イ、エ、オ」 to designate the / v /

consonant has also been established but it's not often used probably due to the fact that Japanese people still have difficulty pronouncing / v /. For instance, while you may guess that "volume" would be pronounced with a / v / sound, the Japanese have opted for the easier to pronounce "bolume" （ボリューム）. In the same way, vodka is written as "wokka" （ウォッカ） and not 「ヴォッカ」. You can write "violin" as either 「バイオリン」 or 「ヴァイオリン」. It really doesn't matter however because almost all Japanese people will pronounce it with a / b / sound anyway. The following table shows the added sounds that were lacking with a highlight. Other sounds that already existed are reused as appropriate.

Additional sounds

v	w	f	ch	d	t	j	sh	
ヴァ	ワ	ファ	チャ	ダ	タ	ジャ	シャ	a
ヴィ	ウィ	フィ	チ	ディ	ティ	ジ	シ	i
ヴ	ウ	フ	チュ	ドゥ	トゥ	ジュ	シュ	u
ヴェ	ウェ	フェ	チェ	デ	テ	ジェ	シェ	e
ヴォ	ウォ	フォ	チョ	ド	ト	ジョ	ショ	o

Notes

1. Notice that there is no / wu / sound. For example, the Katakana for "woman" is written as "u-man" （ウーマン）.
2. While the / tu / sound (as in "too") can technically be produced given the rules as 「トゥ」, foreign words that have become popular before these sounds were available simply used / tsu / to make do. For instance, "tool" is still 「ツール」 and "tour" is similarly still 「ツアー」.
3. Back in the old days, without these new sounds, there was no choice but to just take characters off the regular table without regard for actual pronunciation. On old buildings, you may still see 「ビルヂング」 instead of the modern spelling 「ビルディング」.

Some examples of words in Katakana

Translating English words into Japanese is a knack that requires quite a bit of practice and luck. To give you a sense of how English words become "Japanified", here are a few examples of words in Katakana. Sometimes the words in Katakana may not even be correct English or have a different meaning from the English word it's supposed to represent. Of course, not all Katakana words are derived from English.

Sample Katakana Words

English	Japanese
America	アメリカ
Russia	ロシア
cheating	カンニング (cunning)
tour	ツアー
company employee	サラリーマン (salary man)
Mozart	モーツァルト
car horn	クラクション (klaxon)
sofa	ソファ or ソファー
Halloween	ハロウィーン
French fries	フライドポテト (fried potato)

Kanji

What is Kanji?

In Japanese, nouns and stems of adjectives and verbs are almost all written in Chinese characters called *Kanji*. Adverbs are also fairly frequently written in Kanji as well. This means that you will need to learn Chinese characters to be able to read most of the words in the language. (Children's books or any other material where the audience is not expected to know a lot of Kanji is an exception to this.) Not all words are always written in Kanji however. For example, while the verb "to do" technically has a Kanji associated with it, it is always written in Hiragana.

This guide begins using Kanji from the beginning to help you read "real" Japanese as quickly as possible. Therefore, we will go over some properties of Kanji and discuss some strategies of learning it quickly and efficiently. Mastering Kanji is not easy but it is by no means impossible. The biggest part of the battle is mastering the skills of <u>learning</u> <u>Kanji</u> and <u>time</u>. In short, memorizing Kanji past short-term memory must be done with a great deal of study and, most importantly, for a long time. And by this, I don't mean studying five hours a day but rather reviewing how to write a Kanji once every several months until you are sure you have it down for good. This is another reason why this guide starts using Kanji right away. There is no reason to dump the huge job of learning Kanji at the advanced level. By studying Kanji along with new vocabulary from the beginning, the immense job of learning Kanji is divided into small manageable chunks and the extra time helps settle learned Kanji into permanent memory. In addition, this will help you learn new vocabulary, which will often have combinations of Kanji you already know. If you start learning Kanji later, this benefit will be wasted or reduced.

Learning Kanji

All the resources you need to begin learning Kanji are on the web for free. You can use dictionaries online such as Jim Breen's WWWJDIC or jisho.org. They both have great Kanji dictionaries and stroke order diagrams for most Kanji. Especially for those who are just starting to learn, you will want to repeatedly write out each Kanji to memorize the stroke order. Another important skill is learning how to balance the character so that certain parts are not too big or small. So make sure to copy the characters as close to the original as possible. Eventually, you will naturally develop a sense of the stroke order for certain types of characters allowing you to bypass the drilling stage. All the Kanji used in this guide can be easily looked up by copying and pasting to an online dictionary.

Reading Kanji

Almost every character has two different readings called 音読み （おんよみ） and 訓読み（くんよみ）. 音読み is the original Chinese reading while 訓読み is the Japanese reading. Kanji that appear in a compound or 熟語 is usually read with 音読み while one Kanji by itself is usually read with 訓読み. For example, 「力」（ちから） is read with the 訓読み while the same character in a compound word such as 「能力」 is read with the 音読み （which is 「りょく」 in this case）.

Certain characters (especially the most common ones) can have more than one 音読み or 訓読み. For example, in the word 「怪力」, 「力」 is read here as 「りき」 and not 「りょく」. Certain compound words also have special readings that have nothing to do with the readings of the individual characters. These readings must be individually memorized. Thankfully, these readings are few and far in between.

訓読み is also used in adjectives and verbs in addition to the stand-alone characters. These words often have a string of kana (called okurigana) that come attached to the word. This is so that the reading of the Chinese character stays the same even when the word is conjugated to different forms. For example, the past form of the verb 「食べる」 is 「食べた」 . Even though the verb has changed, the reading for 「食」 remain untouched. (Imagine how difficult things could get if readings for Kanji changed with conjugation or even worse, if the Kanji itself changed.) Okurigana also serves to distinguish between intransitive and transitive verbs (more on this later).

Another concept that is difficult to grasp at first is that the actual readings of Kanji can change slightly in a compound word to make the word easier to say. The more common transformations include the / h / sounds changing to either / b / or / p / sounds or 「つ」 becoming 「っ」 . Examples include: 「一本」 、 「徹底」 、 and 「格好」 .

Yet another fun aspect of Kanji you'll run into are words that practically mean the same thing and use the same reading but have different Kanji to make just a slight difference in meaning. For example 「聞く」 （きく） means to listen and so does 「聴く」 （きく） . The only difference is that 「聴く」 means to pay more attention to what you're listening to. For example, listening to music almost always prefers 「聴く」 over 「聞く」 . 「聞く」 can also mean 'to ask', as well as, "to hear" but 「訊く」 （きく） can only mean "to ask". Yet another example is the common practice of writing 「見る」 as 「観る」 when it applies to watching a show such as a movie. Yet another interesting example is 「書く」 （か く） which means "to write" while 描く （かく） means "to draw". However, when you're depicting an abstract image such as a scene in a book, the reading of the same word 「描く」 becomes 「えが く」 . There's also the case where the meaning and Kanji stays the same but can have multiple readings such as 「今日」 which can be either 「きょう」、「こんじつ」, or 「こんにち」. In this case, it doesn't really matter which reading you choose except that some are preferred over others in certain situations.

Finally, there is one special character 々 that is really not a character. It simply indicates that the previous character is repeated. For example, 「時時」、「様様」、「色色」、「一一」 can and usually are written as 「時々」、「様々」、「色々」、「一々」.

In addition to these "features" of Kanji, you will see a whole slew of delightful perks and surprises Kanji has for you as you advance in Japanese. You can decide for yourself if that statement is sarcasm or not. However, don't be scared into thinking that Japanese is incredibly hard. Most of the words in the language usually only have one Kanji associated with it and a majority of Kanji do not have more than two types of readings.

Why Kanji?

Some people may think that the system of using separate, discrete symbols instead of a sensible alphabet is overly complicated. In fact, it might not have been a good idea to adopt Chinese into Japanese since both languages are fundamentally different in many ways. But the purpose of this guide is not to debate how the language should work but to explain why **you** must learn Kanji in order to learn Japanese. And by this, I mean more than just saying, "That's how it's done so get over it!".

You may wonder why Japanese didn't switched from Chinese to romaji to do away with having to memorize so many characters. In fact, Korea adopted their own alphabet for Korean to greatly simplify their written language with great success. So why shouldn't it work for Japanese? I think anyone who has learned Japanese for a while can easily see why it won't work. At any one time, when you convert typed Hiragana into Kanji, you are presented with almost always at least two choices (two homophones) and sometimes even up to ten. (Try typing "kikan"). The limited number of set sounds in Japanese makes it hard to avoid homophones. Compare this to the Korean alphabet which has 14 consonants and 10 vowels. Any of the consonants can be matched to any of the vowels giving 140 sounds. In addition, a third and sometimes even fourth consonant can be attached to create a single letter. This gives over 1960 sounds that can be created theoretically. (The number of sounds that are actually used is actually much less but it's still much larger than Japanese.)

Since you want to read at a much faster rate than you talk, you need some visual cues to instantly tell you what each word is. You can use the shape of words in English to blaze through text because most words have different shapes. Try this little exercise: Hi, enve thgouh all teh wrods aer seplled icorrenctly, can you sltil udsternand me?" Korean does this too because it has enough characters to make words with distinct and different shapes. However, because the visual cues are not distinct as Kanji, spaces needed to be added to remove ambiguities. (This presents another problem of when and where to set spaces.)

With Kanji, we don't have to worry about spaces and much of the problem of homophones is mostly resolved. Without Kanji, even if spaces were to be added, the ambiguities and lack of visual cues would make Japanese text much more difficult to read.

Basic Grammar

Basic Grammatical Structures

Now that we have learned how to write Japanese, we can begin going over the basic grammatical structure of the language. This section primarily covers all the parts of speech: nouns, adjectives, verbs, and adverbs. It will also describe how to integrate the various parts of speech into a coherent sentence by using particles. By the end of this section, you should have an understanding of how basic sentences are constructed.

Expressing state-of-being

Declaring something is so and so using 「だ」

Vocabulary

1. 人 【ひと】 - person
2. 学生 【がく・せい】 - student
3. 元気 【げん・き】 - healthy; lively
   * Used as a greeting to indicate whether one is well

One of the trickiest part of Japanese is that there is no verb for the state-of-being like the verb "to be" in English. You can, however, declare what something is by attaching the Hiragana character 「だ」 to a noun or na-adjective **only**. (We will learn about na-adjectives in the section on adjectives later.)

Declaring that something is so using 「だ」

- Attach 「だ」 to the noun or na-adjective
  Example: 人 + だ = 人だ

23

Examples

1. 人だ。
   Is person.
2. 学生だ。
   Is student.
3. 元気だ。
   Is well.

Seems easy enough. Here's the real kicker though.

A state-of-being can be implied without using 「だ」！

You can say you're doing well or someone is a student without using 「だ」 at all. For example, below is an example of a very typical greeting among friends. Also notice how the subject isn't even specified when it's obvious from the context.

Typical casual greeting

A：元気?
A: (Are you) well?

B：元気。
B: (I'm) well.

So you may be wondering, "What's the point of using 「だ」?" Well, the main difference is that a declarative statement makes the sentence sound more emphatic and forceful in order to make it more... well declarative. Therefore, it is more common to hear men use 「だ」 at the end of sentences.

The declarative 「だ」 is also needed in various grammatical structures where a state-of-being must be explicitly declared. There are also times when you cannot attach it. It's all quite a pain in the butt really but you don't have to worry about it yet.

Conjugating to the negative state-of-being

Vocabulary

1. 学生 【がく・せい】 - student
2. 友達 【とも・だち】 - friend
3. 元気 【げん・き】 - healthy; lively
   * Used as a greeting to indicate whether one is well

In Japanese, negative and past tense are all expressed by conjugation. We can conjugate a noun or adjective to either its negative or past tense to say that something is *not* [X] or that something *was* [X]. This may be a bit hard to grasp at first but none of these state-of-being conjugations make anything declarative like 「だ」 does. We'll learn how to make these tenses declarative by attaching 「だ」 to the end of the sentence in a later lesson.

First, for the negative, attach 「じゃない」 to the noun or na-adjective.

Conjugation rules for the negative state-of-being

- Attach 「じゃない」 to the noun or na-adjective
  Example: 学生 + じゃない = 学生じゃない

Examples

1. 学生<u>じゃない</u>。
   Is not student.

2. 友達<u>じゃない</u>。
   Is not friend.

3. 元気<u>じゃない</u>。
   Is not well.

Conjugating to the past state-of-being

Vocabulary

1. 学生 【がく・せい】 - student
2. 友達 【とも・だち】 - friend
3. 元気 【げん・き】 - healthy; lively
   * Used as a greeting to indicate whether one is well

We will now learn the past tense of the state-of-being. To say something *was* something, attach 「だった」 to the noun or na-adjective.

In order to say the negative past (*was not*), conjugate the negative to the negative past tense by dropping the 「い」 from 「じゃない」 and adding 「かった」.

Conjugation rules for the past state-of-being

1. **Past state-of-being:** Attach 「だった」 to the noun or na-adjective

   Example: 友達 + だった = 友達だった

2. **Negative past state-of-being:** Conjugate the noun or na-adjective to the negative first and then replace the 「い」 of 「じゃない」 with 「かった」
   Example: 友達じゃない → 友達じゃなかった = 友達じゃなかった

Examples

1. 学生だった。
   Was student.
2. 友達じゃなかった。
   Was not friend.
3. 元気じゃなかった。
   Was not well.

Conjugation summary

We've now learned how to express state-of-being in all four tenses. Next we will learn some particles, which will allow us assign roles to words. Here is a summary chart of the conjugations we learned in this section.

Summary of state-of-being

	Positive		Negative	
Non-Past	学生 （だ）	Is student	学生 じゃ ない	Is not student
Past	学生 だった	Was student	学生 じゃな かった	Was not student

Introduction to Particles

Defining grammatical functions with particles

We want to now make good use of what we learned in the last lesson by associating a noun with another noun. This is done with something called particles. Particles are one or more Hiragana characters that attach to the end of a word to define the grammatical function of that word in the sentence. Using the correct particles is very important because the meaning of a sentence can completely change just by changing the particles. For example, the sentence "Eat fish." can become "The fish eats." simply by changing one particle.

The 「は」 topic particle

Vocabulary

1. 学生 【がく・せい】 - student
2. うん - yes (casual)

3. 明日 【あした】 - tomorrow
4. ううん - no (casual)
5. 今日 【きょう】 - today
6. 試験 【しけん】 - exam

The first particle we will learn is the topic particle. The topic particle identifies what it is that you're talking about, essentially the topic of your sentence. Let's say a person says, "Not student." This is a perfectly valid sentence in Japanese but it doesn't tell us much without knowing what the person is talking about. The topic particle will allow us to express what our sentences are about. The topic particle is the character 「は」. Now, while this character is normally pronounced as /ha/, it is pronounced /wa/ only when it is being used as the topic particle.

Example 1

ボブ：アリスは学生?
Bob: Is Alice (you) student?

アリス：うん、学生。
Alice: Yeah, (I) am.

Here, Bob is indicating that his question is about Alice. Notice that once the topic is established, Alice does not have to repeat the topic to answer the question about herself.

Example 2

ボブ：ジョンは明日?
Bob: John is tomorrow?

アリス：ううん、明日じゃない。
Alice: No, not tomorrow.

Since we have no context, we don't have enough information to make any sense of this conversation. It obviously makes no sense for John to actually **be** tomorrow. Given a context, as long as the sentence has something to do with John and tomorrow, it can mean anything. For instance, they could be talking about when John is taking an exam.

Example 3

アリス：今日は試験だ。
Alice: Today is exam.

ボブ：ジョンは？
Bob: What about John?

アリス：ジョンは明日。
Alice: John is tomorrow. (As for John, the exam is tomorrow.)

The last example shows how generic the topic of a sentence is. A topic can be referring to any action or object from anywhere even including other sentences. For example, in the last sentence from the previous example, even though the sentence is about when the exam is for John, the word "exam" doesn't appear anywhere in the sentence!

We'll see a more specific particle that ties more closely into the sentence at the end of this lesson with the identifier particle.

The 「も」 inclusive topic particle

Vocabulary

1. 学生 【がく・せい】 - student

2. うん - yes (casual)
3. でも - but
4. ううん - no (casual)

Another particle that is very similar to the topic particle is the inclusive topic particle. It is essentially the topic particle with the additional meaning of "also". Basically, it can introduce another topic in addition to the current topic. The inclusive topic particle is the 「も」 character and its use is best explained by an example.

Example 1

ボブ：アリスは学生?
Bob: Is Alice (you) student?

アリス：うん、トムも学生。
Alice: Yeah, and Tom is also student.

The inclusion of 「も」 must be consistent with the answer. It would not make sense to say, "I am a student, and Tom is also not a student." Instead, use the 「は」 particle to make a break from the inclusion as seen in the next example.

Example 2

ボブ：アリスは学生?
Bob: Is Alice (you) student?

アリス：うん、でもトムは学生じゃない。
Alice: Yeah, but Tom is not student.

Below is an example of inclusion with the negative.

Example 3

31

ボブ：アリスは学生?
Bob: Is Alice (you) student?

アリス：ううん、トムも学生じゃない。
Alice: No, and Tom is also not student.

The 「が」 identifier particle

Vocabulary

1. 誰 【だれ】 - who
2. 学生 【がく・せい】 - student
3. 私 【わたし】 - me; myself; I

Ok, so we can make a topic using the 「は」 and 「も」 particle. But what if we don't know what the topic is? What if I wanted to ask, "Who is the student?" What I need is some kind of identifier because I don't know who the student is. If I use the topic particle, the question would become, "Is who the student?" and that doesn't make any sense because "who" is not an actual person.

This is where the 「が」 particle comes into play. It is also referred to as the subject particle but I hate that name since "subject" means something completely different in English grammar. Instead, I call it the *identifier particle* because the particle indicates that the speaker wants to identify something unspecified.

Example 1

ボブ：誰が学生?
Bob: Who is the one that is student?

アリス：ジョンが学生。
Alice: John is the one who is student.

Bob wants to identify who among all the possible candidates is a student. Alice responds that John is the one. Notice, Alice could also have answered with the topic particle to indicate that, speaking of John, she knows that he is *a* student (maybe not *the* student). You can see the difference in the next example.

Example 2

1. 誰が学生?
   Who is the one that is student?
2. 学生は誰?
   (The) student is who?

The first sentence seeks to identify a specific person for "student" while the second sentence is simply talking about the student. You cannot replace 「が」 with 「は」 in the first sentence because "who" would become the topic and the question would become, "Is who a student?"

The two particles 「は」 and 「が」 may seem very similar only because it is impossible to translate them directly into English. For example, the two sentences below have the same English translation.*

Example 3

1. 私は学生。
   I (am) student.
2. 私が学生。
   I (am) student.

However, they only seem similar because English cannot express information about the context as succinctly as Japanese sometimes can. In the first sentence, since 「私」 is the topic, the sentence means, "Speaking about me, I am a student".

However, the second sentence is specifying who the 「学生」 is. If we want to know who the student is, the 「が」 particle tells us it's 「私」. You can also think about the 「が」 particle as always answering a silent question. The second sentence might be answering a question, "Who is the student?" I often translate the topic particle as "as for; about" and the identifier particle as "the one; the thing" to illustrate the difference.

1. 私は学生。
   As for me, (I am) student.
2. 私が学生。
   I (am) the one (that is) student.

The 「は」 and 「が」 particles are actually quite different if you think of it the right way. The 「が」 particle identifies a specific property of something while the 「は」 particle is used only to bring up a new topic of conversation. This is why, in longer sentences, it is common to separate the topic with commas to remove ambiguity about which part of the sentence the topic applies to.

*Well technically, it's the most likely translation given the lack of context.

*Note: The order of topics covered are different in the videos so you may want to read about Adjectives first.

Adjectives

Properties of Adjectives

Now that we can connect two nouns together in various ways using particles, we want to describe our nouns with adjectives. An adjective can directly modify a noun that immediately follows it. It can also be connected in the same way we did with nouns using particles. All adjectives fall under two categories: *na-adjectives* and *i-adjectives*.

The na-adjective

Vocabulary

1. 静か 【しず・か】 (na-adj) - quiet
2. 人 【ひと】 - person
3. きれい (na-adj) - pretty; clean
4. 友達 【とも・だち】 - friend
5. 親切 【しん・せつ】 (na-adj) - kind
6. 魚 【さかな】 - fish
7. 好き 【す・き】 (na-adj) - likable; desirable
8. 肉 【にく】 - meat
9. 野菜 【や・さい】 - vegetables

The na-adjective is very simple to learn because it acts essentially like a noun. All the conjugation rules for both nouns and na-adjectives are the same. One main difference is that a na-adjective can directly modify a noun following it by sticking 「な」 between the adjective and noun. (Hence the name, na-adjective.)

Examples

1. 静かな人。
   Quiet person.
2. きれいな人。
   Pretty person.

You can also use adjectives with particles just like we did in the last lesson with nouns.

Examples

1. 友達は親切。
   Friend is kind.
2. 友達は親切な人だ。
   Friend is kind person.

As shown by the following examples, the conjugation rules for na-adjectives are the same as nouns.

Examples

1. ボブは魚が好きだ。
   Bob likes fish.
2. ボブは魚が好きじゃない。
   Bob does not like fish.
3. ボブは魚が好きだった。
   Bob liked fish.
4. ボブは魚が好きじゃなかった。
   Bob did not like fish.

If it bothers you that "like" is an adjective and not a verb in Japanese, you can think of 「好き」 as meaning "desirable". Also, you can see a good example of the topic and identifier particle working in harmony. The sentence is about the topic "Bob" and "fish" identifies specifically what Bob likes.

You can also use the last three conjugations to directly modify the noun. (Remember to attach 「な」 for positive non-past tense.)

Examples

36

1. 魚が好きな人。
   Person that likes fish.
2. 魚が好きじゃない人。
   Person that does not like fish.
3. 魚が好きだった人。
   Person that liked fish.
4. 魚が好きじゃなかった人。
   Person that did not like fish.

Here, the entire clause 「魚が好き」、「魚が好きじゃない」、etc.
is modifying "person" to talk about people that like or dislike fish. You
can see why this type of sentence is useful because 「人は魚が好き
だ」 would mean "People like fish", which isn't always the case.

We can even treat the whole descriptive noun clause as we would a
single noun. For instance, we can make the whole clause a topic like
the following example.

Examples

1. 魚が好きじゃない人は、肉が好きだ。
   Person who does not like fish like meat.
2. 魚が好きな人は、野菜も好きだ。
   Person who likes fish also like vegetables.

The i-adjective

Vocabulary

1. 嫌い 【きら・い】 (na-adj) - distasteful, hateful
2. 食べ物 【た・べ・もの】 - food
3. おいしい (i-adj) - tasty
4. 高い 【たか・い】 (i-adj) - high; tall; expensive

5. ビル - building
6. 値段 【ね・だん】 - price
7. レストラン - restaurant
8. あまり／あんまり - not very (when used with negative)
9. 好き 【す・き】 (na-adj) - likable; desirable
10. いい (i-adj) - good

All i-adjectives always end in the Hiragana character: 「い」. However, you may have noticed that some na-adjectives also end in 「い」 such as 「きれい（な）」. So how can you tell the difference? There are actually very few na-adjectives that end with 「い」 that is usually not written in Kanji. Two of the most common include: 「きれい」 and 「嫌い」. Almost all other na-adjectives that end in 「い」 are usually written in Kanji and so you can easily tell that it's not an i-adjective. For instance, 「きれい」 written in Kanji looks like 「綺麗」 or 「奇麗」. Since the 「い」 part of 「麗」 is part of a Kanji character, you know that it can't be an i-adjective. That's because the whole point of the 「い」 in i-adjectives is to allow conjugation without changing the Kanji. In fact, 「嫌い」 is one of the rare na-adjectives that ends in 「い」 without a Kanji. This has to do with the fact that 「嫌い」 is actually derived from the verb 「嫌う」.

Unlike na-adjectives, you do **not** need to add 「な」 to directly modify a noun with an i-adjective.

Examples

1. 嫌いな食べ物。
   Hated food.
2. おいしい食べ物。
   Tasty food.

Remember how the negative state-of-being for nouns also ended in 「い」 (じゃない)？Well, just like the negative state-of-being for nouns, you can never attach the declarative 「だ」 to i-adjectives.

Do NOT attach 「だ」 to i-adjectives.

Now that we got that matter cleared up, below are the rules for conjugating i-adjectives. Notice that the rule for conjugating to negative past tense is the same as the rule for the past tense.

Conjugation rules for i-adjectives

Negative: First remove the trailing 「い」 from the i-adjective and then attach 「くない」
Example: 高い → 高くない
Past-tense: First remove the trailing 「い」 from the i-adjective or negative i-adjective and then attach 「かった」
Examples

1. 高い → 高かった
2. 高くない → 高くなかった

Summary of i-adjective conjugations

	Positive	Negative
Non-Past	高い	高くない
Past	高かった	高くなかった

Examples

1. 高いビル。
   Tall building.
2. 高くないビル。
   Not tall building.
3. 高かったビル。
   Building that was tall.
4. 高くなかったビル。
   Building that was not tall.

Note that you can make the same type of descriptive noun clause as we have done with na-adjectives. The only difference is that we don't need 「な」 to directly modify the noun.

Example

- 値段が高いレストランはあまり好きじゃない。
  Don't like high price restaurants very much.

In this example, the descriptive clause 「値段が高い」 is directly modifying 「レストラン」.

An annoying exception

Vocabulary

1. 値段 【ね・だん】 - price
2. あまり／あんまり - not very (when used with negative)
3. いい (i-adj) - good
4. 彼 【かれ】 - he; boyfriend
5. かっこいい (i-adj) - cool; handsome

There is one i-adjective meaning "good" that acts slightly differently from all other i-adjectives. This is a classic case of how learning Japanese is harder for beginners because the most common and useful words also have the most exceptions. The word for "good" was originally 「よい（良い）」. However, with time, it soon became 「いい」. When it is written in Kanji, it is usually read as 「よい」 so 「いい」 is almost always Hiragana. That's all fine and good. Unfortunately, all the conjugations are still derived from 「よい」 and not 「いい」. This is shown in the next table.

Another adjective that acts like this is 「かっこいい」 because it is an abbreviated version of two words merged together: 「格好」 and 「いい」. Since it uses the same 「いい」, you need to use the same conjugations.

Conjugation for 「いい」

	Positive	Negative
Non-Past	いい	よくない
Past	よかった	よくな かった

Conjugation for 「かっこいい」

	Positive	Negative
Non-Past	かっこ いい	かっこよくない
Past	かっこよ かった	かっこよくなかった

Take care to make all the conjugations from 「よい」 not 「いい」.

Examples

1. 値段があんまりよくない。 Price isn't very good.
2. 彼はかっこよかった! He looked really cool!

Verb Basics

Role of Verbs

Vocabulary

1. 食べる　【た・べる】　(ru-verb) - to eat
2. 分かる　【わ・かる】　(u-verb) - to understand
3. 見る　【み・る】　(ru-verb) - to see
4. 寝る　【ね・る】　(ru-verb) - to sleep
5. 起きる　【お・きる】　(ru-verb) - to wake; to occur
6. 考える　【かんが・える】　(ru-verb) - to think
7. 教える　【おし・える】　(ru-verb) - to teach; to inform
8. 出る　【で・る】　(ru-verb) - to come out
9. いる (ru-verb) - to exist (animate)
10. 着る　【き・る】　(ru-verb) - to wear
11. 話す　【はな・す】　(u-verb) - to speak
12. 聞く　【き・く】　(u-verb) - to ask; to listen
13. 泳ぐ　【およ・ぐ】　(u-verb) - to swim
14. 遊ぶ　【あそ・ぶ】　(u-verb) - to play
15. 待つ　【ま・つ】　(u-verb) - to wait
16. 飲む　【の・む】　(u-verb) - to drink
17. 買う　【か・う】　(u-verb) - to buy
18. ある (u-verb) - to exist (inanimate)
19. 死ぬ　【し・ぬ】　(u-verb) - to die
20. する (exception) - to do
21. 来る　【く・る】　(exception) - to come
22. お金　【お・かね】　- money
23. 私　【わたし】　- me, myself, I
24. 猫　【ねこ】　- cat

We've now learned how to describe nouns in various ways with other nouns and adjectives. This gives us quite a bit of expressive power. However, we still cannot express actions. This is where verbs come in. Verbs, in Japanese, always come at the end of clauses.

Since we have not yet learned how to create more than one clause, for now it means that any sentence with a verb must end with the verb. We will now learn the three main categories of verbs, which will allow us to define conjugation rules. Before learning about verbs, there is one important thing to keep in mind.

A grammatically complete sentence requires a verb <u>only</u> (including state-of-being).

Or to rephrase, unlike English, the only thing you need to make a grammatically complete sentence is a verb and nothing else! That's why even the simplest, most basic Japanese sentence cannot be translated into English!

A grammatically complete sentence:

- 食べる。
  Eat. (possible translations include: I eat/she eats/they eat)

Classifying verbs into ru-verbs and u-verbs

Before we can learn any verb conjugations, we first need to learn how verbs are categorized. With the exception of only two exception verbs, all verbs fall into the category of *ru-verb* or *u-verb*.

All ru-verbs end in 「る」 while u-verbs can end in a number of u-vowel sounds including 「る」. Therefore, if a verb does **not** end in 「る」, it will always be an u-verb. For verbs ending in 「る」, if the vowel sound preceding the 「る」 is an /a/, /u/ or /o/ vowel sound, it will always be an u-verb. Otherwise, if the preceding sound is an /i/ or /e/ vowel sound, it will be a ru-verb **in most cases**. A list of common exceptions are at the end of this section.

Examples

1. 食べる - 「べ」 is an e-vowel sound so it is a ru-verb
2. 分かる - 「か」 is an a-vowel sound so it is an u-verb

If you're unsure which category a verb falls in, you can verify which kind it is with most dictionaries. There are only two exception verbs that are neither ru-verbs nor u-verbs as shown in the table below.

Examples of different verb types

ru-verb	u-verb	exception
見る	話す	する
食べる	聞く	来る
寝る	泳ぐ	
起きる	遊ぶ	
考える	待つ	
教える	飲む	
出る	買う	
いる	ある	
着る	死ぬ	

Examples

Here are some example sentences using ru-verbs, u-verbs, and exception verbs.

1. アリスは食べる。
   As for Alice, eat.
2. ジムが来る。
   Jim is the one that comes.
3. ボブもする。
   Bob also do.
4. お金がある。
   There is money. (lit: Money is the thing that exists.)
5. 私は買う。
   As for me, buy.
6. 猫はいる。
   There is cat. (lit: As for cat, it exists.)

Appendix: iru/eru u-verbs

Vocabulary

1. 要る 【い・る】 (u-verb) - to need
2. 帰る 【かえ・る】 (u-verb) - to go home
3. 切る 【き・る】 (u-verb) - to cut
4. しゃべる (u-verb) - to talk
5. 知る 【し・る】 (u-verb) - to know
6. 入る 【はい・る】 (u-verb) - to enter
7. 走る 【はし・る】 (u-verb) - to run
8. 減る 【へ・る】 (u-verb) - to decrease
9. 焦る 【あせ・る】 (u-verb) - to be in a hurry
10. 限る 【かぎ・る】 (u-verb) - to limit
11. 蹴る 【け・る】 (u-verb) - to kick
12. 滑る 【すべ・る】 (u-verb) - to be slippery
13. 握る 【にぎ・る】 (u-verb) - to grasp

14. 練る　【ね・る】　(u-verb) - to knead
15. 参る　【まい・る】　(u-verb) - to go; to come
16. 交じる　【まじ・る】　(u-verb) - to mingle
17. 嘲る　【あざけ・る】　(u-verb) - to ridicule
18. 覆る　【くつがえ・る】　(u-verb) - to overturn
19. 遮る　【さえぎ・る】　(u-verb) - to interrupt
20. 罵る　【ののし・る】　(u-verb) - to abuse verbally
21. 捻る　【ひね・る】　(u-verb) - to twist
22. 翻る　【ひるが・える】　(u-verb) - to turn over; to wave
23. 滅入る　【めい・る】　(u-verb) - to feel depressed
24. 蘇る　【よみがえ・る】　(u-verb) - to be resurrected

Below is a list of u-verbs with a preceding vowel sound of /i/ or /e/ ("iru" or "eru" sound endings). The list is **not** comprehensive but it does include many of the more common verbs categorized roughly into three levels.

iru/eru u-verbs grouped (roughly) by level

Basic	Intermediate	Advanced
要る	焦る	嘲る
帰る	限る	覆る
切る	蹴る	遮る
しゃべる	滑る	罵る
知る	握る	捻る
入る	練る	翻る
走る	参る	滅入る
減る	交じる	蘇る

Negative Verbs

Now that we've seen how to declare things and perform actions with verbs, we want to be able to say the negative. In other words, we want to say that such-and-such action was *not* performed. This is done by conjugating the verb to the negative form just like the state-of-being for nouns and adjectives. However, the rules are a tad more complicated.

Conjugating verbs into the negative

Vocabulary

1. ある (u-verb) - to exist (inanimate)
2. いる (ru-verb) - to exist (animate)
3. 食べる 【た・べる】 (ru-verb) - to eat
4. 買う 【か・う】 (u-verb) - to buy
5. 待つ 【ま・つ】 (u-verb) - to wait
6. する (exception) - to do
7. 来る 【く・る】 (exception) - to come
8. 見る 【み・る】 (ru-verb) - to see
9. 寝る 【ね・る】 (ru-verb) - to sleep
10. 起きる 【お・きる】 (ru-verb) - to wake; to occur
11. 考える 【かんが・える】 (ru-verb) - to think
12. 教える 【おし・える】 (ru-verb) - to teach; to inform
13. 出る 【で・る】 (ru-verb) - to come out
14. 着る 【き・る】 (ru-verb) - to wear
15. 話す 【はな・す】 (u-verb) - to speak
16. 聞く 【き・く】 (u-verb) - to ask; to listen
17. 泳ぐ 【およ・ぐ】 (u-verb) - to swim
18. 遊ぶ 【あそ・ぶ】 (u-verb) - to play
19. 飲む 【の・む】 (u-verb) - to drink
20. 帰る 【かえ・る】 (u-verb) - to go home
21. 死ぬ 【し・ぬ】 (u-verb) - to die
22. お金 【お・かね】 - money
23. 私 【わたし】 - me, myself, I
24. 猫 【ねこ】 - cat

We will now make use of the verb classifications we learned in the last section to define the rules for conjugation. But before we get into that, we need to cover one very important exception to the negative conjugation rules: 「ある」.

- ある (u-verb) - to exist (inanimate)
- いる (ru-verb) - to exist (animate)

「ある」 is an u-verb used to express existence of inanimate objects. The equivalent verb for animate objects (such as people or animals) is 「いる」, which is a normal ru-verb. For example, if you wanted to say that a chair is in the room, you would use the verb 「ある」, but if you wanted to say that a *person* is in the room, you must use the verb 「いる」 instead. These two verbs 「ある」 and 「いる」 are quite different from all other verbs because they describe existence and are not actual actions. You also need to be careful to choose the correct one based on animate or inanimate objects.

Anyway, the reason I bring it up here is because the negative of 「ある」 is 「ない」 (meaning that something does not exist). The conjugation rules for all other verbs are listed below as well as a list of example verbs and their negative forms.

* = exceptions particular to this conjugation

Conjugation rules for negative verbs

- **For ru-verbs:** Drop the 「る」 and attach 「ない」
  Example: 食べる + ない = 食べない
- ***For u-verbs that end in 「う」:** Replace 「う」 with 「わ」 and attach 「ない」
  Example: 買う + わ + ない = 買わない
- **For all other u-verbs:** Replace the u-vowel sound with the a-vowel equivalent and attach 「な

い」

Example: 待つ + た = 待<u>たない</u>

- **Exceptions:**
    1. する → しない
    2. くる → こない
    3. ＊ある → ない

Negative form conjugation examples

ru-verb	u-verb	exception
見る → 見ない	話す → 話さない	する → しない
食べる → 食べない	聞く → 聞かない	くる → こない
寝る → 寝ない	泳ぐ → 泳がない	*ある → ない
起きる → 起きない	遊ぶ → 遊ばない	
考える → 考えない	待つ → 待たない	
教える → 教えない	飲む → 飲まない	
出る → 出ない	*買う → 買わない	
着る → 着ない	帰る → 帰らない	
いる → いない	死ぬ → 死なない	

Examples

Here are the example sentences from the last section conjugated to the negative form.

1. アリスは食べない。
   As for Alice, does not eat.
2. ジムが遊ばない。
   Jim is the one that does not play.
3. ボブもしない。
   Bob also does not do.
4. お金がない。
   There is no money. (lit: Money is the thing that does not exist.)
5. 私は買わない。
   As for me, not buy.
6. 猫はいない。
   There is no cat. (lit: As for cat, does not exist.)

Past Tense

We will finish defining all the basic properties of verbs by learning how to express the past and past-negative tense of actions. I will warn you in advance that the conjugation rules in this section will be the most complex rules you will learn in all of Japanese. On the one hand, once you have this section nailed, all other rules of conjugation will seem simple. On the other hand, you might need to refer back to this section many times before you finally get all the rules. You will probably need a great deal of practice until you can become familiar with all the different conjugations.

Past tense for ru-verbs

Vocabulary

1. 出る 【で・る】 (ru-verb) - to come out
2. 捨てる 【す・てる】 (ru-verb) - to throw away
3. ご飯 【ご・はん】 - rice; meal
4. 食べる 【た・べる】 (ru-verb) - to eat
5. 映画 【えい・が】 - movie
6. 全部 【ぜん・ぶ】 - everything
7. 見る 【み・る】 (ru-verb) - to see

We will start off with the easy ru-verb category. To change a ru-verb from the dictionary form into the past tense, you simply drop the 「る」 and add 「た」.

To change ru-verbs into the past tense

Drop the 「る」 part of the ru-verb and add 「た」
Examples

1. 出る → 出た
2. 捨てる → 捨てた

Examples

1. ご飯は、食べた。
   As for meal, ate.
2. 映画は、全部見た。
   As for movie, saw them all.

Past tense for u-verbs

Vocabulary

1. 話す 【はな・す】 (u-verb) - to speak
2. 書く 【か・く】 (u-verb) - to write
3. 泳ぐ 【およ・ぐ】 (u-verb) - to swim
4. 飲む 【の・む】 (u-verb) - to drink
5. 遊ぶ 【あそ・ぶ】 (u-verb) - to play
6. 死ぬ 【し・ぬ】 (u-verb) - to die
7. 切る 【き・る】 (u-verb) - to cut
8. 買う 【か・う】 (u-verb) - to buy
9. 持つ 【も・つ】 (u-verb) - to hold
10. する (exception) - to do
11. 来る 【く・る】 (exception) - to come
12. 行く 【い・く】 (u-verb) - to go
13. 今日 【きょう】 - today
14. 走る 【はし・る】 (u-verb) - to run
15. 友達 【とも・だち】 - friend
16. 私 【わたし】 - me, myself, I
17. 勉強 【べん・きょう】 - study

Changing a u-verb from dictionary form to the past tense is difficult because we must break up u-verbs into four additional categories. These four categories depend on the last character of the verb. The table below illustrates the different sub-categories. In addition, there is one exception to the rules, which is the verb 「行く」. I've bundled it with the regular exception verbs 「する」 and 「来る」 even though 「行く」 is a regular u-verb in all other conjugations.

Ending	Non-Past	changes to...	Past	Non-Past	Past
す	話す	す→した	話した	する	した
く ぐ	書く 泳ぐ	く→いた ぐ→いだ	書いた 泳いだ	くる	きた
む ぶ ぬ	飲む 遊ぶ 死ぬ	む→んだ ぶ→んだ ぬ→んだ	飲んだ 遊んだ 死んだ	行く	行った*
る う つ	切る 買う 持つ	る→った う→った つ→った	切った 買った 持った		

* exceptions particular to this conjugation

Examples

1. 今日は、走った。
   As for today, ran.
2. 友達が来た。
   Friend is the one that came.

3. 私も遊んだ。
   I also played.

4. 勉強は、した。
   About study, did it.

Past-negative tense for all verbs

Vocabulary

1. 捨てる 【す・てる】 (ru-verb) - to throw away
2. 行く 【い・く】 (u-verb) - to go
3. 食べる 【たべ・る】 (ru-verb) - to eat
4. する (exception) - to do
5. お金 【お・かね】 - money
6. ある (u-verb) - to exist (inanimate)
7. 私 【わたし】 - me, myself, I
8. 買う 【か・う】 (u-verb) - to buy
9. 猫　【ねこ】 - cat
10. いる (ru-verb) - to exist (animate)

The conjugation rules for the past-negative tense are the same for *all* verbs. You might have noticed that the negative of just about everything always end in 「ない」. The conjugation rule for the past-negative tense of verbs is pretty much the same as all the other negatives that end in 「ない」. You simply take the negative of any verb, remove the 「い」 from the 「ない」 ending, and replace it with 「かった」.

To change verbs into the past-negative tense

Change the verb to the negative and replace the 「い」 with 「かった」

Examples

1. 捨て<u>る</u> → 捨てな<u>い</u> → 捨てな<u>かった</u>
2. 行<u>く</u> → 行かな<u>い</u> → 行かな<u>かった</u>

Examples

1. アリスは食べな<u>かった</u>。
   As for Alice, did not eat.
2. ジムがしな<u>かった</u>。
   Jim is the one that did not do.
3. ボブも行かな<u>かった</u>。
   Bob also did not go.
4. お金が<u>なかった</u>。
   There was no money. (lit: As for money, did not exist.)
5. 私は買わな<u>かった</u>。
   As for me, did not buy.
6. 猫は<u>いなかった</u>。
   There was no cat. (lit: As for cat, did not exist.)

Particles used with verbs

In this section, we will learn some new particles essential for using verbs. We will learn how to specify the direct object of a verb and the location where a verb takes place whether it's physical or abstract.

The direct object 「を」 particle

Vocabulary

1. 魚 【さかな】 - fish
2. 食べる 【た・べる】 (ru-verb) - to eat
3. ジュース - juice
4. 飲む 【の・む】 (u-verb) - to drink
5. 街 【まち】 - town
6. ぶらぶら - wandering; aimlessly
7. 歩く 【ある・く】 (u-verb) - to walk
8. 高速 【こう・そく】 - high-speed
9. 道路 【どう・ろ】 - route
10. 走る 【はし・る】 (u-verb) - to run
11. 毎日 【まい・にち】 - everyday
12. 日本語 【に・ほん・ご】 - Japanese (language)
13. 勉強 【べん・きょう】 - study
14. する (exception) - to do
15. メールアドレス - email address
16. 登録 【とう・ろく】 - register

The first particle we will learn is the object particle because it is a very straightforward particle. The 「を」 character is attached to the end of a word to signify that that word is the direct object of the verb. This character is essentially never used anywhere else. That is why the katakana equivalent 「ヲ」 is almost never used since particles are always written in hiragana. The 「を」 character, while technically pronounced as /wo/ essentially sounds like /o/ in real speech. Here are some examples of the direct object particle in action.

Examples

1. 魚を食べる。
   Eat fish.
2. ジュースを飲んだ。
   Drank juice.

Unlike the direct object we're familiar with in English, places can also be the direct object of motion verbs such as 「歩く」 and 「走る」. Since the motion verb is done *to* the location, the concept of direct object is the same in Japanese. However, as you can see by the next examples, it often translates to something different in English due to the slight difference of the concept of direct object.

1. 街をぶらぶら歩く。
   Aimlessly walk through town. (Lit: Aimlessly walk town)
2. 高速道路を走る。
   Run through expressway. (Lit: Run expressway)

When you use 「する」 with a noun, the 「を」 particle is optional and you can treat the whole [noun+する] as one verb.

1. 毎日、日本語を勉強する。
   Study Japanese everyday.
2. メールアドレスを登録した。
   Registered email address.

The target 「に」 particle

Vocabulary

1. 日本 【に・ほん】 - Japan
2. 行く 【い・く】 (u-verb) - to go
3. 家 【1) うち; 2) いえ】 - 1) one's own home; 2) house
4. 帰る 【かえ・る】 (u-verb) - to go home
5. 部屋 【へ・や】 - room
6. 来る 【く・る】 (exception) - to come
7. アメリカ - America
8. 宿題 【しゅく・だい】 - homework
9. 今日 【きょう】 - today

60

10. 明日 【あした】 - tomorrow
11. 猫 【ねこ】 - cat
12. いる (ru-verb) - to exist (animate)
13. いす - chair
14. 台所 【だい・どころ】 - kitchen
15. ある (u-verb) - to exist (inanimate)
16. いい (i-adj) - good
17. 友達 【とも・だち】 - friend
18. 会う 【あう】 (u-verb) - to meet
19. 医者 【い・しゃ】 - doctor
20. なる (u-verb) - to become
21. 先週 【せん・しゅう】 - last week
22. 図書館 【と・しょ・かん】 - library
23. 来年 【らい・ねん】 - next year

The 「に」 particle can specify a target of a verb. This is different from the 「を」 particle in which the verb does something *to* the direct object. With the 「に」 particle, the verb does something *toward* the word associated with the 「に」 particle. For example, the target of any motion verb is specified by the 「に」 particle.

Examples

1. ボブは日本に行った。
   Bob went to Japan.
2. 家に帰らない。
   Not go back home.
3. 部屋にくる。
   Come to room.

As you can see in the last example, the target particle always targets "to" rather than "from". If you wanted to say, "come from" for example, you would need to use 「から」, which means "from". If you used 「に」, it would instead mean "come *to*". 「から」 is also often paired with 「まで」, which means "up to".

1. アリスは、アメリカからきた。
   Alice came from America.
2. 宿題を今日から明日までする。
   Will do homework from today to tomorrow.

The idea of a target in Japanese is very general and is not restricted to motion verbs. For example, the location of an object is defined as the target of the verb for existence （ある and いる）. Time is also a common target. Here are some examples of non-motion verbs and their targets

1. 猫は部屋にいる。
   Cat is in room.
2. いすが台所にあった。
   Chair was in the kitchen.
3. いい友達に会った。
   Met good friend.
4. ジムは医者になる。
   Jim will become doctor.
5. 先週に図書館に行った。
   Went to library last week.

Note: Don't forget to use 「ある」 for inanimate objects such as the chair and 「いる」 for animate objects such as the cat.

While the 「に」 particle is not always required to indicate time, there is a slight difference in meaning between using the target particle and not using anything at all. In the following examples, the target particle makes the date a specific target emphasizing that the friend will go to Japan at that time. Without the particle, there is no special emphasis.

1. 友達は、来年、日本に行く。
   Next year, friend go to Japan.
2. 友達は、来年に日本に行く。
   Friend go to Japan next year.

The directional 「へ」 particle

Vocabulary

1. 日本 【に・ほん】 - Japan
2. 行く 【い・く】 (u-verb) - to go
3. 家 【1) うち; 2) いえ】 - 1) one's own home; 2) house
4. 帰る 【かえ・る】 (u-verb) - to go home
5. 部屋 【へ・や】 - room
6. 来る 【く・る】 (exception) - to come
7. 医者 【い・しゃ】 - doctor
8. なる (u-verb) - to become
9. 勝ち 【か・ち】 - victory
10. 向かう 【むか・う】 (u-verb) - to face; to go towards

While 「へ」 is normally pronounced /he/, when it is being used as a particle, it is always pronounced /e/ （え）. The primary difference between the 「に」 and 「へ」 particle is that 「に」 goes *to* a target as the final, intended destination (both physical or abstract). The 「へ」 particle, on the other hand, is used to express the fact that one is setting out towards *the direction* of the target. As a result, it is only used with directional motion verbs. It also does not guarantee whether the target is the final intended destination, only that one is heading towards that direction. In other words, the 「に」 particle sticks to the destination while the 「へ」 particle is fuzzy about where one is ultimately headed. For example, if we choose to replace 「に」 with 「へ」 in the first three examples of the previous section, the nuance changes slightly.

Examples

1. ボブは日本へ行った。
   Bob <u>headed towards</u> Japan.
2. 家へ帰らない。
   Not go home <u>toward</u> house.
3. 部屋へくる。
   Come <u>towards</u> room.

Note that we cannot use the 「へ」 particle with verbs that have no physical direction. For example, the following is incorrect.

- 医者へなる。

  (Grammatically incorrect version of 「医者になる」.)

This does not mean to say that 「へ」 cannot set out towards an abstract concept. In fact, because of the fuzzy directional meaning of this particle, the 「へ」 particle can also be used to talk about setting out towards certain future goals or expectations.

- 勝ちへ向かう。
  Go towards victory.

The contextual 「で」 particle

Vocabulary

1. 映画館 【えい・が・かん】 - movie theatre
2. 見る 【み・る】 (ru-verb) - to see
3. バス - bus
4. 帰る 【かえ・る】 (u-verb) - to go home
5. レストラン - restaurant
6. 昼ご飯 【ひる・ご・はん】 - lunch

7. 食べる　【た・べる】　(ru-verb) - to eat
8. 何　【なに／なん】　- what
9. 暇　【ひま】　- free　(as in not busy)

The 「で」 particle will allow us to specify the context in which the action is performed. For example, if a person ate a fish, where did he eat it? If a person went to school, by what means did she go? With what will you eat the soup? All of these questions can be answered with the 「で」 particle. Here are some examples.

Examples

1. 映画館で見た。
   Saw at movie theater.
2. バスで帰る。
   Go home by bus.
3. レストランで昼ご飯を食べた。
   Ate lunch at restaurant.

It may help to think of 「で」 as meaning "by way of". This way, the same meaning will kind of translate into what the sentence means. The examples will then read: "Saw by way of movie theater", "Go home by way of bus", and "Ate lunch by way of restaurant."

Using 「で」 with 「何」

The word for "what" (何) is quite annoying because while it's usually read as 「なに」, sometimes it is read as 「なん」 depending on how it's used. And since it's always written in Kanji, you can't tell which it is. I would suggest sticking with 「なに」 until someone corrects you for when it should be 「なん」. With the 「で」 particle, it is read as 「なに」 as well. (Hold the mouse cursor over the word to check the reading.)

1. 何できた？
   Came by the way of what?
2. バスできた。
   Came by the way of bus.

Here's the confusing part. There is a colloquial version of the word "why" that is used much more often than the less colloquial version 「どうして」 or the more forceful 「なぜ」. It is also written as 「何で」 but it is read as 「なんで」. This is a completely separate word and has nothing to do with the 「で」 particle.

1. 何できた？
   Why did you come?
2. 暇だから。
   Because I am free (as in have nothing to do).

The 「から」 here meaning "because" is different from the 「から」 we just learned and will be covered later in the compound sentence section. Basically the point is that the two sentences, while written the same way, are read differently and mean completely different things. Don't worry. This causes less confusion than you think because 95% of the time, the latter is used rather than the former. And even when 「なにで」 is intended, the context will leave no mistake on which one is being used. Even in this short example snippet, you can tell which it is by looking at the answer to the question.

When location is the topic

Vocabulary

1. 学校 【がっ・こう】 - school
2. 行く 【い・く】 (u-verb) - to go

3. 図書館 【と・しょ・かん】 - library
4. どこ - where
5. イタリア - Italy
6. レストラン - restaurant
7. どう - how

There are times when the location of an action is also the topic of a sentence. You can attach the topic particle （「は」 and 「も」） to the three particles that indicate location （「に」、「へ」、「で」） when the location is the topic. We'll see how location might become the topic in the following examples.

Example 1

ボブ：学校に行った？
Bob: (Did you) go to school?

アリス：行かなかった。
Alice: Didn't go.

ボブ：図書館には?
Bob: What about library?

アリス：図書館にも行かなかった。
Alice: Also didn't go to library.

In this example, Bob brings up a new topic (library) and so the location becomes the topic. The sentence is actually an abbreviated version of 「図書館には行った？」 which you can ascertain from the context.

Example 2

ボブ：どこで食べる？
Bob: Eat where?

アリス：イタリアレストランではどう？
Alice: How about Italian restaurant?

Bob asks, "Where shall we eat?" and Alice suggests an Italian restaurant. A sentence like, "How about..." usually brings up a new topic because the person is suggesting something new. In this case, the location (restaurant) is being suggested so it becomes the topic.

When direct object is the topic

Vocabulary

1. 日本語 【に・ほん・ご】 - Japanese (language)
2. 習う 【なら・う】 (u-verb) - to learn

The direct object particle is different from particles related to location in that you cannot use any other particles at the same time. For example, going by the previous section, you might have guessed that you can say 「をは」 to express a direct object that is also the topic but this is not the case. A topic can be a direct object without using the 「を」 particle. In fact, putting the 「を」 particle in will make it wrong.

Examples

1. 日本語を習う。
   Learn Japanese.
2. 日本語は、習う。
   About Japanese, (will) learn it.

Please take care to not make this mistake.

- 日本語をは、習う。
  (This is incorrect.)

Transitive and Intransitive Verbs

In Japanese, sometimes there are two types of the same verb often referred to as *transitive* and *intransitive verbs*. The difference between the two is that one verb is an action done by an active agent while the other is something that occurs without a direct agent. In English, this is sometimes expressed with the same verb, such as: "The ball dropped" vs "I dropped the ball" but in Japanese it becomes 「ボールが落ちた」 vs 「ボールを落とした」. Sometimes, the verbs changes when translated into English such as "To put it in the box" (箱に入れる） vs "To enter the box" （箱に入る） but this is only from the differences in the languages. If you think in Japanese, intransitive and transitive verbs have the same meaning except that one indicates that someone had a direct hand in the action (direct object) while the other does not. While knowing the terminology is not important, it is important to know which is which in order to use the correct particle for the correct verb.

Since the basic meaning and the kanji is the same, you can learn two verbs for the price of just one kanji! Let's look at a sample list of intransitive and transitive verbs.

Transitive and Intransitive Verbs

Transitive		Intransitive	
落とす	to drop	落ちる	to fall
出す	to take out	出る	to come out; to leave
入れる	to insert	入る	to enter
開ける	to open	開く	to be opened
閉める	to close	閉まる	to be closed
つける	to attach	つく	to be attached
消す	to erase	消える	to disappear
抜く	to extract	抜ける	to be extracted

Pay attention to particles!

The important lesson to take away here is to learn how to use the correct particle for the correct type of verb. It might be difficult at first to grasp which is which when learning new verbs or whether there even is a transitive/intransitive distinction. If you're not sure, you can always check whether a verb is transitive or intransitive by using an online dictionary such as jisho.org

Examples

1. 私が電気をつけた。
   I am the one that turned on the lights.
2. 電気がついた。
   The lights turned on.
3. 電気を消す。
   Turn off the lights.
4. 電気が消える。
   Lights turn off.
5. 誰が窓を開けた？
   Who opened the window?
6. 窓がどうして開いた？
   Why has the window opened?

The important thing to remember is that intransitive verbs *cannot* have a direct object because there is no direct acting agent. The following sentences are grammatically incorrect.

1. 電気をついた。
   （「を」 should be replaced with 「が」 or 「は」）
2. 電気を消える。
   （「を」 should be replaced with 「が」 or 「は」）

3. どうして窓を開いた？

（「を」 should be replaced with 「が」 or 「は」）

The only time you can use the 「を」 particle for intransitive verbs is when a location is the direct object of a motion verb as briefly described in the previous section.

1. 部屋を出た。
I left room.

Relative Clauses and Sentence Order

Treating verbs and state-of-being like adjectives

Have you noticed how, many forms of verbs and the state-of-being conjugate in a similar manner to i-adjectives? Well, that is because, in a sense, they are adjectives. For example, consider the sentence: "The person who did not eat went to bank." The "did not eat" describes the person and in Japanese, you can directly modify the noun 'person' with the clause 'did not eat' just like a regular adjective. This very simple realization will allow us to modify a noun with any arbitrary verb phrase!

Using state-of-being clauses as adjectives

Vocabulary

1. 国際 【こく・さい】 - international
2. 教育 【きょう・いく】 - education
3. センター - center
4. 登場 【とう・じょう】 - entry (on stage)

5. 人物 【じん・ぶつ】 - character
6. 立入 【たち・いり】 - entering
7. 禁止 【きん・し】 - prohibition, ban
8. 学生 【がく・せい】 - student
9. 人 【ひと】 - person
10. 学校 【がっ・こう】 - school
11. 行く 【い・く】 (u-verb) - to go
12. 子供 【こ・ども】 - child
13. 立派 【りっ・ぱ】 (na-adj) - fine, elegant
14. 大人 【おとな】 - adult
15. なる (u-verb) - to become
16. 友達 【とも・だち】 - friend
17. いい (i-adj) - good
18. 先週 【せん・しゅう】 - last week
19. 医者 【い・しゃ】 - doctor
20. 仕事 【し・ごと】 - job
21. 辞める 【や・める】 (ru-verb) - to quit

The negative, past, and negative past conjugations of verbs can be used just like adjectives to directly modify nouns. However, we cannot do this with the plain non-past state-of-being using 「だ」. (I told you this was a pain in the butt.) The language has particles for this purpose, which will be covered in the next section.

You cannot use 「だ」 **to directly modify a noun with a noun like you can with** 「だった」、 「じゃない」、 **and** 「じゃなかった」.

You can, however, have a string of nouns placed together when they're not meant to modify each other. For example, in a phrase such as "International Education Center" you can see that it is just a string of nouns without any grammatical modifications between them. It's not an "Education Center that is International" or a "Center for International Education", etc., it's just "International Education Center". In Japanese, you can express this as simply 「国際教育セ ンタ」 (or 「センター」). You will see this chaining of nouns in many combinations. Sometimes a certain combination is so commonly used that it has almost become a separate word and is even listed as a separate entry in some dictionaries. Some examples include: 「登場人物」、 「立入禁止」、 or 「通勤手当」. If you have difficulties in figuring out where to separate the words, you can paste them into the WWWJDICs Translate Words in Japanese Text function and it'll parse the words for you (most of the time).

Examples

Here are some examples of direct noun modifications with a *conjugated* noun clause. The noun clause has been highlighted.

1. 学生じゃない人は、学校に行かない。
   Person who is not student do not go to school.
2. 子供だったアリスが立派な大人になった。
   The Alice that was a child became a fine adult.
3. 友達じゃなかったアリスは、いい友達になった。
   Alice who was not a friend, became a good friend.
4. 先週医者だったボブは、仕事を辞めた。
   Bob who was a doctor last week quit his job.

Using relative verb clauses as adjectives

Vocabulary

1. 先週 【せん・しゅう】 - last week

2. 映画 【えい・が】 - movie
3. 見る 【み・る】 (ru-verb) - to see
4. 人 【ひと】 - person
5. 誰 【だれ】 - who
6. いつも - always
7. 勉強 【べん・きょう】 - study
8. する (exception) - to do
9. 赤い 【あか・い】 (i-adj) - red
10. ズボン - pants
11. 買う 【か・う】 (u-verb) - to buy
12. 友達 【とも・だち】 - friend
13. 晩ご飯 【ばん・ご・はん】 - dinner
14. 食べる 【た・べる】 (ru-verb) - to eat
15. 銀行 【ぎん・こう】 - bank

Verbs clauses can also be used just like adjectives to modify nouns. The following examples show us how this will allow us to make quite detailed and complicated sentences. The verb clause is highlighted.

Examples

1. 先週に映画を見た人は誰?
   Who is person who watched movie last week?

2. ボブは、いつも勉強する人だ。
   Bob is a person who always studies.

3. 赤いズボンを買う友達はボブだ。
   Friend who buy red pants is Bob.

4. 晩ご飯を食べなかった人は、映画で見た銀行に行った。
   Person who did not eat dinner went to the bank she saw at movie.

Japanese Sentence Order

Vocabulary

1. 私 【わたし】 - me; myself; I
2. 公園 【こう・えん】 - (public) park
3. お弁当 【お・べん・とう】 - box lunch
4. 食べる 【た・べる】 (ru-verb) - to eat
5. 学生 【がく・せい】 - student
6. 行く 【い・く】 (u-verb) - to go

Now that we've learned the concept of relative clauses and how they are used as building blocks to make sentences, I can go over how Japanese sentence ordering works. There's this myth that keeps floating around about Japanese sentence order that continues to plague many hapless beginners to Japanese. Here's how it goes.

The most basic sentence structure in English can be described as consisting of the following elements in this specific order: [Subject] [Verb] [Object]. A sentence is not grammatically correct if any of those elements are missing or out of order.

Japanese students will tell you that Japanese, on the other hand, while frothing at the mouth, is completely backwards!! Even some Japanese teacher might tell you that the basic Japanese sentence order is [Subject] [Object] [Verb]. This is a classic example of trying to fit Japanese into an English-based type of thinking. Of course, we all know (right?) that the real order of the fundamental Japanese sentence is: [Verb]. Anything else that comes before the verb doesn't have to come in any particular order and nothing more than the verb is required to make a complete sentence. In addition, the verb must always come at the end. That's the whole point of even having particles so that they can identify what grammatical function a word serves no matter where it is in the sentence. In fact, nothing will stop us from making a sentence with [Object] [Subject] [Verb] or just [Object] [Verb]. The following sentences are all complete and correct because the verb is at the end of the sentence.

Grammatically complete and correctly ordered sentences

1. 私は公園でお弁当を食べた。
2. 公園で私はお弁当を食べた。
3. お弁当を私は公園で食べた。
4. 弁当を食べた。
5. 食べた。

So don't sweat over whether your sentence is in the correct order. Just remember the following rules.

Japanese sentence order

- A complete sentence requires a main verb that must come at the end. This also includes the implied state-of-being. Examples
    1. 食べた
    2. 学生 (だ)
- Complete sentences (relative clauses) can be used to modify nouns to make sentences with nested relative clauses except in the case of 「だ」.
  Example

  お弁当を食べた学生が公園に行った。
  Student who ate lunch went to the park.

Noun-related Particles

The last three particles (Not!)

We have already gone over very powerful constructs that can express almost anything we want. We will see the 「の」 particle will give us even more power by allowing us to define a generic, abstract noun. We will also learn how to modify nouns directly with nouns. The three particles we will cover can group nouns together in different ways.

This is the last lesson that will be specifically focused on particles but that does *not* mean that there are no more particles to learn. We will learn many more particles along the way but they may not be labeled as such. As long as you know what they mean and how to use them, it is not too important to know whether they are particles or not.

The Inclusive 「と」 particle

Vocabulary

1. ナイフ - knife
2. フォーク - fork
3. ステーキ - steak
4. 食べる 【た・べる】 (ru-verb) - to eat
5. 本 【ほん】 - book
6. 雑誌 【ざっ・し】 - magazine
7. 葉書 【はがき】 - postcard
8. 買う 【か・う】 (u-verb) - to buy
9. 友達 【とも・だち】 - friend
10. 話す 【はな・す】 (u-verb) - to speak

11. 先生 【せん・せい】 - teacher
12. 会う 【あ・う】 (u-verb) - to meet

The 「と」 particle is similar to the 「も」 particle in that it contains a meaning of inclusion. It can combine two or more nouns together to mean "and".

1. ナイフとフォークでステーキを食べた。
   Ate steak by means of knife and fork.
2. 本と雑誌と葉書を買った。
   Bought book, magazine, and post card.

Another similar use of the 「と」 particle is to show an action that was done together with someone or something else.

1. 友達と話した。
   Talked with friend.
2. 先生と会った。
   Met with teacher.

The Vague Listing 「や」 and 「とか」 particles

Vocabulary

1. 飲み物 【の・み・もの】 - beverage
2. カップ - cup
3. ナプキン - napkin
4. いる (u-verb) - to need
5. 靴 【くつ】 - shoes
6. シャツ - shirt
7. 買う 【か・う】 (u-verb) - to buy

The 「や」 particle, just like the 「と」 particle, is used to list one or more nouns except that it is much more vague than the 「と」 particle. It implies that there may be other things that are unlisted and that not all items in the list may apply. In English, you might think of this as an "and/or, etc." type of listing.

1. 飲み物やカップやナプキンは、いらない？
   You don't need (things like) drink, cup, or napkin, etc.?
2. 靴やシャツを買う。
   Buy (things like) shoes and shirt, etc...

「とか」 also has the same meaning as 「や」 but is a slightly more colloquial expression.

1. 飲み物とかカップとかナプキンは、いらない？
   You don't need (things like) drink, cup, or napkin, etc.?
2. 靴とかシャツを買う。
   Buy (things like) shoes and shirt, etc...

The 「の」 particle

Vocabulary

1. 本 【ほん】 - book
2. アメリカ - America
3. 大学 【だい・がく】 - college
4. 学生 【がく・せい】 - student
5. それ - that
6. その - abbreviation of 「それの」
7. シャツ - shirt
8. 誰 【だれ】 - who
9. これ - this
10. この - abbreviation of 「これの」

11. あれ - that (over there)
12. あの - abbreviation of 「あれの」
13. 白い 【し・ろい】 (i-adj) - white
14. かわいい (i-adj) - cute
15. 授業 【じゅ・ぎょう】 - class
16. 行く 【い・く】 (u-verb) - to go
17. 忘れる 【わす・れる】 (ru-verb) - to forget
18. こと - event, matter
19. 毎日 【まい・にち】 - every day
20. 勉強 【べん・きょう】 - study
21. する (exception) - to do
22. 大変 【たい・へん】 (na-adj) - tough, hard time
23. 同じ 【おな・じ】 - same
24. 物 【もの】 - object
25. 食べる 【た・べる】 (ru-verb) - to eat
26. 面白い 【おも・し・ろい】 (i-adj) - interesting
27. 静か 【しず・か】 (na-adj) - quiet
28. 部屋 【へ・や】 - room
29. 人 【ひと】 - person
30. 学校 【がっ・こう】 - school

The 「の」 particle has many uses and it is a very powerful particle.
It is introduced here because like the 「と」 and 「や」 particle, it
can be used to connect one or more nouns. Let's look at a few
examples.

1. ボブの本。
   Book of Bob.
2. 本のボブ。
   Bob of book.

The first sentence essentially means, "Bob's book." (not a lost bible
chapter). The second sentence means, "Book's Bob" which is
probably a mistake. I've translated the first example as "book of

Bob" because the 「の」 particle doesn't always imply possession as the next example shows.

1. ボブは、アメリカの大学の学生だ。
   Bob is student of college of America.

In normal English, this would translate to, "Bob is a student of an American college." The order of modification is backwards so Bob is a student of a college that is American. 「学生の大学のアメリカ」 means "America of college of student" which is probably an error and makes little sense. (America of student's college?)

The noun that is being modified can be omitted if the context clearly indicates what is being omitted. The following highlighted redundant words can be omitted.

1. そのシャツは誰のシャツ?
   Whose shirt is that shirt?
2. ボブのシャツだ。
   It is shirt of Bob.

to become:

1. そのシャツは誰の?
   Whose shirt is that?
2. ボブのだ。
   It is of Bob.

(「その」 is an abbreviation of 「それ+の」 so it directly modifies the noun because the 「の」 particle is intrinsically attached. Other words include 「この」 from 「これの」 and 「あの」 from 「あれの」.)

The 「の」 particle in this usage essentially replaces the noun and takes over the role as a noun itself. We can essentially treat adjectives and verbs just like nouns by adding the 「の」 particle to it. The particle then becomes a generic noun, which we can treat just like a regular noun.

1. 白いのは、かわいい。
   Thing that is white is cute.
2. 授業に行くのを忘れた。
   Forgot the event of going to class.

Now we can use the direct object, topic, and identifier particle with verbs and adjectives. We don't necessarily have to use the 「の」 particle here. We can use the noun 「物」, which is a generic object or 「こと」 for a generic event. For example, we can also say:

1. 白い物は、かわいい。
   Thing that is white is cute.
2. 授業に行くことを忘れた。
   Forgot the thing of going to class.

However, the 「の」 particle is very useful in that you don't have to specify a particular noun. In the next examples, the 「の」 particle is not replacing any particular noun, it just allows us to modify verb and adjective clauses like noun clauses. The relative clauses are highlighted.

1. 毎日勉強するのは大変。
   The thing of studying every day is tough.
2. 毎日同じ物を食べるのは、面白くない。
   It's not interesting to eat same thing every day.

Even when substituting 「の」 for a noun, you still need the 「な」 to modify the noun when a na-adjective is being used.

• 静かな部屋が、アリスの部屋だ。
  Quiet room is room of Alice.

becomes:

- 静かなのが、アリスの部屋だ。
  Quiet one is room of Alice.

*Warning: This may make things seem like you can replace any arbitrary nouns with 「の」 but this is not so. It is important to realize that the sentence must be about the clause and not the noun that was replaced. For example, in the last section we had the sentence, 「学生じゃない人は、学校に行かない」. You may think that you can just replace 「人」 with 「の」 to produce 「学生じゃないのは、学校に行かない」. But in fact, this makes no sense because the sentence is now about the clause "Is not student". The sentence becomes, "The thing of not being student does not go to school" which is complete gibberish because not being a student is a state and it doesn't make sense for a state to go anywhere much less school.

The 「の」 particle as explanation

Vocabulary

1. 今 【いま】 - now
2. 忙しい 【いそが・しい】 (i-adj) - busy
3. 学生 【がく・せい】 - student
4. 飲む 【のむ】 - to drink
5. どこ - where
6. 行く 【い・く】 (u-verb) - to go
7. 授業 【じゅ・ぎょう】 - class
8. ある (u-verb) - to exist (inanimate)
9. ううん - casual word for "no" (nah, uh-uh)
10. その - that (abbr. of それの)
11. 人 【ひと】 - person

12. 買う 【か・う】 (u-verb) - to buy
13. 先生 【せん・せい】 - teacher
14. 朝ご飯 【あさ・ご・はん】 - breakfast
15. 食べる 【た・べる】 (ru-verb) - to eat
16. どうして - why

The 「の」 particle attached at the end of the last clause of a sentence can also convey an explanatory tone to your sentence. For example, if someone asked you if you have time, you might respond, "The thing is I'm kind of busy right now." The abstract generic noun of "the thing is..." can also be expressed with the 「の」 particle. This type of sentence has an embedded meaning that explains the reason(s) for something else.

The sentence would be expressed like so:

- 今は忙しいの。
  The thing is that (I'm) busy now.

This sounds very soft and feminine. In fact, adult males will almost always add a declarative 「だ」 unless they want to sound cute for some reason.

- 今は忙しいのだ。
  The thing is that (I'm) busy now.

However, since the declarative 「だ」 cannot be used in a question, the same 「の」 in questions do not carry a feminine tone at all and is used by both males and females.

- 今は忙しいの?
  Is it that (you) are busy now? (gender-neutral)

To express state-of-being, when the 「の」 particle is used to convey this explanatory tone, we need to add 「な」 to distinguish it from the 「の」 particle that simply means "of".

1. ジムのだ。
   It is of Jim. (It is Jim's.)
2. ジムなのだ。
   It is Jim (with explanatory tone).

Besides this one case, everything else remains the same as before.

In actuality, while this type of explanatory tone is used all the time, 「のだ」 is usually substituted by 「んだ」. This is probably due to the fact that 「んだ」 is easier to say than 「のだ」. This grammar can have what seems like many different meaning because not only can it be used with all forms of adjectives, nouns, and verbs it itself can **also** be conjugated just like the state-of-being. A conjugation chart will show you what this means.

There's really nothing new here. The first chart is just adding 「んだ」 (or 「なんだ」) to a conjugated verb, noun, or adjective. The second chart adds 「んだ」 (or 「なんだ」) to a non-conjugated verb, noun, adjective and then conjugates the 「だ」 part of 「んだ」 just like a regular state-of-being for nouns and na-adjectives. Just don't forget to attach the 「な」 for nouns as well as na-adjectives.

「んだ」 attached to different conjugations (Substitute 「の」 or 「のだ」 for 「んだ」)

	Noun/Na-Adj	Verb/I-Adj
Plain	学生なんだ	飲むんだ
Negative	学生じゃないんだ	飲まないんだ
Past	学生だったんだ	飲んだんだ
Past-Neg	学生じゃなかったんだ	飲まなかったんだ

「んだ」 is conjugated (Substitute 「の」 for 「ん」 and 「の」 or 「のだ」 for 「んだ」)

	Noun/Na-Adj	Verb/I-Adj
Plain	学生なんだ	飲むんだ
Negative	学生なんじゃない	飲むんじゃない
Past	学生なんだった	飲むんだった
Past-Neg	学生なんじゃなかった	飲むんじゃなかった

I would say that the past and past-negative forms for noun/na-adjective in the second chart are almost never used (especially with 「の」) but they are presented for completeness.

The crucial difference between using the explanatory 「の」 and not using anything at all is that you are telling the listener, "Look, here's the reason" as opposed to simply imparting new information. For example, if someone asked you, "Are you busy now?" you can simply answer, 「今は忙しい」. However, if someone asked you, "How come you can't talk to me?" since you obviously have some explaining to do, you would answer, 「今は忙しいの」 or 「今は忙しいんだ」. This grammar is indispensable for seeking explanations in questions. For instance, if you want to ask, "Hey, isn't it late?" you can't just ask, 「遅くない？」 because that means, "It's not late?" You need to indicate that you are seeking explanation in the form of 「遅いんじゃない？」.

Let's see some examples of the types of situations where this grammar is used. The examples will have literal translation to make it easier to see how the meaning stays the same and carries over into what would be very different types of sentences in normal English. A more natural English translation is provided as well because the literal translations can get a bit convoluted.

Example 1

アリス：どこに行くの?
Alice: Where is it that (you) are going?

ボブ：授業に行くんだ。
Bob: It is that (I) go to class.

Alice: Where are you going? (Seeking explanation)
Bob: I'm going to class. (Explanatory)

Example 2

アリス：今、授業があるんじゃない?
Alice: Isn't it that there is class now?

ボブ：今は、ないんだ。
Bob: Now it is that there is no class.

Alice: Don't you have class now? (Expecting that there is class)
Bob: No, there is no class now. (Explanatory)

Example 3

アリス：今、授業がないんじゃない？
Alice: Isn't it that there isn't class now?

ボブ：ううん、ある。
Bob: No, there is.

Alice: Don't you not have class now? (Expecting that there is no class)
Bob: No, I do have class.

Example 4

アリス：その人が買うんじゃなかったの？
Alice: Wasn't it that that person was the one to buy?

ボブ：ううん、先生が買うんだ。
Bob: No, it is that teacher is the one to buy.

Alice: Wasn't that person going to buy? (Expecting that the person would buy)
Bob: No, the teacher is going to. (Explanatory)

Example 5

アリス：朝ご飯を食べるんじゃなかった。
Alice: It is that breakfast wasn't to eat.

ボブ：どうして？
Bob: Why?

Alice: Should not have eaten breakfast, you know. (Explaining that breakfast wasn't to be eaten)
Bob: How come?

Don't worry if you are thoroughly confused by now, we will see many more examples along the way. Once you get the sense of how everything works, it's better to forget the English because the double and triple negatives can get quite confusing such as Example 3. However, in Japanese it is a perfectly normal expression, as you will begin to realize once you get accustomed to Japanese.

Adverbs and Sentence-ending particles

Properties of Adverbs

Vocabulary

1. 早い 【はや・い】 (i-adj) - fast; early
2. きれい (na-adj) - pretty; clean
3. 朝ご飯 【あさ・ご・はん】 - breakfast
4. 食べる 【た・べる】 (ru-verb) - to eat
5. 自分 【じ・ぶん】 - oneself
6. 部屋 【へ・や】 - room
7. 映画 【えい・が】 - movie
8. たくさん - a lot (amount)
9. 見る 【み・る】 - to see; to watch
10. 最近 【さい・きん】 - recent; lately
11. 全然 【ぜん・ぜん】 - not at all (when used with negative)
12. 声 【こえ】 - voice
13. 結構 【けっ・こう】 - fairly, reasonably
14. 大きい 【おお・きい】 (i-adj) - big
15. この - this (abbr. of これの)
16. 町 【まち】 - town
17. 変わる 【か・わる】 (u-verb) - to change
18. 図書館 【と・しょ・かん】 - library
19. 中 【なか】 - inside
20. 静か 【しず・か】 (na-adj) - quiet

Unlike English, changing adjectives to adverbs is a very simple and straightforward process. In addition, since the system of particles make sentence ordering flexible, adverbs can be placed anywhere in the clause that it applies to as long as it comes *before* the verb that it refers to. As usual, we have two separate rules: one for i-adjectives, and one for na-adjectives.

How to change an adjective to an adverb

- **For i-adjectives:** Substitute the 「い」 with 「く」.
  Example: 早い → 早く
- **For na-adjectives:** Attach the target particle 「に」.
  Example: きれい → きれいに

- ボブは朝ご飯を早く食べた。
  Bob quickly ate breakfast.

The adverb 「早く」 is a little different from the English word 'fast' in that it can mean quickly in terms of speed *or* time. In other words, Bob may have eaten his breakfast early or he may have eaten it quickly depending on the context. In other types of sentences such as 「早く走った」, it is quite obvious that it probably means quickly and not early. (Of course this also depends on the context.)

- アリスは自分の部屋をきれいにした。
  Alice did her own room toward clean.

The literal translation kind of gives you a sense of why the target particle is used. There is some argument against calling this an adverb at all but it is convenient for us to do so because of the grouping of i-adjectives and na-adjectives. Thinking of it as an adverb, we can interpret the sentence to mean: "Alice did her room cleanly." or less literally: "Alice cleaned her room." (「きれい」 literally means "pretty" but if it helps, you can think of it as, "Alice prettied up her own room.")

Note: Not all adverbs are derived from adjectives. Some words like 「全然」 and 「たくさん」 are adverbs in themselves without any conjugation. These words can be used without particles just like regular adverbs.

1. 映画をたくさん見た。
   Saw a lot of movies.
2. 最近、全然食べない。
   Lately, don't eat at all.

Examples

Here are some more examples of using adverbs.

1. ボブの声は、結構大きい。
   Bob's voice is fairly large.
2. この町は、最近大きく変わった。
   This town had changed greatly lately.
3. 図書館の中では、静かにする。
   Within the library, [we] do things quietly.

Sentence-ending particles

Vocabulary

1. いい (i-adj) - good
2. 天気 【てん・き】 - weather

3. そう - (things are) that way
4. 面白い 【おも・しろ・い】 (i-adj) - interesting
5. 映画 【えい・が】 - movie
6. 全然 【ぜん・ぜん】 - not at all (when used with negative)
7. 時間 【じ・かん】 - time
8. ある (u-verb) - to exist (inanimate)
9. 大丈夫 【だい・じょう・ぶ】 (na-adj) - ok
10. 今日 【きょう】 - today
11. うん - yes (casual)
12. でも - but
13. 明日 【あした】 - tomorrow
14. 雨 【あめ】 - rain
15. 降る 【ふ・る】 (u-verb) - to precipitate
16. 魚 【さかな】 - fish
17. 好き 【す・き】 (na-adj) - likable

Sentence-ending particles are particles that always come at the end of sentences to change the "tone" or "feel" of a sentence. In this section, we will cover the two most commonly used sentence-ending particles.

「ね」 sentence ending

People usually add 「ね」 to the end of their sentence when they are looking for (and expecting) agreement to what they are saying. This is equivalent to saying, "right?" or "isn't it?" in English.

Example 1

ボブ：いい天気だね。
Bob: Good weather, huh?

94

アリス：そうね。
Alice: That is so, <u>isn't it</u>?

The literal translation of 「そうね」 sounds a bit odd but it basically means something like, "Sure is". Males would probably say, 「そうだね」.

Example 2

アリス：おもしろい**映画**だった<u>ね</u>。
Alice: That was interesting movie, <u>wasn't it</u>?

ボブ：え？**全然**おもしろくなかった。
Bob: Huh? No, it wasn't interesting at all.

Since Alice is expecting agreement that the movie was interesting Bob is surprised because he didn't find the movie interesting at all. (「え」 is a
sound of surprise and confusion.)

「よ」 sentence ending

When 「よ」 is attached to the end of a sentence, it means that the speaker is informing the listener of something new. In English, we might say this with a, "You know..." such as the sentence, "You know, I'm actually a genius."

Example 1

アリス：**時間**がない<u>よ</u>。
Alice: <u>You know</u>, there is no time.

ボブ：大丈夫だよ。
Bob: It's ok, you know.

Example 2

アリス：今日はいい天気だね。
Alice: Good weather today, huh?

ボブ：うん。でも、明日雨が降るよ。
Bob: Yeah. But it will rain tomorrow, you know.

Combining both to get 「よね」

You can also combine the two particles we just learned to create 「よね」. This is essentially used when you want to inform the listener of some new point you're trying to make and when you're seeking agreement on it at the same time. When combining the two, the order must always be 「よね」. You cannot reverse the order.

Example

アリス：ボブは、魚が好きなんだよね。
Alice: You know, you like fish, dontcha?

ボブ：そうだね。
Bob: That is so, huh?

Essential Grammar

We have learned the basic foundation of the Japanese language. Now that we have a general knowledge of how Japanese works, we can now extend that by learning specific grammar for various situations. This section will go over what is considered to be essential grammar for basic practical Japanese. You will begin to see fewer literal translations in order to emphasize the new grammar now that you (should) have a good understanding of the basic fundamental grammar. For example, in sentences where the subject has not been specified, I might simply specify the subject in the translation as 'he' even though it may very well be "we" or "them" depending on the context.

This section starts with transforming what we have learned so far into a more unassuming and politer form. In any language, there are ways to word things differently to express a feeling of deference or politeness. Even English has differences such as saying, "May I..." vs "Can I...". You may speak one way to your professor and another way to your friends. However, Japanese is different in that not only does the type of vocabulary change, the grammatical structure for *every sentence* changes as well. There is a distinct and clear line differentiating polite and casual types of speech. On the one hand, the rules clearly tell you how to structure your sentences for different social contexts. On the other hand, every sentence you speak must be conjugated to the proper level of politeness. In section 3, we will cover the polite version of Japanese, which is required for speaking to people of higher social position or to people you are unfamiliar with.

This section will then continue to cover the most useful major types of grammar in Japanese. For this reason, we will learn the most common conjugations such as the te-form, potential, conditional, and volitional. The latter sections are in no particular order and neither does it need to be. The grammar that is presented here is essential which means that you have to learn it all anyway and learn them well.

Polite Form and Verb Stems

Not being rude in Japan

Vocabulary

1. 丁寧語 【てい・ねい・ご】 - polite language
2. 尊敬語 【そん・けい・ご】 - honorific language
3. 謙譲語 【けん・じょう・ご】 - humble language
4. はい - yes (polite)
5. いいえ - no (polite)

The Japanese we have learned so far is all well and good if you're 5-years old. Unfortunately, adults are expected to use a politer version of the language (called 丁寧語) when addressing certain people. People you will probably use 丁寧語 with are: 1) people of higher social rank, and 2) people you are not familiar with. Deciding when to use which language is pretty much a matter of "feel". However, it is a good idea to stick with one form for each person.

Later (probably much later), we will learn an even politer version of the language called honorific （尊敬語） and humble （謙譲語） form. It will be more useful than you may think because store clerks, receptionists, and such will speak to you in those forms. But for now, let's concentrate on just 丁寧語, which is the base for 尊敬語 and 謙譲語.

Fortunately, it is not difficult to change casual speech to polite speech. There may be some slight changes to the vocabulary (for example, "yes" and "no" become 「はい」 and 「いいえ」 respectively in polite speech), and very colloquial types of sentence endings are not used in polite speech. (We will learn about sentence endings in a later section.) Essentially, the only main difference between polite and casual speech comes at the very end of the sentence. You cannot even tell whether a person is speaking in polite or casual speech until the sentence is finished.

The stem of verbs

Vocabulary

1. 食べる 【た・べる】 (ru-verb) - to eat
2. 泳ぐ 【およ・ぐ】 (u-verb) - to swim
3. する (exception) - to do
4. 来る 【く・る】 (exception) - to come
5. 怒る 【おこ・る】 (u-verb) - to get angry
6. 鉄拳 【てっ・けん】 - fist
7. 休み 【やす・み】 - rest; vacation
8. 飲む 【の・む】 (u-verb) - to drink
9. 明日 【あした】 - tomorrow
10. 映画 【えい・が】 - movie
11. 見る 【み・る】 (ru-verb) - to see
12. 行く 【い・く】 (u-verb) - to go
13. 友達 【とも・だち】 - friend
14. 遊ぶ 【あそ・ぶ】 (u-verb) - to play
15. 楽しむ 【たの・しむ】 (u-verb) - to enjoy
16. 出す 【だ・す】 (u-verb) - to bring out
17. 走る 【はし・る】 (u-verb) - to run
18. 走り出す 【はし・り・だ・す】 (u-verb) - to break into a run
19. 着る 【き・る】 (ru-verb) - to wear
20. 替える 【か・える】 (ru-verb) - to switch
21. 着替える 【き・が・える】 (ru-verb) - to change (clothes)
22. 付ける 【つ・ける】 (ru-verb) - to attach
23. 加える 【くわ・える】 (ru-verb) - to add
24. 付け加える 【つ・け・くわ・える】 (ru-verb) - to add one thing to another
25. 言う 【い・う】 (u-verb) - to say

26. 言い出す 【い・い・だ・す】 (u-verb) - to start talking

In order to conjugate all u-verbs and ru-verbs into their respective polite forms, we will first learn about the stem of verbs. This is often called the *masu-stem* in Japanese textbooks but we will call it just the *stem* because it is used in many more conjugations than just its masu-form. The stem is really great because it's very easy to produce and is useful in many different types of grammar.

Rules for extracting the stem of verbs

- **For ru-verbs:** Remove the 「る」
  Example: 食べる → 食べ
- **For u-verbs:** The last vowel sound changes from an / u / vowel sound to an / i / vowel sound.
  Example: 泳ぐ → 泳ぎ
- **Exceptions:**
  1. 「する」 becomes 「し」
  2. 「くる」 becomes 「き」

The stem when used by itself can be a very specialized and limited way of creating nouns from verbs. While the 「の」 particle allows you to talk about verbs as if they were nouns, the stem actually turns verbs into nouns. In fact, in very rare cases, the stem is used more often than the verb itself. For example, the stem of 「怒る」（いかる） is used more often than the verb itself. The movie, "Fists of Fury" is translated as 「怒りの鉄拳」 and not 「怒る鉄拳」. In fact, 「怒る」 will most likely be read as 「おこる」, a completely different verb with the same meaning and kanji! There are a number of specific nouns (such as 「休み」) that are really verb stems that are used like regular nouns. However, in general we cannot take any verb and make it into a noun. For example, the following sentence is wrong.

- 飲みをする。
  (This sentence makes sense but no one talks like this)

However, a useful grammar that works in general for stems of all verbs is using the stem as a target with a motion verb (almost always 「行く」 and 「来る」 in this case). This grammar means, "to go or to come to do [some verb]". Here's an example.

1. 明日、映画を見に行く。 - Tomorrow, go to see movie.

「見に」 is the stem of 「見る」 (which is 見) combined with the target particle 「に」.

The motion target particle 「へ」 sounds like you're literally going or coming to something while the 「に」 particle implies that you are going or coming for the purpose of doing something.

1. 昨日、友達が遊びへきた。
   Yesterday, friend came to a playing activity. (Sounds a bit strange)
2. 昨日、友達が遊びにきた。
   Yesterday, friend came to play.

The expression 「楽しみにする」 meaning "to look forward to" is formed from grammar similar to this but is a special case and should be considered a set expression.

Other verbs are also sometimes attached to the stem to create new verbs. For example, when 「出す」 is attached to the stem of 「走る」, which is 「走り」, you get 「走り出す」 meaning "to break out into a run". Other examples include 「切り替える」, which means "to switch over to something else", and 「付け加える」, which means "to add something by attaching it". You can see how the separate meanings of the two verbs are combined to create the new combined verb. For example, 「言い出す」 means "to start talking", combining the meaning, "to speak" and "to bring out". There are no general rules here, you need to just memorize these combined verbs as separate verbs in their own right.

Things that are written in a formal context such as newspaper articles also use the stem as a conjunctive verb. We will come back to this later in the formal expression lesson.

Using 「〜ます」 to make verbs polite

Vocabulary

1. 明日 【あした】 - tomorrow
2. 大学 【だい・がく】 - college
3. 行く 【い・く】 (u-verb) - to go
4. 先週 【せん・しゅう】 - last week
5. 会う 【あ・う】 (u-verb) - to meet
6. 晩ご飯 【ばん・ご・はん】 - dinner
7. 食べる 【た・べる】 (ru-verb) - to eat
8. 面白い 【おも・しろ・い】 (i-adj) - interesting
9. 映画 【えい・が】 - movie
10. 見る 【み・る】 (ru-verb) - to see

Of course, the reason I introduced the verb stem is to learn how to conjugate verbs into their polite form... the masu-form! The masu-form must always come at the end of a complete sentence and never inside a modifying relative clause. When we learn compound sentences, we will see that each sub-sentence of the compound sentence can end in masu-form as well.

To conjugate verbs into the masu-form, you attach different conjugations of 「ます」 to the stem depending on the tense. Here is a chart.

A conjugation chart with sample stem 「遊び」

	ます conjugations	Stem+ます
Plain	ます	遊びます
Negative	ません	遊びません
Past	ました	遊びました
Past-Neg	ませんでした	遊びませんでした

Examples

1. 明日、大学に行きます。
   Tomorrow, go to college.
2. 先週、ボブに会いましたよ。
   You know, met Bob last week.
3. 晩ご飯を食べませんでしたね。
   Didn't eat dinner, huh?
4. 面白くない映画は見ません。
   About not interesting movies, do not see (them).

Using 「です」 for everything else

Vocabulary

1. かわいい (i-adj) - cute
2. 静か 【しず・か】 (na-adj) - quiet
3. 子犬 【こ・いぬ】 - puppy
4. とても - very
5. 好き 【す・き】 (na-adj) - likable; desirable
6. 昨日 【きのう】 - yesterday
7. 時間 【じ・かん】 - time
8. ある (u-verb) - to exist (inanimate)
9. その - that (abbr of 「それの」)
10. 部屋 【へ・や】 - room
11. 先週 【せん・しゅう】 - last week
12. 見る 【み・る】 (ru-verb) - to see
13. 映画 【えい・が】 - movie
14. 面白い 【おも・しろ・い】 (i-adj) - interesting

For any sentence that does not end in a ru-verb or u-verb, the only thing that needs to be done is to add 「です」 or 「でした」. You can also do this for substituted nouns (both 「の」 and 「ん」) by just treating them like regular nouns. Another important thing to remember is that if there is a declarative 「だ」, it must be removed. In being polite, I guess you can't be so bold as to forwardly declare things the way 「だ」 does. Just like the masu-form, this must also go at the end of a complete sentence. Here is a chart illustrating the conjugations.

i-adjective (だ cannot be used)

	Casual	**Polite**
Plain	かわいい	かわいいです
Negative	かわいくない	かわいくないです
Past	かわいかった	かわいかったです
Past-Neg	かわいくな かった	かわいくな かったです

na-adjective/noun (might have to remove だ)

	Casual	**Polite**
Plain	静か（だ）	静かです
Negative	静かじゃない	静かじゃないです
Past	静かだった	※静かでした
Past-Neg	静かじゃな かった	静かじゃな かったです

※ Notice in the case of noun/na-adjective only, the past tense becomes 「でした」. A very common mistake is to do the same for i-adjectives. Remember 「かわいいでした」 is wrong!

Examples

1. 子犬はとても<u>好きです</u>。
   About puppies, like very much. (The most natural translation is that someone likes puppies very much but there is not enough context to rule out that the puppies like something very much.)
2. 昨日、時間が<u>なかったんです</u>。
   It was that there was no time yesterday.
3. その部屋はあまり<u>静かじゃないです</u>。
   That room is not very quiet.
4. 先週に見た映画は、とても<u>面白かったです</u>。
   Movie saw last week was very interesting.

※ Reality Check

I have heard on a number of occasions that the negative non-past conjugation as given here is not an "officially" correct conjugation. Instead what's considered to be a more "correct" conjugation is to actually replace the 「ないです」 part with 「ありません」. The reasoning is that the polite negative form of the verb 「ある」 is not 「ないです」 but 「ありません」. Therefore, 「かわいくない」 actually becomes 「かわいくありません」 and 「静かじゃない」 becomes 「静かじゃありません」.

The reality of today's Japanese is that what's supposed to be the "official" conjugation sounds rather stiff and formal. In normal everyday conversations, the conjugation presented here will be used almost every time. While you should use the more formal conjugations for written works using the polite form, you'll rarely hear it in actual speech. In conclusion, I recommend studying and becoming familiar with <u>both</u> types of conjugations.

A more formal negative conjugation

	Casual	**Polite**
Negative	かわいくない	かわいくあ りません
Past-Neg	かわいく なかった	かわいくありま せんでした
Negative	静かじゃない	静かじゃあ りません
Past-Neg	静かじゃ なかった	静かじゃありま せんでした

Examples

1. その部屋はあまり静かじゃないですよ。
   You know, that room is not very quiet.
2. その部屋はあまり静かじゃありませんよ。
   You know, that room is not very quiet.

「です」 is NOT the same as 「だ」

Vocabulary

1. そう - so
2. 思う 【おも・う】 (u-verb) - to think

3. はい - yes (polite)
4. 答える 【こた・える】 (ru-verb) - to answer

Many of you who have taken Japanese classes have probably been taught that 「です」 is the polite version of 「だ」. However, I want to point some several key differences here and the reasons why they are in fact completely different things. It is impossible to fully explain the reasons why they are fundamentally different without discussing grammar that have yet to be covered so I would like to target this toward those who have already started learning Japanese and have been incorrectly misinformed that 「だ」 is the casual version of 「です」. For the rest of you new to this, you can easily skip this part.

I'm sure most of you have learned the expression 「そう」 by now. Now, there are four ways to make a complete sentence using the state-of-being with 「そう」 to produce a sentence that says, "That is so."

Different ways to say, "That is so."

1. そう。
2. そうだ。
3. そうです。
4. そうでございます。

The first 「そう」 is the implied state-of-being and 「そうだ」 is the declarative. As I've stated before, the non-assuming soft spoken 「そう」 is often used by females while the more confident 「そうだ」 is often used by males.

「そうです」 is the polite version of 「そう」, created by attaching 「です」 to the noun. 「そうです」 is **not** the polite version of 「そ

うだ」 where the 「だ」 is replaced by 「です」 and I'll explain why.

Perhaps we wanted to make that sentence into a question instead to ask, "Is that so?" There are several ways to do this but some possibilities are given in the following. (This grammar is covered in a later section.)

Different ways to ask, "Is that so?"

1. そう？
2. そうか？
3. そうですか？

As I've explained before, the 「だ」 is used to declare what one believes to be a fact. Therefore, 「そうだか？」 is not a valid way to ask a question because it is declaring a fact and asking a question at the same time. But the fact that 「そうですか」 is a valid question shows that 「です」 and 「だ」 are essentially different. 「そうです」, in showing respect and humbleness, is not as assertive and is merely the polite version of 「そう」.

Besides the difference in nuance between 「だ」 and 「です」, another key difference is that 「だ」 is used in many different types of grammar to delineate a relative clause. 「です」, on the other hand, is only used at the end of a sentence to designate a polite state-of-being. For instance, consider the two following sentences. (This grammar is covered in a later section.)

- そうだと思います
  I think that is so.
- そうですと思います
  (Incorrect sentence)

109

「そうだと思います」 is valid while 「そうですと思います」 is not because 「です」 can only go at the end of the sentence. 「です」 can only be in a relative clause when it is a direct quote of what someone said such as the following.

- 「はい、そうです」と答えた。

In conclusion, replacing 「です」 with 「だ」, thinking one is the polite equivalent of the other or vice-versa will potentially result in grammatically incorrect sentences. It is best to think of them as totally separate things (because they are).

Addressing People

Not only is it important to use the right type of language with the right people, it is also important to address them by the right name. It is also important to address yourself with the proper level of politeness. Japanese is special in that there are so many ways of saying the simple words, "I" and "you". We will go over some of ways to refer to yourself and others.

Referring to yourself

Vocabulary

- 名前 【な・まえ】 - name

There are many ways to say "I" in Japanese. Some of these words are not as common and others are hopelessly outdated. We will go over the most common ones that are in use today. The usages of all the different words for "I" is separated into two categories: gender and politeness. In other words, there are words that are usually used by males and words that are usually only used by females and they all depend on the social context.

Before going into this: a note about the word 「私」. The official reading of the kanji is 「わたくし」. This is the reading you is used in a formal context (for example, a speech by the president of a company). This reading will probably be accompanied with honorific and humble forms, which we will cover later. In all other situations, it is usually read as 「わたし」. This is the most generic reference to "I" in terms of politeness and gender; therefore it is usually one of the first words taught to students of Japanese.

Here is a list of the most common words for "I" and how they are used:

1. 私【わたくし】 - Used by both males and females for formal situations.
2. 私【わたし】 - Used by both males and females for normal polite situations.
3. 僕【ぼく】 - Used primarily by males from fairly polite to fairly casual situations.
4. 俺【おれ】 - A very rough version of "I" used almost exclusively by males in very casual situations.
5. あたし - A very feminine and casual way to refer to oneself. Many girls have decided to opt for 「わたし」 instead because 「あたし」 has a cutesy and girly sound.
6. One's own name - Also a very feminine and kind of childish way to refer to oneself.
7. わし - Usually used by older men well in their middle-ages.

Let's see how different types of sentences use the appropriate version of "I". 「わたくし」 is left out because we have yet to go over very formal grammatical expressions.

1. 私の名前はキムです。
   My name is Kim. (Neutral, polite)
2. 僕の名前はキムです。
   My name is Kim. (Masculine, polite)
3. 僕の名前はボブだ。
   My name is Bob. (Masculine, casual)
4. 俺の名前はボブだ。
   My name is Bob. (Masculine, casual)
5. あたしの名前はアリス。
   My name is Alice. (Feminine, casual)

Referring to others by name

Vocabulary

1. 社長 【しゃ・ちょう】 - company president
2. 課長 【か・ちょう】 - section manager
3. 先生 【せん・せい】 - teacher
4. 田中 【た・なか】 - Tanaka (last name)

Japanese does not require the use of "you" nearly as much as English does. I hope that the examples with Bob, Alice, and Jim have shown that people refer to other people by their names even when they are directly addressing that person. Another common way to address people is by their title such as 「社長」、「課長」、「先生」, etc. The word 「先生」 is used to generally mean any person who has significant knowledge and expertise in something. For example, people usually use 「先生」 when directly addressing doctors or teachers (obviously). You can also include the person's last name such as 「田中先生」 (teacher Tanaka). In the case where your relationship with the person doesn't involve any title, you can use their name (usually their last name) attached with

「さん」 to show politeness. If calling them by their last name

seems a little too polite and distant, the practice of attaching 「さ
ん」 to their first name also exists. More endearing and colloquial
versions of 「さん」 include 「くん」 and 「ちゃん」. 「くん」 is
usually attached to the name of males who are of equal or lower
social position. (For example, my boss sometimes calls me 「キムく
ん」). 「ちゃん」 is a very endearing way to refer to usually
females of equal or lower social position.

Referring to others with "you"

Please do not use 「あなた」 just like you would use the word "you"
in English. In directly addressing people, there are three levels of
politeness: 1) Using the person's name with the appropriate suffix, 2)
Not using anything at all, 3) Using 「あなた」. In fact, by the time
you get to three, you're dangerously in the area of being rude. Most
of the time, you do not need to use anything at all because you are
directly addressing the person. Constantly pounding the listener with
"you" every sentence sounds like you are accusing the person of
something.

「あなた」 is also an old-fashioned way for women to refer to their
husband or lover. Unless you are a middle-aged women with a
Japanese husband, I doubt you will be using 「あなた」 in this
fashion as well.

Here is a list of some words meaning "you" in English. You will rarely
need to use any of these words, especially the ones in the second
half of the list.

1. あなた - Generally only used when there is no way to physically
   address the person or know the person's name. For example,
   direct questions to the reader on a form that the reader must fill
   out would use 「あなた」.

2. 君【きみ】 - Can be a very close and assuming way to address girls (especially by guys). Can also be kind of rude.
3. お前【お・まえ】 - A very rough and coarse way to address someone. Usually used by guys and often changed to 「おめえ」.
4. あんた - A very assuming and familiar way to address someone. The person using this is maybe miffed off about something.
5. 手前【て・めえ】 - Very rude. Like 「お前」, to add extra punch, people will usually say it like, 「てめ〜〜」. Sounds like you want to beat someone up. I've only seen this one used in movies and comic books. In fact, if you try this on your friends, they will probably laugh at you and tell you that you've probably been reading too many comic books.
6. 貴様【き・さま】 - Very, very rude. Sounds like you want to take someone out. I've also only seen this one used in comic books. I only go over it so you can understand and enjoy comic books yourself!

Referring to others in third person

Vocabulary

1. 彼 【かれ】 - he; boyfriend
2. 彼女 【かの・じょ】 - she; girlfriend
3. ガールフレンド - girlfriend
4. ボーイフレンド - boyfriend

You can use 「彼」 and 「彼女」 for "he" and "she" respectively. Notice that 「彼」 and 「彼女」 can also mean "boyfriend" and "girlfriend". So how can you tell which meaning is being used? Context, of course. For example, if someone asks, 「彼女ですか？」 the person is obviously asking if she is your girlfriend because the question, "Is she she?" doesn't make any sense. Another less commonly used alternative is to say 「ガールフレンド」 and 「ボーイフレンド」 for, well, I'm sure you can guess what they mean.

Referring to family members

1. 母 【はは】 - mother
2. お母さん 【お・かあ・さん】 - mother (polite)
3. 両親 【りょう・しん】 - parents
4. 父 【ちち】 - father
5. お父さん 【お・とう・さん】 - father (polite)
6. 妻 【つま】 - wife
7. 奥さん 【おく・さん】 - wife (polite)
8. 夫 【おっと】 - husband
9. 主人 【しゅ・じん】 - husband
10. 姉 【あね】 - older sister
11. お姉さん 【お・ねえ・さん】 - older sister (polite)
12. 兄 【あに】 - older brother
13. お兄さん 【お・にい・さん】 - older brother (polite)
14. 妹 【いもうと】 - younger sister
15. 弟 【おとうと】 - younger brother
16. 息子 【むす・こ】 - son
17. 娘 【むすめ】 - daughter

Referring to family members is a little more complicated than English. (It could be worse, try learning Korean!) For the purpose of brevity, (since this *is* a grammar guide and not a vocabulary guide) we will only go over the immediate family. In Japanese, you refer to members of other people's family more politely than your own. This is only when you are talking about members of your own family to others <u>outside the family</u>. For example, you would refer to your own mother as 「母」 to people outside your family but you might very well call her 「お母さん」 at home within your own family. There is also a distinction between older and younger siblings. The following chart list some of the most common terms for family members. There may also be other possibilities not covered in this chart.

Family member chart

	One's own family	Someone else's family
Parents	両親	ご両親
Mother	母	お母さん
Father	父	お父さん
Wife	妻	奥さん
Husband	夫	ご主人
Older Sister	姉	お姉さん
Older Brother	兄	お兄さん
Younger Sister	妹	妹さん
Younger Brother	弟	弟さん
Son	息子	息子さん
Daughter	娘	娘さん

Another word for wife, 「家内」 is often considered politically incorrect because the kanji used are "house" and "inside" which implies that wives belong in the home. Amen. (Just kidding)

The Question Marker

Questions in polite form

Vocabulary

1. 田中 【た・なか】 - Tanaka (last name)
2. お母さん 【お・かあ・さん】 - mother (polite)
3. どこ - where
4. 鈴木 【すず・き】 - Suzuki (last name)
5. 母 【はは】 - mother
6. 買い物 【か・い・もの】 - shopping
7. 行く 【い・く】 (u-verb) - to go
8. イタリア - Italy
9. 料理 【りょう・り】 - cooking; cuisine; dish
10. 食べる 【た・べる】 (ru-verb) - to eat
11. すみません - sorry (polite)
12. ちょっと - a little
13. お腹 【お・なか】 - stomach
14. いっぱい - full
15. ごめんなさい - sorry (polite)
16. ごめん - sorry

The question marker is covered here because it is primarily used to clearly indicate a question in polite sentences. While it is entirely possible to express a question even in polite form using just intonation, the question marker is often attached to the very end of the sentence to indicate a question. The question marker is simply the hiragana character 「か」 and you don't need to add a question mark. For previously explained reasons, you must not use the declarative 「だ」 with the question marker.

Example 1

田中さん：お母さんはどこです<u>か</u>。
Tanaka-san: Where is (your) mother?

鈴木さん：母は買い物に行きました。
Suzuki-san: (My) mother went shopping.

Example 2

キムさん：イタリア料理を食べに行きません<u>か</u>。
Kim-san: Go to eat Italian food?

鈴木さん：すみません。ちょっと、お腹がいっぱいです。
Suzuki-san: Sorry. (My) stomach is a little full.

Here the question is actually being used as an invitation just like how in English we say, "Won't you come in for a drink?" 「すみません」 is a polite way of apologizing. Slightly less formal is 「ごめんなさい」 while the casual version is simply 「ごめん」.

The question marker in casual speech

Vocabulary

1. こんな - this sort of
2. 本当 【ほん・とう】 - real
3. 食べる 【た・べる】 (ru-verb) - to eat
4. そんな - that sort of
5. ある (u-verb) - to exist (inanimate)

It makes sense to conclude that the question marker would work in exactly the same way in casual speech as it does in polite speech.

However, this is **not** the case. The question marker 「か」 is usually not used with casual speech to make actual questions. It is often used to consider whether something is true or not. Depending on the context and intonation, it can also be used to make rhetorical questions or to express sarcasm. It can sound quite rough so you might want to be careful about using 「か」 for questions in the plain casual form.

Examples

1. こんなのを本当に食べるか?
   Do you think [he/she] will really eat this type of thing?
2. そんなのは、あるかよ！
   Do I look like I would have something like that?!

Instead of 「か」, real questions in casual speech are usually asked with the explanatory の particle or nothing at all except for a rise in intonation, as we have already seen in previous sections.

1. こんなのを本当に食べる？
   Are you really going to eat something like this?
2. そんなのは、あるの?
   Do you have something like that?

「か」 used in relative clauses

Vocabulary

1. 昨日 【きのう】 - yesterday
2. 何 【なに】 - what
3. 食べる 【た・べる】 (ru-verb) - to eat
4. 忘れる 【わす・れる】 (ru-verb) - to forget
5. 彼 【かれ】 - he; boyfriend

6. 言う 【い・う】 (u-verb) - to say
7. 分かる 【わ・かる】 (u-verb) - to understand
8. 先生 【せん・せい】 - teacher
9. 学校 【がっ・こう】 - school
10. 行く 【い・く】 (u-verb) - to go
11. 教える 【おし・える】 (ru-verb) - to teach; to inform
12. どう - how
13. 知る 【し・る】 (u-verb) - to know

Another use of the question marker is simply grammatical and has nothing to do with the politeness. A question marker attached to the end of a relative clause makes a mini-question inside a larger sentence. This allows the speaker to talk about the question. For example, you can talk about the question, "What did I eat today?" In the following examples, the question that is being considered is in red.

1. 昨日何を食べたか忘れた。
   Forgot what I ate yesterday.

2. 彼は何を言ったか分からない。
   Don't understand what he said.

3. 先生が学校に行ったか教えない？
   Won't you inform me whether teacher went to school?

In sentences like example 3 where the question being considered has a yes/no answer, it is common (but not necessary) to attach 「どうか」. This is roughly equivalent to saying, "whether or not" in English. You can also include the alternative as well to mean the same thing.

1. 先生が学校に行ったかどうか知らない。
   Don't know whether or not teacher went to school.

2. 先生が学校に行ったか行かなかったか知らない。
   Don't know whether teacher went to school or didn't.

Using question words

Vocabulary

1. おいしい (i-adj) - tasty
2. クッキー - cookie
3. 全部 【ぜん・ぶ】 - everything
4. 食べる 【た・べる】 (ru-verb) - to eat
5. 誰 【だれ】 - who
6. 盗む 【ぬす・む】 (u-verb) - to steal
7. 知る 【し・る】 (u-verb) - to know
8. 犯人 【はん・にん】 - criminal
9. 見る 【み・る】 (ru-verb) - to see
10. この - this (abbr. of これの)
11. 中 【なか】 - inside
12. 〜から (particle) - from ~
13. 選ぶ 【えら・ぶ】 (u-verb) - to select

While we're on the topic of questions, this is a good time to go over question words (where, who, what, etc.) and what they mean in various contexts. Take a look at what adding the question marker does to the meaning of the words.

Question Words

Word+Question Marker	Meaning
誰か	Someone
何か	Something
いつか	Sometime
どこか	Somewhere
どれか	A certain one from many

Examples

As you can see by the following examples, you can treat these words just like any regular nouns.

1. 誰かがおいしいクッキーを全部食べた。
   Someone ate all the delicious cookies.
2. 誰が盗んだのか、誰か知りませんか。
   Doesn't anybody know who stole it?
3. 犯人をどこかで見ましたか。
   Did you see the criminal somewhere?
4. この中からどれかを選ぶの。
   (Explaining) You are to select a certain one from inside this (selection).

Question words with inclusive meaning

Vocabulary

1. 全部 【ぜん・ぶ】 - everything
2. 皆 【みんな】 - everybody
3. 皆さん 【みな・さん】 - everybody (polite)
4. この - this （abbr. of これの）
5. 質問 【しつ・もん】 - question
6. 答え 【こた・え】 - answer
7. 知る 【し・る】 (u-verb) - to know
8. 友達 【とも・だち】 - friend
9. 遅れる 【おく・れる】 (ru-verb) - to be late
10. ここ - here
11. ある (u-verb) - to exist (inanimate)
12. レストラン - restaurant
13. おいしい (i-adj) - tasty
14. 今週末 【こん・しゅう・まつ】 - this weekend
15. 行く 【い・く】 (u-verb) - to go

The same question words in the chart above can be combined with 「も」 in a negative sentence to mean "nobody" （誰も）, "nothing" （何も）, "nowhere" （どこも）, etc.

「誰も」 and 「何も」 are primarily used only for negative sentences. Curiously, there is no way to say "everything" with question words. Instead, it is conventional to use other words like 「全部」. And although 「誰も」 can sometimes be used to mean "everybody", it is customary to use 「皆」 or 「皆さん」

The remaining three words 「いつも」 (meaning "always") and 「どれも」 (meaning "any and all"), and 「どこも」 (meaning everywhere) can be used in both negative and positive sentences.

Inclusive Words

Word+も	Meaning
誰も	Everybody/Nobody
何も	Nothing (negative only)
いつも	Always
どこも	Everywhere
どれも	Any and all

Examples

1. この質問の答えは、誰も知らない。
   Nobody knows the answer of this question.
2. 友達はいつも遅れる。
   Friend is always late.
3. ここにあるレストランはどれもおいしくない。
   Any and all restaurants that are here are not tasty.
4. 今週末は、どこにも行かなかった。
   Went nowhere this weekend.

(Grammatically, this 「も」 is the same as the topic particle 「も」 so the target particle 「に」 must go before the topic particle 「も」 in ordering.)

Question words to mean "any"

Vocabulary

1. この - this   (abbr. of これの）
2. 質問 【しつ・もん】 - question
3. 答え 【こた・え】 - answer
4. 分かる 【わ・かる】 (u-verb) - to understand
5. 昼ご飯 【ひる・ご・はん】 - lunch
6. いい (i-adj) - good
7. あの - that (over there)   (abbr. of あれの）
8. 人 【ひと】 - person
9. 本当 【ほん・とう】 - real
10. 食べる 【た・べる】 (ru-verb) - to eat

The same question words combined with 「でも」 can be used to mean "any". One thing to be careful about is that 「何でも」 is read as 「なんでも」 and *not* 「なにでも」

Words for "Any"

Word+でも	Meaning
誰でも	Anybody
何でも	Anything
いつでも	Anytime
どこでも	Anywhere
どれでも	Whichever

Examples

1. この質問の答えは、誰でも分かる。
   Anybody understands the answer of this question.
2. 昼ご飯は、どこでもいいです。
   About lunch, anywhere is good.
3. あの人は、本当に何でも食べる。
   That person really eats anything.

Compound Sentences

In this section, we will learn various ways to combine multiple simple sentences into one complex sentence. For example, we will learn how to chain separate sentences together to express multiple actions or states. In other words, if we have two simple sentences with the same subject, "I ran" and "I ate", we will learn how to group them together to mean, "I ran and ate." We will also learn how to do this with adjectives and nouns. (Ex: He is rich, handsome, and charming.)

Expressing a sequence of states

Vocabulary

1. 一般的 【いっ・ぱん・てき】 - in general
2. 静か 【しず・か】 (na-adj) - quiet
3. 狭い 【せま・い】 (i-adj) - narrow
4. 彼女 【かの・じょ】 - she; girlfriend
5. いい (i-adj) - good
6. 私 【わたし】 - me; myself; I
7. 部屋 【へ・や】 - room
8. きれい (na-adj) - pretty; clean
9. とても - very
10. 好き 【す・き】 (na-adj) - likable; desirable

11. 学生 【がく・せい】 - student
12. 先生 【せん・せい】 - teacher
13. 田中 【た・なか】 - Tanaka (last name)
14. お金持ち 【お・かね・も・ち】 - rich
15. かっこいい (i-adj) - cool; handsome
16. 魅力的 【み・りょく・てき】 - charming

It is very easy to combine a chain of nouns and adjectives to describe a person or object. For example, in English if we wanted to say, "He is X. He is Y. He is Z." since all three sentences have the same noun, we would usually say, "He is X, Y, and Z." In Japanese, we can do the same thing by conjugating the noun or adjective. The last noun or adjective remains the same as before.

How to chain nouns and adjectives together

- **For nouns and na-adjectives:** Attach 「で」 to the noun or na-adjective.
  Examples
  1. 一般的 → 一般的で
  2. 静か → 静かで
- **For i-adjectives and negative noun/adjectives:** Replace the 「い」 with 「くて」.
  ※For 「いい」 and 「かっこいい」, the 「い→よ」 exception applies here as well.
  Examples
  1. 狭い → 狭くて
  2. 彼女じゃない → 彼女じゃなくて
  3. いい → よくて

127

Examples

1. 私の部屋は、きれいで、静かで、とても好き。
My room is clean, quiet, and I like it a lot.
2. 彼女は、学生じゃなくて、先生だ。
She is not a student, she is a teacher.
3. 田中さんは、お金持ちで、かっこよくて、魅力的ですね。
Tanaka-san is rich, handsome, and charming, isn't he?

As you can see, the 「で」 attached to 「お金持ち」 obviously cannot be the context particle 「で」 here because there is no verb. It might be helpful to think of 「で」 as merely a substitution for 「だ」 that can be chained together.

Expressing a sequence of verbs with the te-form

Vocabulary

1. 学生 【がく・せい】 - student
2. 買う 【か・う】 (u-verb) - to buy
3. 食べる 【た・べる】 (ru-verb) - to eat
4. 行く 【い・く】 (u-verb) - to go
5. する (exception) - to do
6. 遊ぶ 【あそ・ぶ】 (u-verb) - to play
7. 飲む 【の・む】 (u-verb) - to drink
8. 食堂 【しょく・どう】 - cafeteria
9. 昼ご飯 【ひる・ご・はん】 - lunch
10. 昼寝 【ひる・ね】 - afternoon nap
11. 時間 【じ・かん】 - time
12. ある (u-verb) - to exist (inanimate)
13. 映画 【えい・が】 - movie
14. 見る 【み・る】 (ru-verb) - to see

In a similar fashion, you can express multiple actions. It is usually interpreted as a sequence of event. (I did [X], then I did [Y], then I finally did [Z].) There are two forms: positive and negative. The tense of all the actions is determined by the tense of the last verb.

How to chain verbs together

- **Positive:** Conjugate the verb to its past tense and replace 「た」 with 「て」 or 「だ」 with 「で」. This is often called the *te-form* even though it could sometimes be 'de'.

- **Negative:** Same as i-adjectives, replace 「い」 with 「くて」.

  This rule also works for the polite 「です」 and 「ます」 endings.

  Examples
    1. 学生です → 学生でした → 学生でして
    2. 買います → 買いました → 買いまして

Sample conjugations

Past Tense	Te-form	Negative	Te-form
食べた	食べて	食べない	食べな くて
行った	行って	行かない	行かな くて
した	して	しない	しなくて
遊んだ	遊んで	遊ばない	遊ばな くて
飲んだ	飲んで	飲まない	飲まな くて

Examples

1. 食堂に行って、昼ご飯を食べて、昼寝をする。
   I will go to cafeteria, eat lunch, and take a nap.

2. 食堂に行って、昼ご飯を食べて、昼寝をした。
   I went to cafeteria, ate lunch, and took a nap.

3. 時間がありまして、映画を見ました。
   There was time and I watched a movie.

Expressing reason or causation using 「から」 and 「ので」

Vocabulary

1. 時間 【じ・かん】 - time
2. ある (u-verb) - to exist (inanimate)
3. パーティー - party
4. 行く 【い・く】 (u-verb) - to go
5. 友達 【とも・だち】 - friend
6. プレゼント - present
7. 来る 【く・る】 (exception) - to come
8. 田中 【た・なか】 - Tanaka (last name)
9. どうして - why
10. 山田 【や・まだ】 - Yamada (last name)
11. 一郎 【いち・ろう】 - Ichirou (first name)
12. 直子 【なお・こ】 - Naoko (first name)
13. ちょっと - a little
14. 忙しい 【いそが・しい】 (i-adj) - busy
15. そろそろ - gradually; soon
16. 失礼 【しつ・れい】 - discourtesy
17. する (exception) - to do
18. 学生 【がく・せい】 - student
19. お金 【お・かね】 - money
20. ここ - here
21. 静か 【しず・か】 (na-adj) - quiet
22. とても - very
23. 穏やか 【おだ・やか】 (na-adj) - calm, peaceful
24. 会う 【あ・う】 (u-verb) - to meet

You can connect two complete sentences using 「から」 to indicate a reason for something. The two sentences are always ordered [reason] から [result]. When the reason is a non-conjugated noun or na-adjective, you must add 「だ」 to explicitly declare the reason in the form of 「(noun/na-adjective)だから」 . If you forget to add the declarative 「だ」 to 「から」 , it will end up sounding like the 「か

ら」 meaning "from" which was first introduced in the section on particles, earlier.

Examples

1. 時間がなかったからパーティーに行きませんでした。
   There was no time so didn't go to party.
2. 友達からプレゼントが来た。
   Present came from friend.
3. 友達だからプレゼントが来た。
   Present came because (the person is) friend. (This sentence sounds a bit odd.)

Either the reason or the result can be omitted if it is clear from the context. In the case of polite speech, you would treat 「から」 just like a regular noun and add 「です」.

Example 1

田中さん：どうしてパーティーに行きませんでしたか。
Tanaka-san: Why didn't you go to the party?

山田さん：時間がなかったからです。
Yamada-san: It's because I didn't have time.

Example 2

一郎: パーティーに行かなかったの？
Ichiro: You didn't go to the party?

直子: うん、時間がなかったから。
Naoko: Yeah, because I didn't have time.

Example 3

When you omit the reason, you must include the declarative 「だ」 or 「です」.

直子: 時間がなかった。
Naoko: I didn't have time.

一郎: だからパーティーに行かなかったの？
Ichiro: Is that why you didn't go to the party?

Notice that we could have also used the explanatory 「の」 to express the same thing. In other words, 山田さん could have also said, 「時間がなかったのです」 or 「時間がなかったんです」 while 直子 could have said 「時間がなかったの」 (we'll assume she wants to use the more feminine form). In fact, this is where 「ので」 possibly came from. Let's say you want to combine two sentences: 「時間がなかったのだ」 and 「パーティーに行かなかった」. Remember we can treat the 「の」 just like a noun so we can use what we just learned in the first section of this lesson.

時間がなかったのだ＋パーティーに行かなかった
becomes:

時間がなかったのでパーティーに行かなかった。

In fact, 「ので」 is almost interchangeable with 「から」 with a few subtle differences. 「から」 explicitly states that the sentence preceding is the reason for something while 「ので」 is merely putting two sentences together, the first with an explanatory tone. This is something I call causation where [X] happened, therefore [Y] happened. This is slightly different from 「から」 where [Y] happened explicitly *because* [X] happened. This difference tends to make 「ので」 sound softer and slightly more polite and it is favored over 「から」 when explaining a reason for doing something that is considered discourteous.

- ちょっと忙しいので、そろそろ失礼します。
  Because I'm a little busy, I'll be making my leave soon.

(「失礼します」, which literally means "I'm doing a discourtesy", is commonly used as a polite way to make your leave or disturb someone's time.)

Reminder: Don't forget that the explanatory 「の」 requires a 「な」 for both non-conjugated nouns and na-adjectives. Review Particles 3 to see why.

1. 私は学生なので、お金がないんです。
   Because I'm a student, I have no money (lit: there is no money).
2. ここは静かなので、とても穏やかです。
   It is very calm here because it is quiet.
3. なので、友達に会う時間がない。
   That's why there's no time to meet friend.

Just like how the explanatory 「の」 can be shortened to 「ん」, in speech, the 「ので」 can be changed to 「んで」 simply because it's easier to slur the sounds together rather than pronouncing the / o / syllable.

1. 時間がなかったんでパーティーに行かなかった。
   Didn't go to the party because there was no time.
2. ここは静かなんで、とても穏やかです。
   It is very calm here because it is quiet.
3. なんで、友達に会う時間がない。
   That's why there's no time to meet friend.

Using 「のに」 to mean "despite"

Vocabulary

1. 毎日 【まい・にち】 - everyday
2. 運動 【うん・どう】 - exercise
3. する (exception) - to do
4. 全然 【ぜん・ぜん】 - not at all (when used with negative)
5. 痩せる 【や・せる】 (ru-verb) - to become thin
6. 学生 【がく・せい】 - student
7. 彼女 【かの・じょ】 - she; girlfriend
8. 勉強 【べん・きょう】 - study

Grammatically, 「のに」 is used exactly the same way as 「ので」. When used to combine two simple sentences together, it means " [Sentence 1] despite the fact that [Sentence 2]." However the order is reversed: [Sentence 2]のに[Sentence 1].

Examples

1. 毎日運動したのに、全然痩せなかった。
   Despite exercising every day, I didn't get thinner.
2. 学生なのに、彼女は勉強しない。
   Despite being a student, she does not study.

Expressing contradiction using 「が」 and 「けど」

Vocabulary

1. デパート - department store
2. 行く 【い・く】 (u-verb) - to go

3. 何 【なに／なん】 - what
4. 全然 【ぜん・ぜん】 - not at all (when used with negative)
5. 欲しい 【ほ・しい】 (i-adj) - desirable
6. 友達 【とも・だち】 - friend
7. 聞く 【き・く】 (u-verb) - to ask; to listen
8. 知る 【し・る】 (u-verb) - to know
9. 今日 【きょう】 - today
10. 暇 【ひま】 - free (as in not busy)
11. 明日 【あした】 - tomorrow
12. 忙しい 【いそが・しい】 (i-adj) - busy
13. 彼 【かれ】 - he; boyfriend
14. まだ - yet
15. 好き 【す・き】 (na-adj) - likable; desirable
16. いい (i-adj) - good
17. 物 【もの】 - object
18. たくさん - a lot (amount)
19. ある (u-verb) - to exist (inanimate)
20. 見る 【み・る】 (ru-verb) - to see
21. 面白い 【おも・しろ・い】 (i-adj) - interesting

Used in the same manner as 「から」 and 「ので」, 「が」 and
「けど」 also connect two sentences together but this time to
express a contradiction. Just like 「から」 the declarative 「だ」 is
required for nouns and na-adjectives. And just like 「から」 and
「ので」, either part of the contradiction can be left out.

Examples

1. デパートに行きましたが、何も欲しくなかったです。
   I went to department store but there was nothing I wanted.
2. 友達に聞いたけど、知らなかった。
   I asked (or heard from) a friend but he (or I) didn't know.
3. 今日は暇だけど、明日は忙しい。
   I'm free today but I will be busy tomorrow.

4. だけど、彼がまだ好きなの。
   That may be so, but it is that I still like him. [explanation, feminine tone]

It may seem odd but 「聞く」 can either mean "to listen" or "to ask". You may think this may become confusing but the meaning is usually clear within context. In the second example, we're assuming that the friend didn't know, so the speaker was probably asking the friend. Yet again we see the importance of context in Japanese because this sentence can also mean, "I heard from a friend but I didn't know" since there is neither subject nor topic.

Similar to the difference between 「から」 and 「ので」, 「が」 has a softer tone and is slightly more polite than 「けど」. Though this isn't a rule as such, it is generally common to see 「が」 attached to a 「〜ます」 or 「〜です」 ending and 「けど」 attached to a regular, plain ending. A more formal version of 「けど」 is 「けれど」 and even more formal is 「けれども」, which we may see later when we cover formal expressions.

Unlike the English word for contradiction such as "but" or "however", 「けど」 and 「が」 do not always express a direct contradiction. Often times, especially when introducing a new topic, it is used as a general connector of two separate sentences. For example, in the following sentences, there is no actual contradiction but 「が」 and 「けど」 are used simply to connect the sentences. Sometimes, the English "and" becomes a closer translation than "but".

1. デパートに行きましたが、いい物がたくさんありました。
   I went to the department store and there was a lot of good stuff.
2. マトリックスを見たけど、面白かった。
   I watched the "Matrix" and it was interesting.

Expressing multiple reasons using 「し」

Vocabulary

1. どうして - why
2. 友達 【とも・だち】 - friend
3. 先生 【せん・せい】 - teacher
4. 年上 【とし・うえ】 - older
5. 彼 【かれ】 - he; boyfriend
6. 好き 【す・き】 (na-adj) - likable
7. 優しい 【やさ・しい】 (i-adj) - gentle; kind
8. かっこいい (i-adj) - cool; handsome
9. 面白い 【おも・し・ろい】 (i-adj) - interesting

When you want to list reasons for multiple states or actions you can do so by adding 「し」 to the end of each relative clause. It is very similar to the 「や」 particle except that it lists reasons for verbs and state-of-being. Again, for states of being, 「だ」 must be used to explicitly declare the state-of-being for any non-conjugated noun or na-adjective. Let's look at some examples.

Example 1

A: どうして友達じゃないんですか？
A: Why isn't (he/she) friend [seeking explanation]?

B: 先生だし、年上だし・・・。
B: Well, he's/she's the teacher, and older...

Example 2

A: どうして彼が好きなの？
A: Why (do you) like him?

B: 優しいし、かっこいいし、面白いから。
B: Because he's kind, attractive, and interesting (among other

things).

Notice that 「優しくて、かっこよくて、面白いから。」 could also have worked but much like the difference between the 「と」 and 「や」 particle, 「し」 implies that there may be other reasons.

Expressing multiple actions or states using 「〜たりする」

Vocabulary

1. する (exception) - to do
2. 食べる 【た・べる】 (ru-verb) - to eat
3. 飲む 【の・む】 (u-verb) - to drink
4. 簡単 【かん・たん】 (na-adj) - simple
5. 難しい 【むずか・しい】 (i-adj) - difficult
6. 映画 【えい・が】 - movie
7. 見る 【み・る】 (ru-verb) - to see
8. 本 【ほん】 - book
9. 読む 【よ・む】 (u-verb) - to read
10. 昼寝 【ひる・ね】 - afternoon nap
11. この - this (abbr. of これの)
12. 大学 【だい・がく】 - college
13. 授業 【じゅ・ぎょう】 - class

This is the verb version of the 「や」 particle. You can make an example list of verbs among a possible larger list by conjugating each verb into the past tense and adding 「り」. At the end, you need to attach the verb 「する」. Just like the 「や」 particle, the tense is determined by the last verb, which in this case will always be 「する」 (since you have to attach it at the end).

You can also use this with the state-of-being to say that you are a number of things at various random times among a larger list. Similar to regular verbs, you just take the noun or adjective for each state-of-being and conjugate it to the past state-of-being and then attach 「り」. Then finally, attach 「する」 at the end.

Rules for stating a list of verbs among a larger list using 「～たりする」

- **For verbs:** Conjugate each verb to the past tense and add 「り」. Finally, add 「する」 at the very end.
  Example
  食べる、飲む → 食べた、飲んだ → 食べたり、飲んだり → 食べたり、飲んだりする
- **For state-of-being:** Conjugate the noun or adjective for each state-of-being to the past tense and add 「り」.
  Finally, add 「する」 at the very end.
  Example
  簡単、難しい → 簡単だった、難しかった → 簡単だったり、難しかったり → 簡単だったり、難しかったりする

---

1. 映画を見たり、本を読んだり、昼寝したりする。
   I do things like (among other things) watch movies, read books, and take naps.
2. この大学の授業は簡単だったり、難しかったりする。
   Class of this college is sometimes easy, sometimes difficult (and other times something else maybe).

As you can see, the tense and negative/positive state is controlled by the last 「する」.

1. 映画を見たり、本を読んだりした。
   I <u>did</u> things like (among other things) watch movies, and read books.
2. 映画を見たり、本を読んだりしない。
   I <u>don't do</u> things like (among other things) watch movies, and read books.
3. 映画を見たり、本を読んだりしなかった。
   I <u>didn't do</u> things like (among other things) watch movies, and read books.

Other uses of the te-form

The te-form is incredibly useful as it is used widely in many different types of grammatical expressions. We will learn about enduring states with the 「〜ている」 and 「〜てある」 form. Even though we have learned various conjugations for verbs, they have all been one-time actions. We will now go over how one would say, for example, "I <u>am</u> running." We will also learn how to perform an action for the future using the 「〜ておく」 expression and to express directions of actions using 「〜ていく」 and 「〜てくる」.

Using 「〜ている」 for enduring states

Vocabulary

1. 食べる 【た・べる】 (ru-verb) - to eat
2. 読む 【よ・む】 (u-verb) - to read
3. 友達 【とも・だち】 - friend
4. 何【なに】 - what
5. する (exception) - to do
6. 昼ご飯 【ひる・ご・はん】 - lunch
7. 教科書 【きょう・か・しょ】 - textbook

8. 話 【はなし】 - story
9. 聞く 【き・く】 (u-verb) - to ask; to listen
10. ううん - casual word for "no" (nah, uh-uh)

We already know how to express a state-of-being using 「です」, 「だ」, etc. However, it only indicates a one-time thing; you are something or not. This grammar, however, describes a continuing state of an action verb. This usually translates to the progressive form in English except for a few exceptions, which we will examine later. We can make good use of the te-form we learned in the last section because the only thing left to do is add 「いる」! You can then treat the result as a regular ru-verb.

This 「いる」 is the same ru-verb describing existence, first described in the negative verb section. However, in this case, you don't have to worry about whether the subject is animate or inanimate.

Using 「〜ている」 for enduring states

To describe a continuing action, first conjugate the verb to the te-form and then attach the verb 「いる」. The entire result conjugates as a ru-verb.
Examples

1. 食べる → 食べて → 食べている
2. 読む → 読んで → 読んでいる

The result conjugates as a ru-verb regardless of what the original verb is

	Positive		Negative	
Non-Past	読んでいる	reading	読んでいない	is not reading
Past	読んでいた	was reading	読んでいなかった	was not reading

Example 1

Ａ：友達は何をしているの？
A: What is friend doing?

Ｂ：昼ご飯を食べている。
B: (Friend) is eating lunch.

Note that once you've changed it into a regular ru-verb, you can do all the normal conjugations. The examples below show the masu-form and plain negative conjugations.

Example 2

Ａ：何を読んでいる?
A: What are you reading?

143

Ｂ：　教科書を読ん<u>でいます</u>。
B: I am reading textbook.

Example 3

Ａ：　話を聞い<u>ていますか</u>。
A: Are you listening to me? (lit: Are you listening to story?)

Ｂ：　ううん、聞い<u>ていない</u>。
B: No, I'm not listening.

Since people are usually too lazy to roll their tongues to properly pronounce the 「い」, it is often omitted in conversational Japanese. If you are writing an essay or paper, you should always include the 「い」. Here are the abbreviated versions of the previous examples.

Example 4

Ａ：　友達は何を<u>してる</u>の？
A: What is friend doing?

Ｂ：　昼ご飯を食べ<u>てる</u>。
B: (Friend) is eating lunch.

Example 5

Ａ：　何を読ん<u>でる</u>?
A: What are you reading?

Ｂ：　教科書を読ん<u>でいます</u>。
B: I am reading textbook.

Example 6

A：話を聞いて<u>いますか</u>。
A: Are you listening to me? (lit: Are you listening to story?)

B：ううん、聞い<u>てない</u>。
B: No, I'm not listening.

Notice how I left the 「い」 alone for the polite forms. Though people certainly omit the 「い」 even in polite form, you might want to get used to the proper way of saying things first before getting carried away with casual abbreviations. You will be amazed at the extensive types of abbreviations that exist in casual speech. (You may also be amazed at how long everything gets in super polite speech.) Basically, you will get the abbreviations if you just act lazy and slur everything together. Particles also get punted off left and right.

For example:

1. 何をしているの？(Those particles are such a pain to say all the time...)
2. 何しているの？(Ugh, I hate having to spell out all the vowels.)
3. 何してんの？(Ah, perfect.)

Enduring state-of-being vs enduring state of action

Vocabulary

1. 知る 【し・る】 (u-verb) - to know
2. 分かる 【わ・かる】 (u-verb) - to understand
3. 今日 【きょう】 - today
4. この - this (abbr. of これの)
5. 歌 【うた】 - song

6. 道 【みち】 - road

7. はい - yes (polite)

There are certain cases where an enduring state doesn't translate into the progressive form. In fact, there is an ambiguity in whether one is in a state of *doing* an action versus being in a state that *resulted* from some action. This is usually decided by context and common practices. For example, although 「結婚している」 can technically mean someone is in a chapel currently getting married, it is usually used to refer to someone who is already married and is currently in that married state. We'll now discuss some common verbs that often cause this type of confusion for learners of Japanese.

「知る」

「知る」 means "to know". English is weird in that "know" is supposed to be a verb but is actually describing a state of having knowledge. Japanese is more consistent and 「知る」 is just a regular action verb. In other words, I "knowed" (action) something and so now I know it (state). That's why the English word "to know" is really a continuing state in Japanese, namely: 「知っている」.

「知る」 vs 「分かる」

「分かる」 meaning "to understand" may seem similar to 「知る」 in some cases. However, there is a difference between "knowing" and "understanding". Try not to confuse 「知っている」 with 「分かっている」. 「分かっている」 means that you are already in a state of understanding, in other words, you already get it. If you misuse this, you may sound pompous. ("Yeah, yeah, I got it already.") On the other hand, 「知っている」 simply means you know something.

146

Examples

1. 今日、知りました。
   I found out about it today. (I did the action of knowing today.)
2. この歌を知っていますか？
   Do (you) know this song?
3. 道は分かりますか。
   Do you know the way? (lit: Do (you) understand the road?)
4. はい、はい、分かった、分かった。
   Yes, yes, I got it, I got it.

Motion Verbs (行く、来る、etc.)

Vocabulary

1. 鈴木 【すず・き】 - Suzuki (last name)
2. どこ - where
3. もう - already
4. 家 【1) うち; 2) いえ】 - 1) one's own home; 2) house
5. 帰る 【かえ・る】 (u-verb) - to go home
6. 先 【さき】 - before
7. 行く 【い・く】 (u-verb) - to go
8. 美恵 【み・え】 - Mie (first name)
9. 来る 【く・る】 (exception) - to come

It is reasonable to assume the actions 「行っている」 and 「来ている」 would mean, "going" and "coming" respectively. But unfortunately, this is not the case. The 「～ている」 form of motion verbs is more like a sequence of actions we saw in the last section. You completed the motion, and now you exist in that state. (Remember, 「いる」 is the verb of existence of animate objects.) It might help to think of it as two separate and successive actions:

「行って」、and then 「いる」.

Examples

1. 鈴木さんはどこですか。
   Where is Suzuki-san?
2. もう、家に帰っている。
   He is already at home (went home and is there now).
3. 先に行っているよ。
   I'll go on ahead. (I'll go and be there before you.)
4. 美恵ちゃんは、もう来ているよ。
   Mie-chan is already here, you know. (She came and is here.)

Using 「〜てある」 for resultant states

Vocabulary

1. 準備 【じゅん・び】 - preparations
2. どう - how
3. もう - already
4. する (exception) - to do
5. ある (u-verb) - to exist (inanimate)
6. 旅行 【りょ・こう】 - travel
7. 計画 【けい・かく】 - plans
8. 終わる 【お・わる】 (u-verb) - to end
9. うん - casual word for "yes" (yeah, uh-huh)
10. 切符 【きっ・ぷ】 - ticket
11. 買う 【か・う】 (u-verb) - to buy
12. ホテル - hotel
13. 予約 【よ・やく】 - reservation

Appropriately enough, just like there is an 「ある」 to go with 「い
る」, there is a 「〜てある」 form that also has a special meaning.
By replacing 「いる」 with 「ある」, instead of a continuing action,
it becomes a resultant state after the action has already taken place.

148

Usually, this expression is used to explain that something is in a state of completion. The completed action also carries a nuance of being completed in preparation for something else.

Since this grammar describes the state of a completed action, it is common to see the 「は」 and 「も」 particles instead of the 「を」 particle.

Example 1

Ａ: 準備はどうですか。
A: How are the preparations?

Ｂ: 準備は、もうしてあるよ。
B: The preparations are already done.

Example 2

Ａ: 旅行の計画は終わった？
A: Are the plans for the trip complete?

Ｂ: うん、切符を買ったし、ホテルの予約もしてある。
B: Uh huh, not only did I buy the ticket, I also took care of the hotel reservations.

Using the 「〜ておく」 form as preparation for the future

Vocabulary

1. 晩ご飯 【ばん・ご・はん】 - dinner
2. 作る 【つく・る】 (u-verb) - to make
3. 電池 【でん・ち】 - battery

4. 買う 【か・う】 (u-verb) - to buy

While 「～てある」 carries a nuance of a completed action in preparation for something else, 「～ておく」 explicitly states that the action is done (or will be done) with the future in mind. Imagine this: you have made a delicious pie and you're going to *place* it on the window sill for it to cool so that you can eat it later. This image might help explain why the verb 「おく」 （置く）, meaning "to place", can be used to describe a preparation for the future. (It's just too bad that pies on window sills always seem to go through some kind of mishap especially in cartoons.) While 「置く」 by itself is written in kanji, it is customary to use hiragana when it comes attached to a conjugated verb (such as the te-form).

Examples

1. 晩ご飯を作っておく。
   Make dinner (in advance for the future).
2. 電池を買っておきます。
   I'll buy batteries (in advance for the future).

「ておく」 is also sometimes abbreviated to 「～とく」 for convenience.

1. 晩ご飯を作っとく。
   Make dinner (in advance for the future).
2. 電池を買っときます。
   I'll buy batteries (in advance for the future).

Using motion verbs （行く、来る） with the te-form

Vocabulary

1. えんぴつ - pencil
2. 持つ 【も・つ】 (u-verb) - to hold
3. いる (ru-verb) - to exist (animate)
4. 学校 【がっ・こう】 - school
5. 行く 【い・く】 (u-verb) - to go
6. 家 【1) うち; 2) いえ】 - 1) one's own home; 2) house
7. 来る 【く・る】 (exception) - to come
8. お父さん 【お・とう・さん】 - father (polite)
9. 早い 【はや・い】 (i-adj) - fast; early
10. 帰る 【かえ・る】 (u-verb) - to go home
11. 駅 【えき】 - station
12. 方 【ほう】 - direction, way
13. 走る 【はし・る】 (u-verb) - to run
14. 冬 【ふゆ】 - winter
15. 入る 【はい・る】 (u-verb) - to enter
16. コート - coat
17. 着る 【き・る】 (ru-verb) - to wear
18. 増える 【ふ・える】 (ru-verb) - to increase
19. 一生懸命 【いっ・しょう・けん・めい】 - with all one's might
20. 頑張る 【がん・ば・る】 (u-verb) - to try one's best
21. 色々 【いろ・いろ】 (na-adj) - various
22. 人 【ひと】 - person
23. 付き合う 【つ・き・あ・う】 (u-verb) - to go out with; to keep in company with
24. いい (i-adj) - good
25. まだ - yet
26. 見つかる 【み・つかる】 (u-verb) - to be found
27. 日本語 【に・ほん・ご】 - Japanese (language)
28. ずっと - long; far
29. 前 【まえ】 - front; before
30. 勉強 【べん・きょう】 - study
31. する (exception) - to do
32. 結局 【けっ・きょく】 - eventually
33. やめる (ru-verb) - to stop; to quit

You can also use the motion verbs "to go" （行く） and "to come"
（来る） with the te-form, to show that an action is oriented toward
or from someplace. The most common and useful example of this is
the verb 「持つ」 (to hold). While 「持っている」 means you are in
a state of holding something (in possession of), when the 「いる」
is replaced with 「いく」 or 「くる」, it means you are taking or
bringing something. Of course, the conjugation is the same as the
regular 「行く」 and 「来る」.

Examples

1. えんぴつを持っている?
   Do (you) have a pencil?
2. 鉛筆を学校へ持っていく?
   Are (you) taking pencil to school?
3. 鉛筆を家に持ってくる?
   Are (you) bringing pencil to home?

For these examples, it may make more sense to think of them as a
sequence of actions: hold and go, or hold and come. Here are a
couple more examples.

1. お父さんは、早く帰ってきました。
   Father came back home early.
2. 駅の方へ走っていった。
   Went running toward the direction of station.

The motion verbs can also be used in time expressions to move
forward or come up to the present.

1. 冬に入って、コートを着ている人が増えていきます。
   Entering winter, people wearing coat will increase (toward the
   future).

2. 一生懸命、頑張っていく！
   Will try my hardest (toward the future) with all my might!
3. 色々な人と付き合ってきたけど、いい人はまだ見つからない。
   Went out (up to the present) with various types of people but a good person hasn't been found yet.
4. 日本語をずっと前から勉強してきて、結局はやめた。
   Studied Japanese from way back before and eventually quit.

Potential Form

Expressing the ability to do something

In Japanese, the ability to do a certain action is expressed by conjugating the verb rather than adding a word such as the words "can" or "able to" in the case of English. All verbs conjugated into the potential form become a ru-verb.

The Potential Form

Vocabulary

1. 見る 【み・る】 (ru-verb) - to see
2. 遊ぶ 【あそ・ぶ】 (u-verb) - to play
3. する (exception) - to do
4. 来る 【く・る】 (exception) - to come
5. 出来る 【で・き・る】 (ru-verb) - to be able to do
6. 食べる 【た・べる】 (ru-verb) - to eat
7. 着る 【き・る】 (ru-verb) - to wear
8. 信じる 【しん・じる】 (ru-verb) - to believe
9. 寝る 【ね・る】 (ru-verb) - to sleep
10. 起きる 【お・きる】 (ru-verb) - to wake; to occur
11. 出る 【で・る】 (ru-verb) - to come out

12. 掛ける 【か・ける】 (ru-verb) - to hang
13. 調べる 【しら・べる】 (ru-verb) - to investigate
14. 話す 【はな・す】 (u-verb) - to speak
15. 書く 【か・く】 (u-verb) - to write
16. 待つ 【ま・つ】 (u-verb) - to wait
17. 飲む 【の・む】 (u-verb) - to drink
18. 取る 【と・る】 (u-verb) - to take
19. 死ぬ 【し・ぬ】 (u-verb) - to die
20. 買う 【か・う】 (u-verb) - to buy
21. 漢字 【かん・じ】 - Kanji
22. 残念 【ざん・ねん】 (na-adj) - unfortunate
23. 今週末 【こん・しゅう・まつ】 - this weekend
24. 行く 【い・く】 (u-verb) - to go
25. もう - already

Once again, the conjugation rules can be split into three major groups: ru-verbs, u-verbs, and exception verbs. However, the potential form of the verb 「する」 (meaning "to do") is a special exception because it becomes a completely different verb: 「できる」 (出来る）

Rules for creating potential form

- **For ru-verbs:** Replace the 「る」 with 「られる」.
  Example: 見る → 見られる
- **For u-verbs**: Change the last character from a / u / vowel sound to the equivalent / e / vowel sound and add 「る」.
  Example: 遊ぶ → 遊べ → 遊べる
- **Exceptions:**
  1. 「する」 becomes 「できる」

---

2. 「くる」 becomes 「こられる」

※Remember that all potential verbs become ru-verbs.

Plain	Potential	Plain	Potential	Plain	Potential
食べる	食べられる	話す	話せる	する	できる
着る	着られる	書く	書ける	くる	こられる
信じる	信じられる	遊ぶ	遊べる		
寝る	寝られる	待つ	待てる		
起きる	起きられる	飲む	飲める		
出る	出られる	取る	取れる		
掛ける	掛けられる	死ぬ	死ねる		
調べる	調べられる	買う	買える		

It is also possible to just add 「れる」 instead of the full 「られる」 for ru-verbs. For example, 「食べる」 becomes 「食べれる」 instead of 「食べられる」. I suggest learning the official 「られる」 conjugation first because laziness can be a hard habit to break and the shorter version, though common, is considered to be slang.

155

Examples

1. 漢字は書けますか?
   Can you write kanji?
2. 残念だが、今週末は行けない。
   It's unfortunate, but can't go this weekend.
3. もう信じられない。
   I can't believe it already.

Potential forms do not have direct objects

Vocabulary

1. 富士山 【ふ・じ・さん】 - Mt. Fuji
2. 登る 【のぼ・る】 (u-verb) - to climb
3. 重い 【おも・い】 (i-adj) - heavy
4. 荷物 【に・もつ】 - baggage
5. 持つ 【も・つ】 (u-verb) - to hold

The potential form indicates that something is possible but no actual action is actually taken. While the potential form is still a verb, because it is describing the state of feasibility, in general, you don't want to use the direct object 「を」 as you would with the non-potential form of the verb. For example the following sentences sound unnatural.

1. 富士山を登れた。
2. 重い荷物を持てます。

Here are the versions using either 「が」 or 「は」 instead:

1. 富士山が登れた。
   Was able to climb Fuji-san.

2. 重い荷物<u>は</u>持てます。
   Am able to hold heavy baggage.

Are 「見える」 and 「聞こえる」 exceptions?

Vocabulary

1. 見える 【み・える】 (ru-verb) - to be visible
2. 聞こえる 【き・こえる】 (ru-verb) - to be audible
3. 今日 【きょう】 - today
4. 晴れる 【は・れる】 (ru-verb) - to be sunny
5. 富士山 【ふ・じ・さん】 - Mt. Fuji
6. 友達 【とも・だち】 - friend
7. おかげ - thanks to
8. 映画 【えい・が】 - movie
9. ただ - free of charge; only
10. 見る 【み・る】 (ru-verb) - to see
11. こと - event, matter
12. 出来る 【で・き・る】 (ru-verb) - to be able to do
13. 久しぶり 【ひさ・しぶり】 - after a long time
14. 彼 【かれ】 - he; boyfriend
15. 声 【こえ】 - voice
16. 聞く 【き・く】 (u-verb) - to ask; to listen
17. 周り 【まわ・り】 - surroundings
18. うるさい (i-adj) - noisy
19. 言う 【い・う】 (u-verb) - to say
20. あまり／あんまり - not very (when used with negative)

There are two verbs 「見える」 and 「聞こえる」 that mean that
something is visible and audible, respectively. When you want to say
that you can see or hear something, you'll want to use these verbs.
If however, you wanted to say that you were given the opportunity to
see or hear something, you would use the regular potential form.

However, in this case, it is more common to use the type of expression as seen in example 3.

Examples

1. 今日は晴れて、富士山が見える。
   (It) cleared up today and Fuji-san is visible.
2. 友達のおかげで、映画はただで見られた。
   Thanks to (my) friend, (I) was able to watch the movie for free.
3. 友達のおかげで、映画をただで見ることができた。
   Thanks to (my) friend, (I) was able to watch the movie for free.

You can see that example 3 uses the generic noun for an event to say literally, "The event of seeing movie was able to be done." which essentially means the same thing as 「見られる」. You can also just use generic noun substitution to substitute for 「こと」.

1. 友達のおかげで、映画をただで見るのができた。

Here's some more examples using 「聞く」, can you tell the difference? Notice that 「聞こえる」 always means "audible" and never "able to ask".

1. 久しぶりに彼の声が聞けた。
   I was able to hear his voice for the first time in a long time.
2. 周りがうるさくて、彼が言っていることがあんまり聞こえなかった。
   The surroundings were noisy and I couldn't hear what he was saying very well.

「ある」, yet another exception

Vocabulary

1. そんな - that sort of
2. こと - event, matter
3. 有り得る 【あ・り・え・る／あ・り・う・る】 (ru-verb) - to possibly exist
4. 彼 【かれ】 - he; boyfriend
5. 寝坊【ね・ぼう】 - oversleep
6. する (exception) - to do
7. それ - that
8. 話 【はなし】 - story

You can say that something has a possibility of existing by combining 「ある」 and the verb 「得る」 to produce 「あり得る」. This essentially means 「あることができる」 except that nobody actually says that, they just use 「あり得る」. This verb is very curious in that it can be read as either 「ありうる」 or 「ありえる」, *however*, all the other conjugations such as 「ありえない」、「ありえた」、and 「ありえなかった」 only have one possible reading using 「え」.

Examples

1. そんなことはありうる。
   That kind of situation/event is possible (lit: can exist).
2. そんなことはありえる。
   That kind of situation/event is possible (lit: can exist).
3. そんなことはありえない。
   That kind of situation/event is not possible (lit: cannot exist).
4. 彼が寝坊したこともありうるね。
   It's also possible that he overslept. (lit: The event that he overslept also possibly exists.)
5. それは、ありえない話だよ。
   That's an impossible story/scenario. (lit: That story/scenario cannot exist.)

Using する and なる with the に particle

We can use the verbs 「する」 and 「なる」 in conjunction with the 「に」 particle to make various useful expressions. We are used to using the object particle with 「する」 because something is usually done <u>to</u> something else. We will see how the meaning changes when we change the particle to 「に」. As for 「なる」, it is always used with the 「に」 particle because "becoming" is not an action done to something else but rather a target of change. The only grammatical point of interest here is using 「なる」 with i-adjectives and verbs.

Using 「なる」 and 「する」 for nouns and na-adjectives

Vocabulary

1. 彼 【かれ】 - he; boyfriend
2. 日本語 【に・ほん・ご】 - Japanese (language)
3. 上手 【じょう・ず】 (na-adj) - skillful
4. なる (u-verb) - to become
5. 私 【わたし】 - me, myself, I
6. 医者 【い・しゃ】 - doctor
7. 有名 【ゆう・めい】 (na-adj) - famous
8. 人 【ひと】 - person
9. ハンバーガー - hamburger
10. サラダ - salad
11. する (exception) - to do
12. 他 【ほか】 - other
13. いい (i-adj) - good
14. 物 【もの】 - object
15. たくさん - a lot (amount)

160

16. ある (u-verb) - to exist (inanimate)
17. やはり／やっぱり - as I thought
18. これ - this

As already explained, using 「なる」 with nouns and na-adjectives presents nothing new and acts pretty much the way you'd expect.

1. 彼の日本語が上手になった。
   His Japanese has become skillful.

2. 私は医者になった。
   I became a doctor.

3. 私は有名な人になる。
   I will become a famous person.

For adjectives, using the verb 「する」 with the 「に」 particle is just a review back to the lesson on adverbs. However, for nouns, when you use the verb 「する」 with the 「に」 particle, it means that you are going to do things toward something. This changes the meaning of 「する」 to mean, "to decide on [X]". This is a common expression to use, for instance, when you are ordering items on a menu.

1. 私は、ハンバーガーとサラダにします。
   I'll have the hamburger and salad. (lit: I'll do toward hamburger and salad.)

2. 他にいいものがたくさんあるけど、やっぱりこれにする。
   There are a lot of other good things, but as I thought, I'll go with this one.

If you think this expression is strange, think about the English expression, "I'll go with the hamburger." Exactly where are you going with the hamburger?

Using 「なる」 with i-adjectives

Vocabulary

1. 去年 【きょ・ねん】 - last year
2. ～から (particle) - from ~
3. 背 【せ】 - height
4. 高い 【たか・い】 (i-adj) - high; tall; expensive
5. なる (u-verb) - to become
6. 運動 【うん・どう】 - exercise
7. する (exception) - to do
8. ～から (particle) - ~ so
9. 強い 【つよ・い】 (i-adj) - strong
10. 勉強 【べん・きょう】 - study
11. たくさん - a lot (amount)
12. 頭 【あたま】 - head
13. いい (i-adj) - good

Because the 「に」 particle is a target particle that is used for nouns and by extension na-adjectives, we need to use something else to show that something is becoming an i-adjective. Since "becoming" expresses a change in state, it makes sense to describe this process using an adverb. In fact, you'll notice that we were already using adverbs (of a sort) in the previous section by using 「に」 with na-adjectives.

1. 去年から背が高くなったね。
   Your height has gotten taller from last year, huh?

2. 運動しているから、強くなる。
   I will become stronger because I am exercising.

3. 勉強をたくさんしたから、頭がよくなった。
   Since I studied a lot, I became smarter. (lit: head became better)

Using 「なる」 and 「する」 with verbs

Vocabulary

1. 海外 【かい・がい】 - overseas
2. 行く 【い・く】 (u-verb) - to go
3. こと - event, matter
4. なる (u-verb) - to become
5. 毎日 【まい・にち】 - everyday
6. 肉 【にく】 - meat
7. 食べる 【た・べる】 (ru-verb) - to eat
8. する (exception) - to do
9. 日本 【に・ほん】 - Japan
10. 来る 【く・る】 (exception) - to come
11. 寿司 【すし】 - sushi
12. 一年間 【いち・ねん・かん】 - span of 1 year
13. 練習 【れん・しゅう】 - practice
14. ピアノ - piano
15. 弾く 【ひ・く】 (u-verb) - to play (piano, guitar)
16. 地下 【ち・か】 - underground
17. 入る 【はい・る】 (u-verb) - to enter
18. 富士山 【ふ・じ・さん】 - Mt. Fuji
19. 見える 【み・える】 (ru-verb) - to be visible

You may be wondering how to use 「なる」 and 「する」 with verbs since there's no way to directly modify a verb with another verb. The simple solution is to add a generic noun such as a generic event: こと （事） or an appearance/manner: よう （様）. These nouns don't refer to anything specific and are used to describe something else. In this case, they allow us to describe verbs in the same manner as nouns. Here are some examples of how to use these generic nouns with 「する」 and 「なる」.

1. 海外に行くことになった。
It's been decided that I will go abroad. (lit: It became the event of going abroad.)

2. 毎日、肉を食べるようになった。
   It became so that I eat meat everyday. (lit: It became the appearance of eating meat everyday.)

3. 海外に行くことにした。
   I decided I will go abroad. (lit: I did toward the event of going abroad.)

4. 毎日、肉を食べるようにする。
   I will try to eat meat everyday. (lit: I will do toward the manner of eating meat everyday.)

You can modify a verb with 「なる」 or 「する」 by first making it into a noun clause and then treating it just like a regular noun. Pretty clever, huh? I hope the literal translations give you a sense of why the example sentences mean what they do. For instance, in the fourth example, 「～ようにする」 translates into "to make an effort toward..." but in Japanese, it's really only a target towards acting in a certain manner.

Since potential verbs describe a state of feasibility rather than an action (remember, that's why the 「を」 particle couldn't be used), it is often used in conjunction with 「～ようになる」 to describe a change in manner to a state of feasibility. Let's take this opportunity to get some potential conjugation practice in.

1. 日本に来て、寿司が食べられるようになった。
   After coming to Japan, I became able to eat sushi.

2. 一年間練習したから、ピアノが弾けるようになった。
   Because I practiced for one year, I became able to play the piano.

3. 地下に入って、富士山が見えなくなった。
   After going underground, Fuji-san became not visible.

Conditionals

How to say "if" in Japanese

This whole section is dedicated to learning how to say "if" in Japanese. Oh, if only it was as simple as English. In Japanese, there's four (count them, four) ways to say "if"! Thankfully, the conjugations are sparse and easy especially since you don't have to deal with tenses.

Expressing natural consequence using 「と」

Vocabulary

1. ボール - ball
2. 落とす 【お・とす】 (u-verb) - to drop
3. 落ちる 【お・ちる】 (ru-verb) - to fall
4. 電気 【でん・き】 - electricity; (electric) light
5. 消す 【け・す】 (u-verb) - to erase
6. 暗い 【くら・い】 (i-adj) - dark
7. 学校 【がっ・こう】 - school
8. 行く 【い・く】 (u-verb) - to go
9. 友達 【とも・だち】 - friend
10. 会う 【あ・う】 (u-verb) - to meet
11. たくさん - a lot (amount)
12. 太る 【ふと・る】 (u-verb) - to become fatter
13. 先生 【せん・せい】 - teacher
14. きっと - for sure
15. 年上 【とし・うえ】 - older

We'll first cover the simplest type of "if" which is the natural consequence conditional. This means that if [X] happens, [Y] will happen as a natural consequence. No question about it. If I drop a ball, it will fall to the ground. If I turn off the lights at night, it will get dark. We can express this type of condition in the following format.

Examples

1. ボールを落すと落ちる。
   If you drop the ball, it will fall.

2. 電気を消すと暗くなる。
   If you turn off the lights, it will get dark.

These examples are designed to show how 「と」 is used to express natural consequence. However, even if the statement isn't a natural consequence in itself, the 「と」 will tell the audience that it is nevertheless expected to be a natural consequence.

1. 学校に行かないと友達と会えないよ。
   If you don't go to school, you can't meet your friends.

2. たくさん食べると太るよ。
   If you eat a lot, you will get fat, for sure.

3. 先生だと、きっと年上なんじゃないですか？
   If he's a teacher, he must be older for sure, right?

The "for sure" part is the implied meaning supplied by the 「と」. The speaker is saying that the following condition will occur in that situation, no matter what. As you can see from the last example, if the condition is a state-of-being, it must be expressed so explicitly using 「だ」. This applies to all non-conjugated nouns and na-adjectives as I'm sure you're used to by now. This will also help prevent confusion with other types of 「と」.

Contextual conditionals using 「なら（ば）」

Vocabulary

1. 皆 【みんな】 - everybody
2. 行く 【い・く】 (u-verb) - to go
3. 私 【わたし】 - me, myself, I
4. 言う 【い・う】 (u-verb) - to say
5. 問題 【もん・だい】 - problem
6. ある (u-verb) - to exist (inanimate)
7. 図書館 【と・しょ・かん】 - library
8. あそこ - over there

Another relatively easy to understand type of "if" is the contextual conditional. You can use this particle to express what will happen given a certain context. For example, if you wanted to say, "Well, if everybody's going, I'm going too" you would use the 「なら」 conditional because you are saying that you will go in the context of everybody else going. The contextual conditional always requires a context in which the conditional occurs. For instance, you would use it for saying things like, "If *that's* what you are talking about..." or "If *that's* the case, then..."

In a sense, you are explaining what would occur if you assume a certain condition is satisfied. In other words, you are saying "if given a certain context, here is what will happen." You will see this reflected in the English translations as the phrase "if given" in the examples.

The 「なら」 is attached to the context in which the conditional occurs. The format is the same as the 「と」 conditional, however, you <u>must not</u> attach the declarative 「だ」.

Rules for using the contextual conditional 「なら」

1. Attach 「なら」 to the context in which the conditional would occur
   = [Assumed Context] + なら + [Result]
2. You <u>must not</u> attach the declarative 「だ」.

Examples

1. みんなが行くなら私も行く。
   If given that everybody is going, then I'll go too.
2. アリスさんが言うなら問題ないよ。
   If given that Alice-san says so, there's no problem.

Example Dialogue

アリス：図書館はどこですか。
Alice: Where is the library?

ボブ：図書館なら、あそこです。
Bob: If given that you're talking about the library, then it's over there.

The following is incorrect.

- 図書館だならあそこです。

You can also decide to use 「ならば」 instead of just 「なら」. This means exactly the same thing except that it has a more formal nuance.

General conditionals using 「ば」

Vocabulary

1. 食べる 【た・べる】 (ru-verb) - to eat
2. 待つ 【ま・つ】 (u-verb) - to wait
3. おかしい (i-adj) - funny
4. ある (u-verb) - to exist (inanimate)
5. 学生 【がく・せい】 - student
6. 暇 【ひま】 - free (as in not busy)
7. 友達 【とも・だち】 - friend
8. 会う 【あ・う】 (u-verb) - to meet
9. 買い物 【か・い・もの】 - shopping
10. 行く 【い・く】 (u-verb) - to go
11. お金 【お・かね】 - money
12. いい (i-adj) - good
13. 楽しい 【たの・しい】 (i-adj) - fun
14. 私 【わたし】 - me; myself; I
15. 病気 【びょう・き】 - disease; sickness
16. なる (u-verb) - to become

The next type of conditional just expresses a regular "if" condition without any assumptions or embedded meanings. The conjugation rules for the 「ば」 conditional is below. Note, the conjugation rule for nouns and na-adjectives is actually using the verb 「ある」 in 「である」, a formal expression we'll learn much later.

Conjugation Rules for 「ば」

- **For verbs:** Change the last /u/ vowel sound to the equivalent /e/ vowel sound and attach 「ば」
  Examples
    1. 食べる　→　食べれ→食べれば
    2. 待つ　→　待て→待てば
- **For i-adjectives or negatives ending in** 「ない」**:** Drop the last 「い」 and attach 「ければ」.
  Examples
    1. おかしい　→　おかしければ
    2. ない　→　なければ
- **For nouns and na-adjectives:** Attach 「であれば」
  Examples
    1. 学生　→　学生であれば
    2. 暇　→　暇であれば

Examples

1. 友達に会えれば、買い物に行きます。
   If I can meet with my friend, we will go shopping.
2. お金があればいいね。
   If I had money, it would be good, huh?
3. 楽しければ、私も行く。
   If it's fun, I'll go too.
4. 楽しくなければ、私も行かない。
   If it's not fun, I'll also not go.
5. 食べなければ病気になるよ。
   If you don't eat, you will become sick.

Past conditional using 「たら（ば）」

Vocabulary

1. 自動 【じ・どう】 - automatic
2. 待つ 【ま・つ】 (u-verb) - to wait
3. 読む 【よ・む】 (u-verb) - to read
4. 忙しい 【いそが・しい】 (i-adj) - busy
5. 暇 【ひま】 - free (as in not busy)
6. 遊ぶ 【あそ・ぶ】 (u-verb) - to play
7. 行く 【い・く】 (u-verb) - to go
8. 学生 【がく・せい】 - student
9. 割引 【わり・びき】 - discount
10. 買う 【か・う】 (u-verb) - to buy
11. 友達 【とも・だち】 - friend
12. 会う 【あ・う】 (u-verb) - to meet
13. 買い物 【か・い・もの】 - shopping
14. お金 【お・かね】 - money
15. ある (u-verb) - to exist (inanimate)
16. いい (i-adj) - good
17. 家 【1) うち; 2) いえ】 - 1) one's own home; 2) house
18. 帰る 【かえ・る】 (u-verb) - to go home
19. 誰 【だれ】 - who
20. いる (ru-verb) - to exist (animate)
21. アメリカ - America
22. たくさん - a lot (amount)
23. 太る 【ふと・る】 (u-verb) - to become fatter

I call this next conditional the past conditional because it is produced
by taking the past tense and just adding 「ら」. It is commonly
called the 「たら」 conditional because all past-tense ends with
「た／だ」 and so it always becomes 「たら／だら」. Like the
「ば」 conditional, it is also a general conditional.

Examples

1. 暇だったら、遊びに行くよ。
   If I am free, I will go play.
2. 学生だったら、学生割引で買えます。
   If you're a student, you can buy with a student discount.

For i-adjectives and verbs, it is very difficult to differentiate between the two types of conditionals, and you can make life easier for yourself by considering them to be the same. However there is a small difference in that the 「たら」 conditional focuses on what happens after the condition. This is another reason why I call this the past conditional because the condition is "in the past" (not literally) and we're interested in the result not the condition. The 「ば」 conditional, on the other hand, focuses on the conditional part.

Let's compare the difference in nuance.

Example 1

A：友達に会えれば、買い物に行きます。
A: We will go shopping, if I can meet with my friend.

B：友達に会えたら、買い物に行きます。
B: If I can meet with my friend, we will go shopping.

Example 2

A：お金があればいいね。
A: It would be good, if I had money, huh?

B：お金があったらいいね。
B: If I had money, it would be good, huh?

Going by the context, the 「～たら」 form sounds more natural for both examples because it doesn't seem like we're really focusing on the condition itself. We're probably more interested in what's going to happen once we meet the friend or how nice it would be if we had money.

The past conditional is the only type of conditional where the result can be in the past. It may seem strange to have an "if" when the result has already taken place. Indeed, in this usage, there really is no "if", it's just a way of expressing surprise at the result of the condition. This has little to do with conditionals but it is explained here because the grammatical structure is the same.

1. 家に帰ったら、誰もいなかった。
   When I went home, there was no one there. (unexpected result)
2. アメリカに行ったら、たくさん太りました。
   As a result of going to America, I got really fat. (unexpected result)

You can also use 「たらば」 instead of 「たら」. Similar to 「なら ば」, this means exactly the same thing except that it has a more formal nuance.

How does 「もし」 fit into all of this?

Vocabulary

1. もし - if by any chance
2. いい (i-adj) - good
3. 映画 【えい・が】 - movie
4. 観る 【み・る】 (ru-verb) - to watch
5. 行く 【い・く】 (u-verb) - to go
6. 時間 【じ・かん】 - time
7. ある (u-verb) - to exist (inanimate)
8. 明日 【あした】 - tomorrow

Some of you may be aware of the word 「もし」 which means "if" and may be wondering how it fits into all of this. Well, if you want to say a conditional, you need to use one of the conditionals discussed above. 「もし」 is really a supplement to add a sense of uncertainty on whether the condition is true. For instance, you might use it when you want to make an invitation and you don't want to presume like the following example.

1. もしよかったら、映画を観に行きますか？
   If by any chance it's ok with you, go to watch movie?
2. もし時間がないなら、明日でもいいよ。
   If given that there's no time, tomorrow is fine as well. (Not certain whether there is no time)

Expressing "must" or "have to"

When there's something that must or must not be done

In life, there are things that we must or must not do whether it's taking out the trash or doing our homework. We will cover how to say this in Japanese because it is a useful expression and it also ties in well with the previous section. We will also learn how to the say the expression, "You don't have to..." to finish off this section.

Using 「だめ」, 「いけない」, and 「ならない」 for things that must not be done

Vocabulary

1. 駄目 【だめ】 - no good
2. ここ - here
3. 入る 【はい・る】 (u-verb) - to enter
4. それ - that
5. 食べる 【たべ・る】 (ru-verb) - to eat
6. 夜 【よる】 - evening
7. 遅い 【おそ・い】 (i-adj) - late
8. ～まで (particle) - until ~
9. 電話 【でん・わ】 - phone
10. する (exception) - to do
11. 早い 【はや・い】 (i-adj) - fast; early
12. 寝る 【ね・る】 (ru-verb) - to sleep

If you're not familiar with the word 「だめ」 (駄目), though it can be used in many different ways it essentially means "no good". The other two key words in this section are 「いけない」 and 「ならない」 and they have essentially the same basic meaning as 「だめ」. However, while 「いけない」 can be used by itself, 「ならな

175

い」 must only be used in the grammar presented here. In addition, while 「いけない」 and 「ならない」 conjugate like i-adjectives they are not actual adjectives. Let's learn how to use these words to express things that must not be done.

How to say: Must not [verb]

- Take the te-form of the verb, add the 「は」 (wa) particle and finally attach either 「だめ」、「いけない」、or 「ならない」.
  Example
  入る → 入って ＋ は ＋ だめ／いけない／ならない ＝ 入ってはだめ／入ってはいけない／入ってはならない

---

1. ここに入ってはいけません。
   You must not enter here.

2. それを食べてはだめ！
   You can't (must not) eat that!

3. 夜、遅くまで電話してはならない。
   You must not use the phone until late at night.

4. 早く寝てはなりませんでした。
   Wasn't allowed to sleep early.

The difference between 「だめ」、「いけない」、and 「ならない」 is that, first of all, 「だめ」 is casual. While 「いけない」 and 「ならない」 are basically identical, 「ならない」 is generally more for things that apply to more than one person like rules and policies.

Expressing things that must be done

176

Vocabulary

1. 毎日 【まい・にち】 - everyday
2. 学校 【がっ・こう】 - school
3. 行く 【い・く】 (u-verb) - to go
4. 宿題 【しゅく・だい】 - homework
5. する (exception) - to do

You may have predicted that the opposite of "You must not do" would use 「いける」 or 「なる」 because they look like the positive version of 「いけない」 and 「ならない」. However, 「いけない」 and 「ならない」 must always be negative, so this is not correct. In actuality, we still use the same 「だめ／いけない／ならない」 and use the opposite of the verb that goes in front of it instead. This double negative can be kind of confusing at first but you will get used to it with practice. There are three ways to conjugate the verb before adding 「だめ／いけない／ならない」 and two of them involve conditionals so aren't you glad that you just learned conditionals in the previous section?

How to say: Must [verb]

1. Negative te-form + 「は」 (wa) particle + だめ／いけない／ならない
2. Negative verb + 「と」 conditional + だめ／いけない／ならない
3. Negative verb + 「ば」 conditional + だめ／いけない／ならない

The first method is the same as the "must not do" grammar form except that we simply negated the verb.

1. 毎日学校に行かなくてはなりません。
   Must go to school everyday.
2. 宿題をしなくてはいけなかった
   Had to do homework.

The second method uses the natural conditional that we learned in the last lesson. Literally, it means if you don't do something, then it automatically leads to the fact that it is no good. (In other words, you must do it.) However, people tend to use it for situations beyond the natural consequence characterization that we learned from the last section because it's shorter and easier to use than the other two types of grammar.

1. 毎日学校に行かないとだめです。
   Must go to school everyday.
2. 宿題をしないといけない
   Have to do homework.

The third method is similar to the second except that it uses a different type of conditional as explained in the last lesson. With the 「ば」 conditional, it can be used for a wider range of situations. Note that since the verb is always negative, for the 「ば」 conditional, we will always be removing the last 「い」 and adding 「ければ」.

1. 毎日学校に行かなければいけません。
   Must go to school everyday.
2. 宿題をしなければだめだった。
   Had to do homework.

It may seem like I just breezed through a whole lot of material because there are three grammar forms and 「だめ／いけない／ならない」 adding up to nine possible combinations (3x3). However, some combinations are more common than others but I did not explicitly point out which were more common because any combination is technically correct and going over style would merely confuse at this point. Also, keep in mind that there is nothing essentially new in terms of conjugation rules. We already covered conditionals in the last lesson and adding the wa particle to the te-form in the beginning of this section.

※ **Reality Check**

Although we spent the last section explaining 「〜なければ」 and 「〜なくては」, the reality is that because they are so long, they are practically never used in real conversations. While they are often used in a written context, in actual speech, people usually use the 「と」 conditional or the various shortcuts described below. In casual speech, the 「と」 conditional is the most prevalent type of conditional. Though I explained in depth the meaning associated with the 「と」 conditional, you have to take it with a grain of salt here because people are inherently lazy.

Various short-cuts for the lazy

Vocabulary

1. 勉強 【べん・きょう】 - study
2. する (exception) - to do
3. ご飯 【ご・はん】 - rice; meal
4. 食べる 【た・べる】 (ru-verb) - to eat
5. 学校 【がっ・こう】 - school
6. 行く 【い・く】 (u-verb) - to go

7. ここ - here
8. 入る 【はい・る】 (u-verb) - to enter
9. 駄目 【だめ】 - no good
10. 死ぬ 【し・ぬ】 (u-verb) - to die

You may have been grumbling and complaining about how long most of the expressions are just to say you must do something. You can end up with up to eight additional syllables just to say "I have to..."!

Well, others have thought the same before and people usually use short abbreviated versions of 「なくては」 and 「なければ」 in casual speech. Teachers are often reluctant to teach these overly familiar expressions because they are so much easier to use which is bad for times when they might not be appropriate. But, on the other hand, if you don't learn casual expressions, it makes it difficult to understand your friends (or would-be friends if you only knew how to speak less stiffly!). So here they are but take care to properly practice the longer forms so that you will be able to use them for the appropriate occasions.

Casual abbreviations for things that must be done

1. Simply replace 「なくて」 with 「なくちゃ」
2. Simply replace 「なければ」 with 「なきゃ」

Right now, you may be saying, "What the?" because the "abbreviations" are about the same length as what we've already covered. The secret here is that, unlike the expressions we learned so far, you can just leave the 「だめ／いけない／ならない」 part out altogether!

1. 勉強しなくちゃ。
   Gotta study.
2. ご飯を食べなきゃ。
   Gotta eat.

The 「と」 conditional is also used by itself to imply 「だめ／いけない／ならない」.

- 学校に行かないと。
  Gotta go to school.

There is another 「ちゃ」 abbreviation for things that you must <u>not do</u>. However, in this case, you cannot leave out 「だめ／いけない／ならない」. Since this *is* a casual abbreviation, 「だめ」 is used in most cases.

One very important difference for this casual form is that verbs that end in 「む」、「ぶ」、「ぬ」 use 「じゃ」 instead of 「ちゃ」. Essentially, all the verbs that end in 「んだ」 for past tense fall in this category.

Casual abbreviations for things that must <u>not</u> be done

1. Replace 「ては」 with 「ちゃ」
2. Replace 「では」 with 「じゃ」

---

1. ここに入っちゃだめだよ。
   You can't enter here.

2. 死んじゃだめだよ！ - You can't die!

On a final note, in general,「ちゃ」sounds a bit cutesy or girly.
You've already seen an example of this with the「ちゃん」suffix.
Similarly,「なくちゃ」also sounds a bit cutesy or childish.

Saying something is ok to do or not do

Vocabulary

1. 全部 【ぜん・ぶ】 - everything
2. 食べる 【た・べる】 (ru-verb) - to eat
3. いい (i-adj) - good
4. 飲む 【の・む】 (u-verb) - to drink
5. 大丈夫 【だい・じょう・ぶ】 (na-adj) - ok
6. 構う 【かま・う】 (u-verb) - to mind; to be concerned about
7. もう - already
8. 帰る 【かえ・る】 (u-verb) - to go home
9. これ - this
10. ちょっと - just a little
11. 見る 【み・る】 (ru-verb) - to see

Now let's learn how to say either that it's ok to do or not do
something. I decided to shove this section in here because in
Japanese, this is essential how to say that you don't have to
something (by saying it's ok to not do it). The grammar itself is also
relatively easy to pick up and makes for a short section.

By simply using the te-form and the「も」particle, you are
essentially saying, "even if you do X..." Common words that come

after this include 「いい」, 「大丈夫」, or 「構わない」. Some examples will come in handy.

1. 全部食べ<u>ても</u>いいよ。
   You can go ahead and eat it all. (lit: Even if you eat it all, it's good, you know.)
2. 全部食べなく<u>ても</u>いいよ。
   You don't have to eat it all. (lit: Even if you don't eat it all, it's good, you know.)
3. 全部飲ん<u>でも</u>**大丈夫**だよ。
   It's ok if you drink it all. (lit: Even if you drink it all, it's OK, you know.)
4. 全部飲ん<u>でも</u>**構わない**よ。
   I don't mind if you drink it all. (lit: Even if you drink it all, I don't mind, you know.)

In casual speech, 「〜てもいい」 sometimes get shortened to just 「〜ていい」 (or 「〜でいい」 instead of 「〜でもいい」).

1. もう帰っ<u>ていい</u>?
   Can I go home already?
2. これ、ちょっと見<u>ていい</u>?
   Can I take a quick look at this?

Desire and Suggestions

How to get your way in Japan

We will now learn how to say what you want either by just coming out and saying it or by making discreet suggestions. The major topics we will cover will be the 「たい」 conjugation and the volitional form. We will also learn specialized uses of the 「たら」 and 「ば」 conditionals to offer advice.

Verbs you want to do with 「たい」

Vocabulary

1. 行く 【い・く】 (u-verb) - to go
2. 何 【なに】 - what
3. する (exception) - to do
4. 温泉 【おん・せん】 - hotspring
5. ケーキ - cake
6. 食べる 【た・べる】 (ru-verb) - to eat
7. ずっと - long; far
8. 一緒 【いっ・しょ】 - together
9. いる (ru-verb) - to exist (animate)
10. 犬 【いぬ】 - dog
11. 遊ぶ 【あそ・ぶ】 (u-verb) - to play

You can express verbs that you *want* to perform with the 「たい」 form. All you need to do is add 「たい」 to the stem of the verb. However, unlike most conjugations we learned where the verb turns into a ru-verb, this form actually transforms the verb into an i-adjective (notice how 「たい」 conveniently ends in 「い」). This makes sense because the conjugated form is a description of something that you want to do. Once you have the 「たい」 form, you can then conjugate it the same as you would any other i-adjective. However, the 「たい」 form is different from regular i-adjectives because it is derived from a verb. This means that all the particles we normally associate with verbs such as 「を」、 「に」、 「へ」、 or 「で」 can all be used with the 「たい」 form, which is not true for regular i-adjectives. Here's a chart just for you.

「たい」 conjugations

	Positive	**Negative**
Non-Past	行きたい	行きたくない
Past	行きたかった	行きたくなかった

Examples

1. 何を<u>したい</u>ですか。 What do you want to do?
2. 温泉に<u>行きたい</u>。 I want to go to hot spring.
3. ケーキ、<u>食べたくない</u>の？ You don't want to eat cake?
4. <u>食べたくなかった</u>けど<u>食べたく</u>なった。 I didn't want to eat it but I became wanting to eat.

Example 4 was very awkward to translate but is quite simple in Japanese if you refer to the section about using 「なる」 with i-adjectives". The past tense of the verb 「なる」 was used to create "became want to eat". Here's a tongue twister using the negative 「〜たくない」 and past-tense of 「なる」： 「食べたくなくなった」 meaning "became not wanting to eat".

This may seem obvious but 「ある」 cannot have a 「たい」 form because inanimate objects cannot want anything. However, 「いる」 can be used with the 「たい」 form in examples like the one below.

- ずっと一緒にいたい。 I want to be together forever. (lit: Want to exist together for long time.)

Also, you can only use the 「たい」 form for the first-person because you cannot read other people's mind to see what they want to do. For referring to anyone beside yourself, it is normal to use expressions such as, "I think he wants to..." or "She said that she wants to..." We will learn how to say such expressions in a later lesson. Of course, if you're asking a question, you can just use the 「たい」 form because you're not presuming to know anything.

- 犬と遊びたいですか。 Do you want to play with dog?

Indicating things you want or want done using 「欲しい」

Vocabulary

1. 欲しい 【ほ・しい】 (i-adj) - wanted; desirable
2. 好き 【す・き】 (na-adj) - likable; desirable
3. 大きい 【おお・きい】 (i-adj) - big
4. 縫いぐるみ 【ぬ・いぐるみ】 - stuffed doll
5. 全部 【ぜん・ぶ】 - everything
6. 食べる 【た・べる】 (ru-verb) - to eat
7. 部屋 【へ・や】 - room
8. きれい (na-adj) - pretty; clean

In English, we employ a verb to say that we want something. In Japanese, "to want" is actually an i-adjective and not a verb. We saw something similar with 「好き」 which is an adjective while "to like" in English is a verb. While I didn't get too much into the workings of 「好き」, I have dedicated a whole section to 「欲しい」 because it means, "to want something done" when combined with the te-form of a verb. We will learn a more polite and appropriate way to make requests in the "Making Requests" lesson instead of saying, "I want this done."

Though not a set rule, whenever words come attached to the te-form of a verb to serve a special grammatical function, it is customary to write it in hiragana. This is because kanji is already used for the verb and the attached word becomes part of that verb.

Examples

1. 大きい縫いぐるみが欲しい！　I want a big stuffed doll!
2. 全部食べてほしいんだけど・・・。　I want it all eaten but...
3. 部屋をきれいにしてほしいのよ。　It is that I want the room cleaned up, you know.

Like I mentioned, there are more appropriate ways to ask for things which we won't go into until later. This grammar is not used too often but is included for completeness.

Making a motion to do something using the volitional form (casual)

Vocabulary

1. 食べる　【た・べる】　(ru-verb) - to eat
2. 入る　【はい・る】　(u-verb) - to enter
3. 着る　【き・る】　(ru-verb) - to wear
4. 信じる　【しん・じる】　(ru-verb) - to believe
5. 寝る　【ね・る】　(ru-verb) - to sleep
6. 起きる　【お・きる】　(ru-verb) - to wake; to occur
7. 出る　【で・る】　(ru-verb) - to come out
8. 掛ける　【か・ける】　(ru-verb) - to hang

9. 捨てる 【す・てる】 (ru-verb) - to throw away
10. 調べる 【しら・べる】 (ru-verb) - to investigate
11. 話す 【はな・す】 (u-verb) - to speak
12. 書く 【か・く】 (u-verb) - to write
13. 待つ 【ま・つ】 (u-verb) - to wait
14. 飲む 【の・む】 (u-verb) - to drink
15. 取る 【と・る】 (u-verb) - to take
16. 聞く 【き・く】 (u-verb) - to ask; to listen
17. 泳ぐ 【およ・ぐ】 (u-verb) - to swim
18. 遊ぶ 【あそ・ぶ】 (u-verb) - to play
19. 直る 【なお・る】 (u-verb) - to be fixed
20. 死ぬ 【し・ぬ】 (u-verb) - to die
21. 買う 【か・う】 (u-verb) - to buy
22. する (exception) - to do
23. 来る 【く・る】 (exception) - to come
24. 今日 【きょう】 - today
25. 何 【なに】 - what
26. テーマパーク - theme park
27. 行く 【い・く】 (u-verb) - to go
28. 明日 【あした】 - tomorrow
29. カレー - curry

The term volitional here means a will to do something. In other words, the volitional form indicates that someone is setting out to do something. In the most common example, this simply translates into the English "let's" or "shall we?" but we'll also see how this form can be used to express an effort to do something in a lesson further along.

To conjugate verbs into the volitional form for casual speech, there are two different rules for ru-verbs and u-verbs. For ru-verbs, you simply remove the 「る」 and add 「よう」. For u-verbs, you replace the / u / vowel sound with the / o / vowel sound and add 「う」.

```
Conjugations rules for the casual volitional form

  • For ru-verbs: Remove the 「る」 and add 「よ
    う」 Example: 食べる → 食べ + よう → 食べよう
  • For u-verbs: Replace the / u / vowel sound with
    the / o / vowel sound and add 「う」 Example: 入
    る → 入ろ + う → 入ろう
```

Here is a list of verbs you should be used to seeing by now.

Plain	Volitional	Plain	Volitional	Plain	Volitional
食べる	食べよう	話す	話そう	する	しよう
着る	着よう	聞く	聞こう	くる	こよう
信じる	信じよう	泳ぐ	泳ごう		
寝る	寝よう	遊ぶ	遊ぼう		
起きる	起きよう	待つ	待とう		
出る	出よう	飲む	飲もう		
掛ける	掛けよう	直る	直ろう		
捨てる	捨てよう	死ぬ	死のう		
調べる	調べよう	買う	買おう		

Examples

I doubt you will ever use 「死のう」 (let's die) but I left it in for completeness. Here are some more realistic examples.

1. 今日は何を<u>しよう</u>か？ What shall (we) do today?
2. テーマパークに<u>行こう</u>！ Let's go to theme park!
3. 明日は何を<u>食べよう</u>か？ What shall (we) eat tomorrow?
4. カレーを<u>食べよう</u>！ Let's eat curry!

Remember, since you're setting out to do something, it doesn't make sense to have this verb in the past tense. Therefore, there is only one tense and if you were to replace 「明日」 in the third example with, let's say, 「昨日」 then the sentence would make no sense.

Making a motion to do something using the volitional form (polite)

Vocabulary

1. 食べる 【た・べる】 (ru-verb) - to eat
2. 入る 【はい・る】 (u-verb) - to enter
3. する (exception) - to do
4. 来る 【く・る】 (exception) - to come
5. 寝る 【ね・る】 (ru-verb) - to sleep
6. 行く 【い・く】 (u-verb) - to go
7. 遊ぶ 【あそ・ぶ】 (u-verb) - to play
8. 今日 【きょう】 - today
9. 何 【なに】 - what
10. テーマパーク - theme park

11. 明日 【あした】 - tomorrow

12. カレー - curry

The conjugation for the polite form is even simpler. All you have to do is add 「〜ましょう」 to the stem of the verb. Similar to the masu-form, verbs in this form must always come at the end of the sentence. In fact, all polite endings must always come at the end and nowhere else as we've already seen.

Conjugations rules for the polite volitional form

- **For all verbs:** Add 「〜ましょう」 to the stem of the verb
    1. 食べる → 食べ + ましょう → 食べましょう
    2. 入る → 入り + ましょう → 入りましょう

Sample verbs

Plain	Volitional
する	しましょう
くる	きましょう
寝る	寝ましょう
行く	行きましょう
遊ぶ	遊びましょう

Examples

Again, there's nothing new here, just the polite version of the volitional form.

1. 今日は何をしましょうか？ What shall (we) do today?
2. テーマパークに行きましょう！ Let's go to theme park!
3. 明日は何を食べましょうか？ What shall (we) eat tomorrow?
4. カレーを食べましょう！ Let's eat curry!

Making Suggestions using the 「ば」 or 「たら」 conditional

Vocabulary

1. 銀行 【ぎん・こう】 - bank
2. 行く 【い・く】 (u-verb) - to go
3. たまに - once in a while
4. 両親 【りょう・しん】 - parents
5. 話す 【はな・す】 (u-verb) - to speak

You can make suggestions by using the 「ば」 or 「たら」 conditional and adding 「どう」. This literally means, "If you do [X], how is it?" In English, this would become, "How about doing [X]?" Grammatically, there's nothing new here but it is a commonly used set phrase.

Examples

1. 銀行に行ったらどうですか。 How about going to bank?
2. たまにご両親と話せばどう？ How about talking with your parents once in a while?

Acting on relative clauses

In the section about modifying relative clauses, we learned how to treat a relative clause like an adjective to directly modify a noun. We will extend the functionality of relative clauses by learning how to perform an action on a relative clause. Obviously, we cannot simply attach the 「を」 particle to a relative clause because the 「を」 particle only applies to noun phrases. We need something to encapsulate the relative clause into a unit that we can perform actions on. This is done by making a quoted phrase.

While in English, you can just add quotes and a comma to make a quotation, Japanese requires attaching 「と」 at the end of the quote. This is completely different from the 「と」 particle and the 「と」 conditional. Unlike quotes in English, we can perform many different types of actions on the quote besides the standard "he said", "she said", etc. For example, we can perform the action, "to think" or "to hear" to produce phrases such as, "I think [clause]" or "I heard [clause]" This is very important in Japanese because Japanese people seldom affirm definite statements. This also why we will have to eventually cover many other types of grammar to express uncertainty or probability.

The direct quote

Vocabulary

1. 言う 【い・う】 (u-verb) - to say
2. 聞く 【き・く】 (u-verb) - to ask; to listen
3. 叫ぶ 【さけ・ぶ】 (u-verb) - to scream
4. 呼ぶ 【よ・ぶ】 (u-verb) - to call
5. 呟く 【つぶや・く】 (u-verb) - to mutter
6. 寒い 【さむ・い】 (i-adj) - cold
7. 今日 【きょう】 - today
8. 授業 【じゅ・ぎょう】 - class
9. 先生 【せん・せい】 - teacher
10. 田中 【た・なか】 - Tanaka (last name)

We'll learn the simplest type of quoted phrase, which is the direct quote. Basically, you are directly quoting something that was said. This is done by simply enclosing the statement in quotes, adding 「と」 and then inserting the appropriate verb. The most common verbs associated with a direct quote would be 「言う」 and 「聞く」 but you may use any verbs related to direct quotation such as: 「叫ぶ」, 「呼ぶ」, 「呟く」, etc. This type of quotation is often used for dialogue in novels and other narrative works.

Examples

1. アリスが、「寒い」と言った。
   Alice said, "Cold".

2. 「今日は授業がない」と先生から聞いたんだけど。
   It is that I heard from the teacher, "There is no class today."

The verb does not need to be directly connected to the relative clause. As long as the verb that applies to the relative clause comes before any other verb, you can have any number of adjectives, adverbs or nouns in between.

- 「寒い」とアリスが田中に言った。
  "Cold," Alice said to Tanaka.

The interpreted quote

Vocabulary

1. 先生 【せん・せい】 - teacher
2. 今日 【きょう】 - today
3. 授業 【じゅ・ぎょう】 - class
4. 聞く 【き・く】 (u-verb) - to ask; to listen
5. これ - this
6. 日本語 【に・ほん・ご】 - Japanese (language)
7. 何 【なに／なん】 - what
8. 言う 【い・う】 (u-verb) - to say
9. 私 【わたし】 - me; myself; I
10. カレー - curry
11. 食べる 【た・べる】 (ru-verb) - to eat
12. 思う 【おも・う】 (u-verb) - to think
13. 時間 【じ・かん】 - time
14. 今 【いま】 - now
15. どこ - where
16. 行く 【い・く】 (u-verb) - to go

17. 考える 【かんが・える】 (ru-verb) - to think
18. 彼 【かれ】 - he; boyfriend
19. 高校生 【こう・こう・せい】 - high school student
20. 信じる 【しん・じる】 (ru-verb) - to believe

The second type of quote is the quote along the lines of what someone actually said. It's not a word-for-word quote. Since this is not a direct quote, no quotations are needed. You can also express thoughts as an interpreted quote as well. By using this and the verb 「思う」 you can say you think that something is so-and-so. You will hear Japanese people use this all the time. You can also use the verb 「考える」 when you are considering something.

Examples

1. 先生から今日は授業がないと聞いたんだけど。
   I heard from the teacher that there is no class today.
2. これは、日本語で何と言いますか。
   What do you call this in Japanese? (lit: About this, what do you say in Japanese?)
3. 私は、アリスと言います。
   I am called Alice. (lit: As for me, you say Alice.)

In an interpreted quote, the meaning of 「言う」 may change as you see in examples 2 and 3. Actually, as you can see from the literal translation, the meaning remains the same in Japanese but changes only when translated to normal English. (We'll learn more about various ways to use 「いう」 in the next lesson.)

Here are some examples of thoughts being used as quoted relative clauses. In example 2 below, the question marker is used with the volitional to insert an embedded question.

1. カレーを食べようと思ったけど、食べる時間がなかった。
   I thought about setting out to eat curry but I didn't have time to eat.
2. 今、どこに行こうかと考えている。
   Now, I'm considering where to set out to go.

Unlike the direct quotation, which you can just copy as is, if the quoted relative clause is a state-of-being for a noun or na-adjective, you have to explicitly include the declarative 「だ」 to show this.

1. 彼は、これは何だと言いましたか。
   What did he say this is?
2. 彼は高校生だと聞いたけど、信じられない。
   I heard that he is a high school student but I can't believe it.

Notice how 「だ」 was added to explicitly declare the state-of-being that is highlighted in the English translation. You can really see how important the 「だ」 is here by comparing the following two sentences.

- これは何だと言いましたか。
  What did (he) say this is?

- 何と言いましたか。
  What did (he) say?

Using 「って」 as a casual version of 「と」

Vocabulary

1. 智子 【とも・こ】 - Tomoko (first name)
2. 来年 【らい・ねん】 - next year
3. 海外 【かい・がい】 - overseas
4. もう - already

5. お金 【お・かね】 - money
6. ある (u-verb) - to exist (inanimate)
7. 本当 【ほん・とう】 - real
8. 明日 【あした】 - tomorrow
9. 雨 【あめ】 - rain
10. 降る 【ふ・る】 (u-verb) - to precipitate
11. すごい (i-adj) - to a great extent
12. いい (i-adj) - good
13. 人 【ひと】 - person

You may be surprised to hear that there is a shorter and casual version of the quoted relative clause since it's already only one hiragana character, 「と」. However, the important point here is that by using this casual shortcut, you can drop the rest of the sentence and hope your audience can understand everything from context.

Examples

1. 智子は来年、海外に行くんだって。
   Tomoko said that she's going overseas next year.

2. もうお金がないって。
   I already told you I have no money.

3. え？何だって？
   Huh? What did you say?

4. 今、時間がないって聞いたんだけど、本当？
   I heard you don't have time now, is that true?

5. 今、時間がないって、本当？
   You don't have time now (I heard), is that true?

「って」 can also be used to talk about practically anything, not just to quote something that was said. You can hear 「って」 being used just about everywhere in casual speech. Most of the time it is used in place of the 「は」 particle to simply bring up a topic.

1. 明日って、雨が降るんだって。
About tomorrow, I hear that it's going to rain.

2. アリスって、すごくいい人でしょ？
About Alice, she's a very good person, right?

Defining and Describing

The various uses of 「いう」

In the previous lesson, we learned how to quote a relative clause by encasing it with 「と」. This allowed us to talk about things that people have said, heard, thought, and more. We also took a look at some examples sentences that used 「と」 and 「言う」 to describe how to say something in Japanese and even what to call oneself. In this section, we will learn that with 「と」, we can use 「いう」 in a similar fashion to define, describe, and generally just talk about the thing itself. We'll also see how to do the same thing with the casual 「って」 version we first learned about in the last lesson.

Using 「いう」 to define

Vocabulary

1. 言う 【い・う】 (u-verb) - to say
2. これ - this
3. 何 【なに／なん】 - what
4. 魚 【さかな】 - fish
5. この - this (abbr. of これの)
6. 鯛 【たい】 - tai (type of fish)
7. デパート - department store
8. どこ - where

9. ある (u-verb) - to exist (inanimate)
10. 知る 【し・る】 (u-verb) - to know
11. 友達 【とも・だち】 - friend
12. 英語 【えい・ご】 - English (language)
13. 意味 【い・み】 - meaning

In the last lesson, we briefly looked at how to introduce ourselves by using 「と」 and 「いう」. For instance, we had the following example, which Alice used to introduce herself.

- 私はアリス<u>といいます</u>。
  I am called Alice. (lit: As for me, you say Alice.)

This sentence pattern is probably one of the first things beginner Japanese students learn in the classroom. In this case, the verb 「いう」 doesn't mean that somebody actually said something. Rather, Alice is saying that people in general say "Alice" when referring to her. While using kanji for 「いう」 is perfectly acceptable, in this case, since nothing is actually being said, using hiragana is also common.

This idea of describing what a person is known or referred to as can also be extended to objects and places. We can essentially define and identify anything we want by using 「という」 in this manner. As you can imagine, this is particularly useful for us because it allows us to ask what things are called in Japanese and for the definition of words we don't know yet.

Examples

1. これは、<u>なんという魚</u>ですか。
   What is this fish referred to as?
2. この魚は、<u>鯛といいます</u>。
   This fish is known as "*Tai*".

200

3. ルミネというデパートはどこにあるか、知っていますか？
Do you know where the department store called "Lumine" is?

4. 「友達」は、英語で [friend] という意味です。
The meaning of "*tomodachi*" in English is "friend".

Using 「いう」 to describe anything

Vocabulary

1. 主人公 【しゅ・じん・こう】 - main character
2. 犯人 【はん・にん】 - criminal
3. 一番 【いち・ばん】 - best; first
4. 面白い 【おも・しろ・い】 (i-adj) - interesting
5. 日本人 【に・ほん・じん】 - Japanese person
6. お酒 【お・さけ】 - alcohol
7. 弱い 【よわ・い】 (i-adj) - weak
8. 言う 【い・う】 (u-verb) - to say
9. 本当 【ほん・とう】 - real
10. 独身 【どく・しん】 - single; unmarried
11. 嘘 【うそ】 - lie
12. リブート - reboot
13. パソコン - computer, PC
14. こう - (things are) this way
15. そう - (things are) that way
16. ああ - (things are) that way
17. どう - how
18. 再起動 【さい・き・どう】 - reboot
19. あんた - you (slang)
20. いつも - always
21. 時 【とき】 - time
22. 来る 【く・る】 (exception) - to come
23. 困る 【こま・る】 (u-verb) - to be bothered, troubled
24. 人 【ひと】 - person

25. 結婚 【けっ・こん】 - marriage
26. 出来る 【で・き・る】 (ru-verb) - to be able to do
27. 幸せ 【しあわ・せ】 - happiness
28. なる (u-verb) - to become
29. 思う 【おも・う】 (u-verb) - to think
30. 大学 【だい・がく】 - college
31. 行く 【い・く】 (u-verb) - to go
32. 意味 【い・み】 - meaning

We learned how to use 「という」 to describe what something is known or referred to as. However, we can take this idea even further by attaching two relative clauses. At this point, 「いう」 is so abstract that it doesn't even really have a meaning. When a relative clause is encapsulated with 「と」, you must have a verb to go along with it and 「いう」 is simply being used as a generic verb to enable us to talk about any relative clause. This allows us to describe and explain just about anything ranging from a single word to complete sentences. As you can imagine, this construction is quite useful and employed quite often in Japanese.

Examples

1. 主人公が犯人だったというのが一番面白かった。
   The most interesting thing was that the main character was the criminal.
2. 日本人はお酒に弱いというのは本当?
   Is it true that Japanese people are weak to alcohol?
3. 独身だというのは、嘘だったの？
   It was a lie that you were single?
4. リブートというのは、パソコンを再起動するということです。
   Reboot means to restart your computer.

We can abstract it even further by replacing the relative clause with a generic way of doing something. In this case, we use 「こう」、

「そう」、「ああ」、and 「どう」, which when combined with 「いう」 means "this way, "that way", "that way (far away in an abstract sense)" and "what way" respectively.

Examples

1. あんたは、いつもこういう時に来るんだから、困るんだよ。
   It's because you always come at times like these that I'm troubled.
2. そういう人と一緒に仕事をするのは、嫌だよね。
   (Anybody would) dislike doing work together with that type of person, huh?
3. ああいう人と結婚できたら、幸せになれると思います。
   I think you can become happy if you could marry that type of person.
4. 大学に行かないって、どういう意味なの？
   What do you mean, "You're not going to go to college?"

Rephrasing and making conclusions with 「という」

Vocabulary

1. あんた - you (slang)
2. 彼女 【かの・じょ】 - she; girlfriend
3. 友達 【とも・だち】 - friend
4. 言う 【い・う】 (u-verb) - to say
5. 何 【なに／なん】 - what
6. お酒 【お・さけ】 - alcohol
7. 好き 【す・き】 (na-adj) - likable
8. ある (u-verb) - to exist (inanimate)
9. 生きる 【い・きる】 (ru-verb) - to live

10. 多分 【た・ぶん】 - maybe
11. 行く 【い・く】 (u-verb) - to go
12. 思う 【おも・う】 (u-verb) - to think
13. お金 【お・かね】 - money
14. もう - already
15. 帰る 【かえ・る】 (u-verb) - to go home
16. 駄目 【だめ】 - no good
17. 洋介 【よう・すけ】 - Yousuke (first name)
18. 別れる 【わか・れる】 (ru-verb) - to separate; to break up
19. こと - event, matter
20. 今 【いま】 - now
21. 彼氏【かれ・し】 - boyfriend
22. いる (ru-verb) - to exist (animate)
23. そう - (things are) that way

We can attach the question marker 「か」 to 「という」 in order to add a questioning element. This construction is used when you want to rephrase or redefine something such as the following dialogue.

Example Dialogue

A: みきちゃんは、あんたの彼女でしょう？
A: Miki-chan is your girlfriend, right?

B: う～ん、彼女というか、友達というか、なんというか・・・
B: Um, you might say girlfriend, or friend, or something…

This construction is used all the time, particularly in casual conversations. It can be used to correct something, come to a different conclusion, or even as an interjection.

Examples

1. お酒は好きというか、ないと生きていけない。
   I like alcohol or rather, can't live on without it.
2. 多分行かないと思う。というか、お金がないから、行けない。
   Don't think I'll go. Or rather, can't because there's no money.
3. というか、もう帰らないとだめですけど。
   Rather than that, I have to go home already.

Rather than using 「か」 to rephrase a conclusion, we can also simply use 「こと」 to sum up something without rephrasing anything.

Example Dialogue

A: みきちゃんが洋介と別れたんだって。
A: I heard that Miki-chan broke up with Yousuke.

B: ということは、みきちゃんは、今彼氏がいないということ?
B: Does that mean Miki-chan doesn't have a boyfriend now?

A: そう。そういうこと。
A: That's right. That's what it means.

Using 「って」 or 「て」 for 「という」

Vocabulary

1. 来年 【らい・ねん】 - next year
2. 留学 【りゅう・がく】 - study abroad
3. する (exception) - to do
4. 言う 【い・う】 (u-verb) - to say
5. 智子 【とも・こ】 - Tomoko (first name)
6. こと - event, matter
7. 駄目 【だめ】 - no good

8. 時間 【じ・かん】 - time
9. ある (u-verb) - to exist (inanimate)
10. 出来る 【で・き・る】 (ru-verb) - to be able to do
11. 行く 【い・く】 (u-verb) - to go
12. いい (i-adj) - good
13. 皆 【みんな】 - everybody
14. 私 【わたし】 - me; myself; I
15. 今 【いま】 - now
16. 彼氏 【かれ・し】 - boyfriend
17. いる (ru-verb) - to exist (animate)
18. もう - already
19. 帰る 【かえ・る】 (u-verb) - to go home

As mentioned in the previous lesson, 「って」 is very often used in causal slang in place of 「と」, because it allows us to leave out the rest of the sentence and assume context (or just plain assumption) will take care of the rest. We already saw that we can use 「って」 to replace 「という」 as well. However, since we just learned how to use 「という」 to do much more than just simply say something, there is a limit to just how much you can leave out. In any case, 「って」 will allow us to leave out not only 「いう」 but also any accompanying particles as you can see in the following example.

Examples

1. 来年留学するというのは、智子のこと？
   The studying abroad next year thing, is that Tomoko?
2. 来年留学するって智子のこと？
   The studying abroad next year thing, is that Tomoko?

「だって」 is also another phrase that leaves out just about everything. By convention, it is used to express disagreement or dissatisfaction usually to whine, complain, or to make an excuse but you can't tell what it means just from looking at it. It is an abbreviation of something along the lines of 「とはいっても」 meaning, "even if that was the case".

Example 1

A: しないとだめだよ。
A: Have to do it, you know.

B: だって、時間がないからできないよ。
B: But (even so), can't do it because there is no time.

Example 2

A: 行かなくてもいいよ。
A: Don't have to go, you know.

B: だって、みんな行くって。私も行かないと。
B: But (even so), everybody said they're going. I have to go too.

In some cases, the small 「つ」 is left out and just 「て」 is used instead of 「って」. This is done (as is usually the case for slang) in order to make things easier to say. In general, this is when there is nothing before the 「て」 or when the sound that comes before it doesn't require the explicit separation the 「っ」 gives us in order to be understood.

Examples

1. てことは、みきちゃんは、今彼氏がいないてこと？
   Does that mean Miki-chan doesn't have a boyfriend now?
2. ていうか、もう帰らないとだめですけど。
   Rather than that, I have to go home already.

Since slang tends to be used in whichever way the person feels like, there are no definite rules defining whether you should use 「って」 or 「て」. However, 「て」 is generally not used to express what people have actually said or heard, which is why it wasn't covered in the last lesson.

- みきちゃんが、明日こない<u>そ</u>。

  (Can't use 「て」 for something actually said)

- みきちゃんが、明日こない<u>って</u>。
  Miki-chan says she isn't coming tomorrow.

Saying 「ゆう」 instead of 「いう」

Vocabulary

1. もう - already
2. 帰る 【かえ・る】 (u-verb) - to go home
3. そう - (things are) that way
4. こと - event, matter

Because the 「という」 construction is used so often, there are a lot of different variations and slang based on it. While I do not plan on covering all of them here, you can check out casual patterns and slang in the miscellaneous section for yet even more slang derived from 「という」.

The last thing I'm am going to briefly mention here is the use of 「ゆう」 instead of 「いう」. In conversations, it is quite normal to say 「ゆう」 instead of 「いう」. 「ゆう」 is easier to say because it is simply one letter with a long vowel sound instead of the two different vowel sounds of 「いう」.

Examples

1. てゆうか、もう帰らないとだめですけど。
   Rather than that, I have to go home already.
2. そうゆうことじゃないって！
   I said it's not like that (lit: it's not that type of thing)!

Trying or attempting something

Let's try some stuff

In English, we use the word, "try" to mean both "to try something out" and "to make an effort to do something". In Japanese, these are separate grammatical expressions. For instance, "I tried the cherry flavor" and "I tried to do homework" mean quite different things and though English does not make a distinction, Japanese does.

To try something out

Vocabulary

1. 見る 【み・る】 - to see; to watch
2. 切る 【き・る】 (u-verb) - to cut
3. お好み焼き 【お・この・み・や・き】 - okonomiyaki (Japanese-style pancake)
4. 初めて 【はじ・めて】 - for the first time
5. 食べる 【た・べる】 (ru-verb) - to eat
6. とても - very
7. おいしい (i-adj) - tasty
8. お酒 【お・さけ】 - alcohol
9. 飲む 【の・む】 (u-verb) - to drink
10. すごい (i-adj) - to a great extent

11. 眠い 【ねむ・い】 (i-adj) - sleepy
12. なる (u-verb) - to become
13. 新しい 【あたら・しい】 (i-adj) - new
14. デパート - department store
15. 行く 【い・く】 (u-verb) - to go
16. 広島 【ひろ・しま】 - Hiroshima

To try something out, you simply need to change the verb to the te-form and add 「みる」. If it helps you to remember, you can think of it as a sequence of an action and then seeing the result. In fact 「みる」 conjugates just like 「見る」. However, just like the 「～てほしい」 grammar we learned, this is a set phrase and 「みる」 is usually written in hiragana.

To try something out

Conjugate the verb to the te-form and add 「みる」.
Example: 切る → 切って → 切ってみる
You can treat the whole result as a regular verb just as you would with 「見る」.
Example: 切ってみる、切ってみた、切ってみない、切ってみなかった

Examples

1. お好み焼きを初めて食べてみたけど、とてもおいしかった！
   I tried eating okonomiyaki for the first time and it was very tasty!
2. お酒を飲んでみましたが、すごく眠くなりました。
   I tried drinking alcohol and I became extremely sleepy.

3. 新しいデパートに行ってみる。
I'm going to check out the new department store.

4. 広島のお好み焼きを食べてみたい！
I want to try eating Hiroshima okonomiyaki!

To attempt to do something

Vocabulary

1. する (exception) - to do
2. 言う 【い・う】 (u-verb) - to say
3. 思う 【おも・う】 (u-verb) - to think
4. 考える 【かんが・える】 (ru-verb) - to think
5. 見る 【み・る】 (ru-verb) - to see
6. 行く 【い・く】 (u-verb) - to go
7. 毎日 【まい・にち】 - everyday
8. 勉強 【べん・きょう】 - study
9. 避ける 【さ・ける】 (ru-verb) - to avoid
10. 無理矢理 【む・り・や・り】 - forcibly
11. 部屋 【へ・や】 - room
12. 入る 【はい・る】 (u-verb) - to enter
13. 早い 【はや・い】 (i-adj) - fast; early
14. 寝る 【ね・る】 (ru-verb) - to sleep
15. 結局 【けっ・きょく】 - eventually
16. 徹夜 【てつ・や】 - staying up all night
17. お酒 【お・さけ】 - alcohol
18. 飲む 【の・む】 (u-verb) - to drink
19. 奥さん 【おく・さん】 - wife (polite)
20. 止める 【と・める】 (ru-verb) - to stop
21. なるべく - as much as possible
22. ジム - gym
23. 決める 【き・める】 (ru-verb) - to decide

We already learned that the volitional form was used to indicate a will to set out to do something. If you guessed that this next grammar for attempting to do something would involve the volitional form, you were right. To say that you tried (as in attempted) to do something, you need to conjugate the verb into the volitional, enclose it in a quotation (so that we can perform an action on the clause) and finally add the verb 「する」. Or put more simply, you just add 「とする」 to the volitional form of the verb. This is simply an extension of the quoted relative clause from the last section. Instead of saying the quote （言う） or treating it as a thought （思う、考える）, we are simply doing it with 「する」.

Attempting a certain action

Change the verb to the volitional form and add 「とする」.
Examples

1. 見る → 見よう → 見ようとする
2. 行く → 行こう → 行こうとする

Examples

1. 毎日、勉強を避けようとする。
   Everyday, she attempts to avoid study.
2. 無理矢理に部屋に入ろうとしている。
   He is attempting to force his way into the room.
3. 早く寝ようとしたけど、結局は徹夜した。
   I attempted to sleep early but ended up staying up all night.
4. お酒を飲もうとしたが、奥さんが止めた。
   He tried to drink alcohol but his wife stopped him.

212

Though we use the verb 「する」 to say, "to do attempt", we can use different verbs to do other things with the attempt. For instance, we can use the verb 「決める」 to say, "decide to attempt to do [X]". Here are some examples of other actions carried out on the attempt.

1. 勉強をなるべく避けようと思った。
   I thought I would attempt to avoid studying as much as possible.
2. 毎日ジムに行こうと決めた。
   Decided to attempt to go to gym everyday.

Giving and Receiving

Japanese people like gifts

Vocabulary

1. お歳暮 【お・せい・ぼ】 - year-end presents
2. お中元 【お・ちゅう・げん】 - Bon festival gifts
3. あげる (ru-verb) - to give; to raise
4. くれる (ru-verb) - to give
5. もらう (u-verb) - to receive

One thing about Japanese culture is that they're big on giving gifts. There are many different customs involving giving and receiving gifts (お歳暮、お中元、etc.) and when Japanese people go traveling, you can be sure that they're going to be picking up souvenirs to take back as gifts. Even when attending marriages or funerals, people are expected to give a certain amount of money as a gift to help fund the ceremony. You can see why properly learning how to express the giving and receiving of favors and items is a very important and useful skill. For some reason, the proper use of 「あげる」、「くれる」、and 「もらう」 has always haunted people studying Japanese as being horribly complex and intractable. I hope to prove in this section that it is conceptually quite straightforward and simple.

When to use 「あげる」

Vocabulary

1. あげる (ru-verb) - to give; to raise
2. 私 【わたし】 - me; myself; I
3. 友達 【とも・だち】 - friend
4. プレゼント - present
5. これ - this
6. 先生 【せん・せい】 - teacher
7. 車 【くるま】 - car
8. 買う 【か・う】 (u-verb) - to buy
9. 代わり 【か・わり】 - substitute
10. 行く 【い・く】 (u-verb) - to go
11. 学生 【がく・せい】 - student
12. 父 【ちち】 - father
13. いい (i-adj) - good
14. こと - event, matter
15. 教える 【おし・える】 (ru-verb) - to teach; to inform

「あげる」 is the Japanese word for "to give" seen from the speaker's point of view. You must use this verb when you are giving something or doing something for someone else.

Examples

1. 私が友達にプレゼントをあげた。
I gave present to friend.

2. これは**先生**にあげる。
   I'll give this to teacher.

In order to express the giving of a favor (verb) you must use the ever useful te-form and then attach 「あげる」. This applies to all the other sections in this lesson as well.

1. **車**を**買**ってあげるよ。
   I'll give you the favor of buying a car.
2. **代**わりに**行**ってあげる。
   I'll give you the favor of going in your place.

For third-person, this verb is used when the speaker is looking at it from the giver's point of view. We'll see the significance of this when we examine the verb 「くれる」 next.

1. **学生**がこれを**先生**にあげる。
   The student give this to teacher. (looking at it from the student's point of view)
2. **友達**が**父**にいいことを**教**えてあげた。
   Friend gave the favor of teaching something good to my dad. (looking at it from the friend's point of view)

Using 「やる」 to mean 「あげる」

Vocabulary

1. **犬** 【いぬ】 - dog
2. **餌** 【えさ】 - food for animals
3. やる (u-verb) - to do

Usually used for pets, animals, and such, you can substitute 「やる」, which normally means "to do", for 「あげる」. You shouldn't use this type of 「やる」 for people because it is used when looking down on someone and can be offensive.

- 犬に餌を<u>やった</u>?
  Did you give the dog food?

Here, 「やる」 does not mean "to do" but "to give". You can tell because "doing food to dog" doesn't make any sense.

When to use 「くれる」

Vocabulary

1. くれる (ru-verb) - to give
2. 友達 【とも・だち】 - friend
3. 私 【わたし】 - me; myself; I
4. プレゼント - present
5. これ - this
6. 先生 【せん・せい】 - teacher
7. 車 【くるま】 - car
8. 買う 【か・う】 (u-verb) - to buy
9. 代わり 【か・わり】 - substitute
10. 行く 【い・く】 (u-verb) - to go
11. 学生 【がく・せい】 - student
12. 父 【ちち】 - father
13. いい (i-adj) - good
14. こと - event, matter
15. 教える 【おし・える】 (ru-verb) - to teach; to inform
16. あげる (ru-verb) - to give; to raise
17. 全部 【ぜん・ぶ】 - everything
18. 食べる 【た・べる】 (ru-verb) - to eat

「くれる」 is also a verb meaning "to give" but unlike 「あげる」, it is from the receiver's point of view. You must use this verb when someone *else* is giving something or doing something for you (effectively the opposite of 「あげる」).

Examples

1. 友達が私にプレゼントをくれた。
   Friend gave present to me.
2. これは、先生がくれた。
   Teacher gave this to me.
3. 車を買ってくれるの？
   You'll give me the favor of buying a car for me?
4. 代わりに行ってくれる?
   Will you give me the favor of going in my place?

Similarly, when used in the third-person, the speaker is speaking from the receiver's point of view and not the giver.

1. 先生がこれを学生にくれる。
   The teacher give this to student. (looking at it from the student's point of view)
2. 友達が父にいいことを教えてくれた。
   Friend gave favor of teaching something good to my dad. (looking at it from the dad's point of view)

The following diagram illustrates the direction of giving from the point of view of the speaker.

From the speaker's point of view, all the giving done to others "go up" to everybody else while the giving done by everybody else "goes down" to the speaker. This is probably related to the fact that there is an identical verb 「上げる」 meaning "to raise" that contains the character for "above" （上） and that the honorific version of 「くれる」 is 「下さる」 with the character for down （下）. This restriction allows us to make certain deductions from vague sentences like the following:

- 先生が教えてあげるんですか。
  Teacher, will you be the one to give favor of teaching to...
  [anybody other than the speaker]?

Because all giving done to the speaker must always use 「くれる」, we know that the teacher must be doing it for someone else and *not the speaker*. The speaker is also looking at it from the teacher's point of view as doing a favor for someone else.

- 先生が教えてくれるんですか。
  Teacher, will you be the one to give favor of teaching to...
  [anybody including the speaker]?

Because the giver is not the speaker, the teacher is either giving to the speaker or anyone else. The speaker is viewing it from the receiver's point of view as receiving a favor done by the teacher.

Let's see some mistakes to watch out for.

- 私が全部食べてくれました。
  「くれる」 is being used as giving done by the speaker.
  (Wrong)
- 私が全部食べてあげました。
  I gave favor of eating it all. (Correct)

- 友達がプレゼントを私に<u>あげた</u>。
  「あげる」 is being used as giving to the speaker. (Wrong)
- 友達がプレゼントを私に<u>くれた</u>。 - Friend gave present to me. (Correct)

When to use 「もらう」

Vocabulary

1. 私 【わたし】 - me; myself; I
2. 友達 【とも・だち】 - friend
3. プレゼント - present
4. もらう (u-verb) - to receive
5. これ - this
6. 買う 【か・う】 (u-verb) - to buy
7. 宿題 【しゅく・だい】 - homework
8. チェック - check
9. する (exception) - to do
10. 時間 【じ・かん】 - time
11. ある (u-verb) - to exist (inanimate)
12. 無理 【む・り】 - impossible
13. その - that　(abbr. of それの)
14. 時計 【と・けい】 - watch; clock

「もらう」 meaning, "to receive" has only one version unlike 「あげる／くれる」 so there's very little to explain. One thing to point out is that since you receive *from* someone, 「から」 is also appropriate in addition to the 「に」 target particle.

Examples

1. 私が友達にプレゼントを<u>もらった</u>。
   I received present from friend.

2. 友達からプレゼントをもらった。
   I received present from friend.
3. これは友達に買ってもらった。
   About this, received the favor of buying it from friend.
4. 宿題をチェックしてもらいたかったけど、時間がなくて無理だった。
   I wanted to receive the favor of checking homework but there was no time and it was impossible.

「もらう」 is seen from the perspective of the receiver, so in the case of first-person, others usually don't receive things from you. However, you might want to use 「私からもらう」 when you want to emphasize that fact that the other person received it from you. For instance, if you wanted to say, "Hey, I gave you that!" you would use 「あげる」. However, you would use 「もらう」 if you wanted to say, "Hey, you got that from me!"

- その時計は私からもらったのよ。
  (He) received that watch from me.

Asking favors with 「くれる」 or 「もらえる」

Vocabulary

1. 千円 【せん・えん】 - 1,000 yen
2. 貸す 【か・す】 (u-verb) - lend
3. する (exception) - to do
4. くれる (ru-verb) - to give
5. もらう (u-verb) - to receive
6. あなた - you
7. 私 【わたし】 - me; myself; I
8. ちょっと - a little
9. 静か 【しず・か】 (na-adj) - quiet

10. 漢字 【かん・じ】 - Kanji

11. 書く 【か・く】 (u-verb) - to write

You can make requests by using 「くれる」 and the potential form of 「もらう」 (can I receive the favor of...). We've already seen an example of this in example 4 of the 「くれる」 section. Because requests are favors done for the speaker, you cannot use 「あげる」 in this situation.

Examples

1. 千円を貸してくれる？
   Will you give me the favor of lending 1000 yen?

2. 千円を貸してもらえる？
   Can I receive the favor of you lending 1000 yen?

Notice that the two sentences essentially mean the same thing. This is because the giver and receiver has been omitted because it is obvious from the context. If we were to write out the full sentence, it would look like this:

1. あなたが、私に千円を貸してくれる？
   Will you give me the favor of lending 1000 yen?

2. 私が、あなたに千円を貸してもらえる？
   Can I receive the favor of you lending 1000 yen?

It is not normal to explicitly include the subject and target like this when directly addressing someone but is provided here to illustrate the change of subject and target depending on the verb 「くれる」 and 「もらえる」.

You can use the negative to make the request a little softer. You'll see that this is true in many other types of grammar.

1. ちょっと静かにして<u>くれない</u>?
   Won't you be a little quieter?

2. 漢字で書いて<u>もらえません</u>か。
   Can you write this in kanji for me?

Asking someone to not do something

Vocabulary

1. 全部 【ぜん・ぶ】 - everything
2. 食べる 【た・べる】 (ru-verb) - to eat
3. くれる (ru-verb) - to give
4. 高い 【たか・い】 (i-adj) - high; tall; expensive
5. 物 【もの】 - object
6. 買う 【か・う】 (u-verb) - to buy

In order to request that someone *not* do something, you simply attach 「で」 to the negative form of the verb and proceed as before.

1. 全部食べない<u>で</u>くれますか。
   Can you not eat it all?

2. 高い物を買わない<u>で</u>くれる?
   Can you not buy expensive thing(s)?

Making Requests

Politely (and not so politely) making requests

Similar to asking for favors, which we learned in the last lesson, there are also various ways to make requests in Japanese. This is effectively the Japanese way of saying, "please do X". We'll first learn the most common way to make requests using a special

conjugation of the verb 「くださる」 and the firmer 「なさる」.
Finally, we'll learn the rarely used excessively strong command form
for the sake of completeness. You can safely skip the last part
unless you're an avid reader of manga.

「〜ください」 - a special conjugation of 「くださる」

Vocabulary

1. それ - that
2. くれる (ru-verb) - to give
3. 漢字 【かん・じ】 - Kanji
4. 書く 【か・く】 (u-verb) - to write
5. ここ - here
6. 来る 【く・る】 (exception) - to come
7. 日本語 【に・ほん・ご】 - Japanese (language)
8. 話す 【はな・す】 (u-verb) - to speak
9. 消しゴム 【け・し・ごむ】 - eraser
10. 貸す 【か・す】 (u-verb) - lend
11. 遠い 【とお・い】 (i-adj) - far
12. 所 【ところ】 - place
13. 行く 【い・く】 (u-verb) - to go
14. お父さん 【お・とう・さん】 - father (polite)
15. 時計 【と・けい】 - watch; clock
16. 壊れる 【こわ・れる】 (ru-verb) - to break
17. 言う 【い・う】 (u-verb) - to say

「ください」 is a special conjugation of 「くださる」, which is the
honorific form of 「くれる」. We will learn more about honorific and
humble forms in the beginning of the next major section. We are
going over 「ください」 here because it has a slight difference in
meaning from the normal 「くれる」 and the honorific 「くださ

る」．「ください」 is different from 「くれる」 in the following fashion:

1. それをください。
   Please give me that.
2. それをくれる?
   Can you give me that?

As you can see 「ください」 is a direct request for something while 「くれる」 is used as a question asking for someone to give something. However, it is similar to 「くれる」 in that you can make a request for an action by simply attaching it to the te-form of the verb.

1. 漢字で書いてください。
   Please write it in kanji.
2. ゆっくり話してください。
   Please speak slowly.

The rules for negative requests are same as the rules for 「くれる」 as well.

1. 落書きを書かないでください。
   Please don't write graffiti.
2. ここにこないでください。
   Please don't come here.

In casual speech, it is often common to simply drop the 「ください」 part.

1. 日本語で話して。
   Please speak in Japanese.
2. 消しゴムを貸して。
   Please lend me the eraser.

3. 遠い所に行かないで。
Please don't go to a far place.

For those who want to sound particularly commanding and manly, it is also possible to use 「くれる」 with the 「る」 removed.

1. 日本語で話してくれ。
Speak in Japanese.
2. 消しゴムを貸してくれ。
Lend me the eraser.
3. 遠い所に行かないでくれ。
Don't go to a far place.

Because 「ください」 like the masu-form must always come at the end sentence or a relative clause, you cannot use it to directly modify a noun. For example, the following is not possible with 「ください」.

• お父さんがくれた時計が壊れた。
The clock that father gave broke.

Of course, since direct quotes is merely repeating something someone said in verbatim, you can put practically anything in a direct quote.

• 「それをください」とお父さんが言った。
Father said, "Please give me that."

Using 「～ちょうだい」 as a casual request

Vocabulary

1. 頂戴 【ちょうだい】 - receiving (humble)
2. 致す 【いたす】 (u-verb) - to do (humble)

3. スプーン - spoon
4. ここ - here
5. 名前 【な・まえ】 - name
6. 書く 【か・く】 (u-verb) - to write

A casual alternative of 「ください」 is 「ちょうだい」. While it can be used by anyone, it has a slightly feminine and childish nuance and is always written in Hiragana. Written in Kanji, it is usually used in a very formal expression such as 「頂戴致します」.

Grammatically, it's used exactly the same way as 「ください」.

Examples

1. スプーンをちょうだい。
   Please give me the spoon.
2. ここに名前を書いてちょうだい。
   Please write your name here.

Using 「～なさい」 to make firm but polite requests

Vocabulary

1. 食べる 【たべ・る】 (ru-verb) - to eat
2. 飲む 【の・む】 (u-verb) - to drink
3. する (exception) - to do
4. いい (i-adj) - good
5. 聞く 【き・く】 (u-verb) - to ask; to listen
6. ここ - here
7. 座る 【すわ・る】 (ru-verb) - to sit
8. まだ - yet
9. いっぱい - full
10. ある (u-verb) - to exist (inanimate)

11. たくさん - a lot (amount)
12. それ - that
13. 思う 【おも・う】 (u-verb) - to think
14. そう - (things are) that way

「なさい」 is a special honorific conjugation of 「する」. It is a soft yet firm way of issuing a command. It is used, for example, when a mother is scolding her child or when a teacher wants a delinquent student to pay attention. Unlike 「ください」, 「なさい」 only applies to positive verbs and uses the stem of the verb instead of the te-form. It also cannot be used by itself but must be attached to another verb.

Using 「なさい」 to make firm but polite requests

Conjugate the verb to its stem and attach 「なさい」
Examples

1. 食べる → 食べなさい
2. 飲む → 飲み → 飲みなさい
3. する → し → しなさい

Examples

1. よく聞きなさい！
   Listen well!

2. ここに座りなさい。
   Sit here.

You can also drop 「さい」 portion of the 「なさい」 to make a casual version of this grammar.

1. まだいっぱいあるから、たくさん<u>食べな</u>。
There's still a lot, so eat a lot.
2. それでいいと思うなら、そう<u>しな</u>よ。
If you think that's fine, then go ahead and do it.

The Command Form

Vocabulary

1. くれる (ru-verb) - to give
2. 死ぬ 【し・ぬ】 (u-verb) - to die
3. する (exception) - to do
4. 来る 【く・る】 (exception) - to come
5. 食べる 【た・べる】 (ru-verb) - to eat
6. 着る 【き・る】 (ru-verb) - to wear
7. 信じる 【しん・じる】 (ru-verb) - to believe
8. 寝る 【ね・る】 (ru-verb) - to sleep
9. 起きる 【お・きる】 (ru-verb) - to wake; to occur
10. 出る 【で・る】 (ru-verb) - to come out
11. 掛ける 【か・ける】 (ru-verb) - to hang
12. 捨てる 【す・てる】 (ru-verb) - to throw away
13. 話す 【はな・す】 (u-verb) - to speak
14. 聞く 【き・く】 (u-verb) - to ask; to listen
15. 遊ぶ 【あそ・ぶ】 (u-verb) - to play
16. 待つ 【ま・つ】 (u-verb) - to wait
17. 飲む 【の・む】 (u-verb) - to drink
18. 直る 【なお・る】 (u-verb) - to be fixed
19. 買う 【か・う】 (u-verb) - to buy
20. 好き 【す・き】 (na-adj) - likable
21. あっち - that way (over there)　(abbr of あちら)

22. 行く 【い・く】 (u-verb) - to go
23. 早い 【はや・い】 (i-adj) - fast; early
24. 酒 【さけ】 - alcohol
25. 持つ 【も・つ】 (u-verb) - to hold

We will go over the command form in the interest of covering all the possible verb conjugations. In reality, the command form is rarely used as Japanese people tend to be too polite to use imperatives. Also, this coarse type of speech is rarely, if indeed at all, used by females who tend to use 「なさい」 or an exasperated 「くれる」 when angry or irritated. This form is only really useful for reading or watching fictional works. You may often see or hear 「死ね！」 ("Die!") in fiction which, of course, you'll never hear in real life. (I hope!)

Be sure to note that, in addition to the familiar 「する」, 「くる」 exception verbs, 「くれる」 is also an exception for the command form.

Rules for creating command form

- **For ru-verbs:** Replace the 「る」 with 「ろ」
- **For u-verbs:** Change the last character from an / u / vowel to an / e / vowel
- **Exceptions:**
    1. する → しろ
    2. くる → こい
    3. くれる → くれ

Plain	Command	Plain	Command	Plain	Command
食べる	食べろ	話す	話せ	する	しろ
着る	着ろ	聞く	聞け	くる	こい
信じる	信じろ	遊ぶ	遊べ	くれる	くれ
寝る	寝ろ	待つ	待て		
起きる	起きろ	飲む	飲め		
出る	出ろ	直る	直れ		
掛ける	掛けろ	死ぬ	死ね		
捨てる	捨てろ	買う	買え		

Examples

1. 好きにしろ。
   Do as you please.
2. あっち行け！
   Go away!
3. 早く酒を持ってきてくれ。
   Hurry up and bring me some alcohol.

Negative Command

Vocabulary

1. 行く 【い・く】 (u-verb) - to go
2. する (exception) - to do
3. それ - that
4. 食べる 【た・べる】 (ru-verb) - to eat
5. 変 【へん】 (na-adj) - strange
6. こと - event, matter
7. 言う 【い・う】 (u-verb) - to say

The negative command form is very simple: simply attach 「な」 to either ru-verbs or u-verbs. Don't confuse this with the 「な」 sentence-ending particle we will be learning at the end of this section. The intonation is totally different.

Using the negative command form

Attach 「な」 to the verb
Examples

1. 行く → 行く<u>な</u>
2. する → する<u>な</u>

Examples

1. それを食べる<u>な</u>！
   Don't eat that!
2. 変なことを言う<u>な</u>！
   Don't say such weird things!

This is not to be confused with the shortened version of 「～なさい」 we just learned in the last section. The most obvious difference (besides the clear difference in tone) is that in 「〜なさい」, the verb is first converted to the stem while the negative command has no conjugation. For example, for 「する」, 「しな」 would be the short version of 「しなさい」 while 「するな」 would be a negative command.

Numbers and Counting

Numbers and counting in Japanese are difficult enough to require its own section. First of all, the number system is in units of four instead of three, which can make converting into English quite difficult. Also, there are things called counters, which are required to count different types of objects, animals, or people. We will learn the most generic and widely used counters to get you started so that you can learn more on your own. To be honest, counters might be the only thing that'll make you want to quit learning Japanese, it's that bad. I recommend you digest only a little bit of this section at a time because it's an awful lot of things to memorize.

The Number System

The Japanese number system is spread into units of four. So a number such as 10,000,000 is actually split up as 1000,0000. However, thanks to the strong influence of the Western world and the standardization of numbers, when numbers are actually written, the split-off is three digits. Here are the first ten numbers.

Kanji and readings for numbers 1 to 10

1	2	3	4	5	6	7	8	9	10
一	二	三	四	五	六	七	八	九	十
いち	に	さん	し／よん	ご	ろく	しち／なな	はち	きゅう	じゅう

As the chart indicates, 4 can either be 「し」 or 「よん」 and 7 can either be 「しち」 or 「なな」. Basically, both are acceptable up to 10. However, past ten, the reading is almost always 「よん」 and 「なな」. In general, 「よん」 and 「なな」 are preferred over 「し」 and 「しち」 in most circumstances.

You can simply count from 1 to 99 with just these ten numbers. Japanese is easier than English in this respect because you do not have to memorize separate words such as "twenty" or "fifty". In Japanese, it's simply just "two ten" and "five ten".

1. 三十一 （さんじゅういち） = 31
2. 五十四 （ごじゅうよん） = 54
3. 七十七 （ななじゅうなな） = 77
4. 二十 （にじゅう） = 20

Notice that numbers are either always written in kanji or numerals because hiragana can get rather long and hard to decipher.

Numbers past 99

Here are the higher numbers:

Numerals	100	1,000	10,000	10^8	10^12
漢字	百	千	万	億	兆
ひらがな	ひゃく	せん	まん	おく	ちょう

Notice how the numbers jumped four digits from 10^4 to 10^8 between 万 and 億? That's because Japanese is divided into units of four. Once you get past 1万 (10,000), you start all over until you reach 9,999万, then it rotates to 1億 (100,000,000). By the way, 百 is 100 and 千 is 1,000, but anything past that, and you need to attach a 1 so the rest of the units become 一万 (10^4)、一億 (10^8)、一兆 (10^12).

Now you can count up to 9,999,999,999,999,999 just by chaining the numbers same as before. This is where the problems start, however. Try saying 「いちちょう」 、 「ろくひゃく」、or 「さんせん」 really quickly, you'll notice it's difficult because of the repetition of similar consonant sounds. Therefore, Japanese people have decided to make it easier on themselves by pronouncing them as 「いっちょう」 、 「ろっぴゃく」 、and 「さんぜん」. Unfortunately, it makes it all the harder for you to remember how to pronounce everything. Here are all the slight sound changes.

Numerals	漢字	ひらがな
300	三百	さんびゃく
600	六百	ろっぴゃく
800	八	はっぴゃ

	百	く
3000	三千	さんぜん
8000	八千	はっせん
10^12	一兆	いっちょう

1. 四万三千七十六 （よんまんさんぜんななじゅうろく） 43,076
2. 七億六百二十四万九千二百二十二 （ななおくろっぴゃくにじゅうよんまんきゅうせんにひゃくにじゅうに） 706,249,222
3. 五百兆二万一 （ごひゃくちょうにまんいち） 500,000,000,020,001

Notice that it is customary to write large numbers only in numerals as even kanji can become difficult to decipher.

Numbers smaller or less than 1

Vocabulary

1. 零 【れい】 - zero
2. ゼロ - zero
3. マル - circle; zero
4. 点 【てん】 - period; point
5. マイナス - minus

Zero in Japanese is 「零」 but 「ゼロ」 or 「マル」 is more common in modern Japanese. There is no special method for reading decimals, you simply say 「点」 for the dot and read each individual number after the decimal point. Here's an example:

- 0.0021 = ゼロ、点、ゼロ、ゼロ、二、一。

For negative numbers, everything is the same as positive numbers except that you say 「マイナス」 first.

- マイナス二十九 = -29

Counting and Counters

Ah, and now we come to the fun part. In Japanese, when you are simply counting numbers, everything is just as you would expect, 一、二、三、 and so on. However, if you want to count any type of object, you have to use something called a counter which depends on what type of object you are counting and on top of this, there are various sound changes similar to the ones we saw with 六百, etc.. The counter themselves are usually single kanji characters that often have a special reading just for the counter. First, let's learn the counters for dates

Dates

Vocabulary

1. 平成 【へい・せい】 - Heisei era
2. 昭和 【しょう・わ】 - Showa era
3. 和暦 【わ・れき】 - Japanese calendar
4. 一日 【いち・にち】 - one day

The year is very easy. All you have to do is say the number and add 「年」 which is pronounced here as 「ねん」. For example, Year 2003 becomes 2003年 (にせんさんねん) . The catch is that there is another calendar which starts over every time a new emperor ascends the throne. The year is preceded by the era, for example the year 2000 is: 平成12年. My birthday, 1981 is 昭和56年 (The Showa era lasted from 1926 to 1989). You may think that you don't need to know this but if you're going to be filling out forms in Japan, they often ask you for your birthday or the current date in the Japanese calendar （和暦）. So here's a <u>neat converter</u> you can use to convert to the Japanese calendar.

Saying the months is actually easier than English because all you have to do is write the number (either in numerals or kanji) of the month and add 「月」 which is read as 「がつ」. However, you need to pay attention to April （４月）, July （７月）, and September （９月） which are pronounced 「しがつ」、「しちがつ」、and 「くがつ」 respectively.

Finally, we get to the days of the month, which is where the headache starts. The first day of the month is 「ついたち」 （一日）; *different* from 「いちにち」 （一日）, which means "one day". Besides this and some other exceptions we'll soon cover, you can simply say the number and add 「日」 which is pronounced here as 「にち」. For example, the 26th becomes 26日 （にじゅうろくにち）. Pretty simple, *however*, the first 10 days, the 14th, 19th, 20th, 29th have special readings that you must separately memorize. If you like memorizing things, you'll have a ball here. Notice that the kanji doesn't change but the reading does.

Days of the month

Day	Kanji	Reading
What day	何日	なん・にち
1st	一日	ついたち
2nd	二日	ふつ・か
3rd	三日	みっ・か
4th	四日	よっ・か
5th	五日	いつ・か
6th	六日	むい・か
7th	七日	なの・か
8th	八日	よう・か
9th	九日	ここの・か
10th	十日	とお・か
11th	十一日	じゅう・いち・にち
12th	十二日	じゅう・に・にち
13th	十三日	じゅう・さん・にち
14th	十四日	じゅう・よっ・か
15th	十五日	じゅう・ご・にち
16th	十六日	じゅう・ろく・にち

17th	十七日	じゅう・しち・にち
18th	十八日	じゅう・はち・にち
19th	十九日	じゅう・く・にち
20th	二十日	はつ・か
21st	二十一日	に・じゅう・いち・にち
22nd	二十二日	に・じゅう・に・にち
23rd	二十三日	に・じゅう・さん・にち
24th	二十四日	に・じゅう・よっ・か
25th	二十五日	に・じゅう・ご・にち
26th	二十六日	に・じゅう・ろく・にち
27th	二十七日	に・じゅう・しち・にち
28th	二十八日	に・じゅう・はち・にち
29th	二十	に・じゅう・く・にち

	九日	
30th	三十日	さん・じゅう・にち
31st	三十 一日	さん・じゅう・ いち・にち

In Japan, the full format for dates follows the international date format and looks like: XXXX年YY月ZZ日. For example, today's date would be: 2003年12月 2日

Time

Now, we'll learn how to tell time. The hour is given by saying the number and adding 「時」 which is pronounced here as 「じ」. Here is a chart of exceptions to look out for.

英語	4 o'clock	7 o'clock	9 o'clock
漢字	四時	七時	九時
ひらがな	よじ	しちじ	くじ

Notice how the numbers 4, 7, and 9 keep coming up to be a pain in the butt? Well, those and sometimes 1, 6 and 8 are the numbers to watch out for. The minutes are given by adding 「分」 which usually read as 「ふん」 with the following exceptions:

英語	1 min	3 min	4 min	6 min	8 min	10 min
漢字	一分	三分	四分	六分	八分	十分
ひらがな	いっぷん	さんぷん	よんぷん	ろっぷん	はっぷん	じゅっぷん

For higher number, you use the normal pronunciation for the higher digits and rotate around the same readings for 1 to 10. For instance, 24 minutes is 「にじゅうよんぷん」 （二十四分） while 30 minutes is 「さんじゅっぷん」 （三十分） . There are also other less common but still correct pronunciations such as 「はちふん」 for 「八分」 and 「じっぷん」 for 「十分」 (this one is almost never used).

All readings for seconds consists of the number plus 「秒」 , which is read as 「びょう」 . There are no exceptions for seconds and all the readings are the same.

Some examples of time.

1. 1時24分 （いちじ・にじゅうよんぷん） 1:24
2. 午後4時10分 （ごご・よじ・じゅっぷん） 4:10 PM
3. 午前9時16分 （ごぜん・くじ・じゅうろっぷん） 9:16 AM
4. 13時16分 （じゅうさんじ・じゅうろっぷん） 13:16
5. 2時18分13秒 （にじ・じゅうはっぷん・じゅうさんびょう） 2:18:13

A Span of Time

Ha! I bet you thought you were done with dates and time, well guess again. This time we will learn counters for counting spans of time, days, months, and years. The basic counter for a span of time is

「間」, which is read as 「かん」. You can attach it to the end of hours, days, weeks, and years. Minutes (in general) and seconds do not need this counter and months have a separate counter, which we will cover next.

1. 二時間四十分 （にじかん・よんじゅっぷん） 2 hours and 40 minutes
2. 二十日間 （はつかかん） 20 days
3. 十五日間 （じゅうごにちかん） 15 days
4. 二年間 （にねんかん） two years
5. 三週間 （さんしゅうかん） three weeks
6. 一日 （いちにち） 1 day

As mentioned before, a period of one day is 「一日」 （いちにち） which is different from the 1st of the month: 「ついたち」.

Pronunciations to watch out for when counting weeks is one week: 「一週間」 （いっしゅうかん） and 8 weeks: 「八週間」 （はっしゅうかん）.

To count the number of months, you simple take a regular number and add 「か」 and 「月」 which is pronounced here as 「げつ」 and *not* 「がつ」. The 「か」 used in this counter is usually written as a small katakana 「ヶ」 which is confusing because it's still pronounced as 「か」 and not 「け」. The small 「ヶ」 is actually totally different from the katakana 「ケ」 and is really an abbreviation for the kanji 「箇」, the original kanji for the counter. This small 「ヶ」 is also used in some place names such as 「千駄ヶ谷」 and other counters, such as the counter for location described in the "Other Counters" section below.

In counting months, you should watch out for the following sound changes:

英語	1 month	6 months	10 months
漢字	一ヶ月	六ヶ月	十ヶ月
ひらがな	いっかげつ	ろっかげつ	じゅっかげつ

Just like minutes, the high numbers rotate back using the same sounds for 1 to 10.

1. 十一ヶ月 （じゅういっかげつ） Eleven months
2. 二十ヶ月 （にじゅっかげつ） Twenty months
3. 三十三ヶ月 （さんじゅうさんかげつ） Thirty three months

Other Counters

We'll cover some of the most common counters so that you'll be familiar with how counters work. This will hopefully allow you to learn other counters on your own because there are too many to even consider covering them all. The important thing to remember is that using the wrong counter is grammatically incorrect. If you are counting people, you **must** use the people counter, etc. Sometimes, it is acceptable to use a more generic counter when a less commonly used counter applies. Here are some counters.

日本語	When to Use
人	To count the number of people
本	To count long, cylindrical objects such as bottles or chopsticks
枚	To count thin objects such as paper or shirts
冊	To count bound objects usually books
匹	To count small animals like cats or dogs
歳	To count the age of a living creatures such as people
個	To count small (often round) objects

回	To count number of times
ヶ所（箇所）	To count number of locations
つ	To count any generic object that has a rare or no counter

Counting 1 to 10 (some variations might exist)

	人	本	枚	冊	匹	歳	個	回	ヶ所（箇所）	つ
1	ひとり	いっぽん	いちまい	いっさつ	いっぴき	いっさい	いっこ	いっかい	いっかしょ	ひとつ
2	ふたり	にほん	にまい	にさつ	にひき	にさい	にこ	にかい	にかしょ	ふたつ
3	さんにん	さんぼん	さんまい	さんさつ	さんびき	さんさい	さんこ	さんかい	さんかしょ	みっつ
4	よにん	よんほん	よんまい	よんさつ	よんひき	よんさい	よんこ	よんかい	よんかしょ	よっつ
5	ごにん	ごほん	ごまい	ごさつ	ごひき	ごさい	ごこ	ごかい	ごかしょ	いつつ
6	ろくにん	ろっぽん	ろくまい	ろくさつ	ろっぴき	ろくさい	ろっこ	ろっかい	ろっかしょ	むっつ
7	しちにん	ななほん	ななまい	ななさつ	ななひき	ななさい	ななこ	ななかい	ななかしょ	ななつ
8	はちにん	はちほん	はちまい	はっさつ	はっぴき	はっさい	はっこ	はちかい	はっかしょ	やっつ
9	きゅうにん	きゅうほん	きゅうまい	きゅうさつ	きゅうひき	きゅうさい	きゅうこ	きゅうかい	きゅうかしょ	ここのつ
10	じゅうにん	じゅっぽん	じゅうまい	じゅっさつ	じゅっぴき	じゅっさい	じゅっこ	じゅっかい	じゅっかしょ	とお

The changed sounds have been highlighted. You don't count 0 because there is nothing to count. You can simply use 「ない」 or 「いない」. The chart has hiragana for pronunciation but, as before, it is usually written with either numbers or kanji plus the counter with the single exception of 「とお」 which is simply written as 「十」.

For higher numbers, it's the same as before, you use the normal pronunciation for the higher digits and rotate around the same readings for 1 to 10 except for 「一人」 and 「二人」 which transforms to the normal 「いち」 and 「に」 once you get past the first two. So 「一人」 is 「ひとり」 while 「11人」 is 「じゅういちにん」. Also, the generic counter 「〜つ」 only applies up to exactly ten items. Past that, you can just use regular plain numbers.

Note: The counter for age is often sometimes written as 「才」 for those who don't have the time to write out the more complex kanji. Plus, age 20 is usually read as 「はたち」 and not 「にじゅっさい」.

Using 「目」 to show order

You can attach 「目」 (read as 「め」) to various counters to indicate the order. The most common example is the 「番」 counter. For example, 「一番」 which means "number one" becomes "the first" when you add 「目」 (一番目). Similarly, 「一回目」 is the first time, 「二回目」 is the second time, 「四人目」 is the fourth person, and so on.

Casual Patterns and Slang

So far, for every grammar we have covered, we also went over all the casual variations as well. However, even though we have already covered all the casual forms, truly mastering casual speech in Japanese requires far more than just learning the various casual forms. There are countless numbers of ways in which wordings and pronunciations change as well as differences between male and female speech. Understanding slang also requires knowing various vocabulary that is also growing with every new generation. Many adults would be hard-pressed to understand the kind of slang being used by kids today.

While comprehensively covering slang and relevant vocabulary would require a book in and of itself (a book that would soon become out of date), I'll instead cover some broad patterns and common phenomenon which will at least help you get started in understanding the most common aspects of Japanese slang. There is no particular order in the material presented here and I expect this page to grow continuously as I find different things to cover.

Please note that slang is also heavily influenced by local dialects. Although all the material presented here is valid for the greater Tokyo area, your mileage may vary depending on where you are located.

Basic Principles of Slang

In the world of slang, anything goes and rules that apply to written Japanese are often broken. The most difficult part is that, of course, you can't just say whatever you want. When you break the rules, you have to break it the correct way. Taking what you learned from textbooks or Japanese classes and applying it to the real world is not so easy because it is impossible to teach all the possible ways things can get jumbled up in the spoken language. Learning how to speak naturally with all the correct idiosyncrasies and inconsistencies in a language is something that requires practice with real people in real-world situations. In this section, we'll look at some common patterns and themes that will at least help you get an idea of where the majority of slang originates from.

One thing you'll soon realize when you first start talking to Japanese people in real life is that many sounds are slurred together. This is especially true for males. The fact is voices in instructional material such as language tapes often exaggerate the pronunciation of each letter in order to make aural comprehension easier. In reality, not all the sounds are pronounced as clearly as it should be and things end up sounding different from how it's written on paper.

There is one major driving factor behind the majority of slang in Japanese. The primary goal of most slang is to make things easier to say. In other words, the goal is to reduce or simplify the movement of your mouth. There are two primary ways in which this is accomplished, 1) By making things shorter or, 2) By slurring the sounds together. We have already seen many examples of the first method such as shortening 「かもしれない」 to 「かも」 or preferring 「と」 to the longer conditional forms. The second method makes things easier to say usually by substituting parts of words with sounds that fit better with the sounds surrounding it or by merging two or more sounds together. For example, the same 「かもしれない」 might be pronounced 「かもしんない」 since 「しん」 requires less movement than 「しれ」.

The fundamental goal of slang is to reduce mouth movement

Let's see some more examples of words that get shortened or slurred. Try saying both versions to get a feel for how the slang saves space and some calories for your mouth.

Examples

Vocabulary

1. ここ - here
2. つまらない (i-adj) - boring

3. 私 【わたし】 - me; myself; I
4. 家 【1) うち; 2) いえ】 - 1) one's own home; 2) house
5. 行く 【い・く】 (u-verb) - to go
6. まったく - entirely; indeed; good grief (expression of exasperation)
7. いつ - when
8. こんな - this sort of
9. 所 【ところ】 - place
10. ぐずぐず - tardily; hesitatingly
11. する (exception) - to do

1. ここはつまらないから私の家に行こう。
2. ここつまんないから、私んち行こう。

1. まったく、いつまでこんなところで、ぐずぐずするんだよ。
2. ったく、いつまでこんなとこで、ぐずぐずすんだよ。

You'll see that a great deal of slang in Japanese stems from this single principle of making things easier to say. It's very natural because it's guided by how your mouth moves. With a fair amount of practice, you should be able to naturally pick up shorter, alternative pronunciations and incorporate them into your own speech.

Sentence ordering and particles (or the lack thereof)

Vocabulary

1. それ - that
2. 何 【なに／なん】 - what
3. 見る 【み・る】 (ru-verb) - to see
4. あの - that (over there) (abbr. of あれの)
5. 人 【ひと】 - person

6. もう - already
7. 食べる 【たべ・る】 (ru-verb) - to eat
8. 昨日【きのう】 - yesterday
9. 買う 【か・う】 (u-verb) - to buy
10. アイス - ice (short for ice cream)

While written Japanese already has fairly loose rules regarding sentence order, casual spoken Japanese takes it one step further. A complete sentence requires a verb at the end of the sentence to complete the thought. However, we'll see how this rule is bent in casual conversations.

Conversations are sporadic and chaotic in any language and it's common for people to say the first thing that pops into their head without thinking out the whole proper sentence.

For example, if you wanted to ask what something was, the normal, proper way would be to ask, 「それは何? 」 However, if the first thing that popped into your head, "What the?" then it would be more natural to say 「何」 first. However, since 「何はそれ？」 doesn't make any sense (Is what that?), you can simply break it up into what are essentially two sentence fragments asking "what" first （何? ）, and then following it up with the explanation of what you were talking about （「それ」 in this case） . For the sake of convenience, this is lumped into what looks like one sentence.

Examples

1. それは何?
   What is that?
2. 何それ？
   What? That. (Two sentences lumped into one)

Sometimes, the first thing that pops into your head might be main verb. But if the main verb has already slipped out of your mouth, you're now left with the rest of the sentence without a verb to complete the thought. In conversational Japanese, it's perfectly acceptable to have the verb come first using the same technique we just saw by breaking them into two sentences. The second sentence is incomplete of course, but that kind of thing is common in the speech of any language.

1. 見た？ あの人?
   Did you see? That guy?
2. もう食べた？昨日買ったアイス。
   You ate it already? The ice cream I bought yesterday.

Using 「じゃん」 instead of 「じゃない」 to confirm

Vocabulary

1. サラリーマン - office worker (salary man)
2. 残業 【ざん・ぎょう】 - overtime
3. たくさん - a lot (amount)
4. する (exception) - to do
5. まあ - well
6. いい (i-adj) - good
7. ほら - look
8. やはり／やっぱり - as I thought
9. レポート - report
10. 書く 【か・く】 (u-verb) - to write
11. 駄目 【だめ】 - no good
12. 誰 【だれ】 - who
13. いる (ru-verb) - to exist (animate)
14. ここ - here

15. 着替える 【きが・える】 (ru-verb) - to change clothes
16. ～君 【～くん】 - name suffix
17. 知る 【し・る】 (u-verb) - to know
18. やはり／やっぱり／やっぱ - as I thought
19. 駅 【えき】 - station
20. 近い 【ちか・い】 (i-adj) - close, near
21. カラオケ - karaoke
22. ある (u-verb) - to exist (inanimate)
23. うん - yes (casual)
24. あそこ - over there
25. すぐ - soon; nearby
26. 隣 【となり】 - next to

「じゃん」 is an abbreviation of 「じゃない」, the negative conjugation for nouns and na-adjectives. However, this only applies to 「じゃない」 used in the following fashion.

- サラリーマンだから、残業はたくさんするんじゃない?
  Because he's a salaryman, doesn't he do a lot of overtime?

The important thing to note about the example above is that 「じゃない」 here is actually confirming the positive. In fact, a closer translation is, "Because he's a salaryman, he *probably does* a lot of overtime." But it's still a question so there's a slight nuance that you are seeking confirmation even though you are relatively sure.

「じゃん」 is a shorter slang for expressing the same type of thing except it doesn't even bother to ask a question to confirm. It's completely affirmative in tone.

In fact, the closest equivalent to 「じゃん」 is 「じゃない」 used in the following fashion.

- まあ、いいじゃない。
  Well, it's probably fine (don't you think?).

This type of expression is the **only** case where you can attach 「じ
ゃない」 directly to i-adjectives and verbs. Once you actually hear
this expression in real life, you'll see that it has a distinct
pronunciation that is different from simply using the negative. Plus,
you have to realize that this type of 「じゃない」 sounds rather
mature and feminine, unlike 「じゃん」, which is gender-neutral.

Like the above, specialized use of 「じゃない」, you can also
attach 「じゃん」 directly to verbs and i-adjectives as well as the
usual nouns and na-adjectives. Because slang is usually created to
make things easier, it's not surprising that the rules for using 「じゃ
ん」 are so lax and easy.

Summary

- Though derived from 「じゃない」, 「じゃん」 is always
  used to confirm the positive.
- It can be attached to the end of any sentence regardless of
  whether it ends in a noun, adjective, verb, or adverb.

Finally, let's get to the examples. Hopefully, you can see that 「じゃ
ん」 is basically saying something along the lines of, "See, I'm right,
aren't I?"

Examples

1. ほら、やっぱりレポートを書かないとだめ<u>じゃん</u>。
   See, as I thought, you have to write the report.
2. 誰もいないからここで着替えてもいい<u>じゃん</u>。
   Since there's nobody, it's probably fine to change here.

A：たかし君は、ここにいる？
A: Is Takashi here?

B：知らない。
B: Dunno.

A：あっ！やっぱ、いる<u>じゃん</u>！
A: Ah! See, he is here!

There's also another variation, which attaches the question marker as well. The meaning is mostly the same but it adds more to the questioning, confirming tone.

A：駅の近くにカラオケがある<u>じゃんか</u>。
A: There's a karaoke place near the station, right?

B：うん。
B: Yeah.

A：あそこのすぐ隣だ。
A: It's right next to there.

Using 「つ」 for 「という」

Vocabulary

1. 言う 【い・う】 (u-verb) - to say
2. 何で 【なん・で】 - why; how
3. お前 【お・まえ】 - you (casual)

254

4. ここ - here
5. いる (ru-verb) - to exist (animate)
6. 宿題 【しゅく・だい】 - homework
7. 時間 【じ・かん】 - time
8. ある (u-verb) - to exist (inanimate)
9. デート - date
10. する (exception) - to do
11. 行く 【い・く】 (u-verb) - to go
12. 聞く 【き・く】 (u-verb) - to ask; to listen
13. 明日 【あした】 - tomorrow
14. 試験 【し・けん】 - exam
15. 勉強 【べん・きょう】 - study
16. 違う 【ちが・う】 (u-verb) - to be different

As we learned in the defining and describing section, 「いう」 serves many more functions than the equivalent English verb, "to say". It is used all the time and therefore, it's not too surprising that a number of variations and slang have developed. Here's one more that I felt was too "slangy" to cover so early at that point of the guide.

This may sound hard to believe but if you really slur 「という」 together, it becomes something resembling 「つ」. Or least, that's what somebody thought when he or she began replacing 「という」 with 「つ」 or in some case 「つう」.

Now, in my opinion, 「つ」 is a lot harder to say than 「という」 so using it like a native might take a bit of practice. Rather than making things easier to say, as is usually the case, the real purpose of this substitution is to sound rougher because 「つ」 has a harder, hissing sound. This is ideal for when you're pissed or for that young and rough image you've always wanted. As you might expect, this type of speech is usually used by males or very tough females.

Examples

1. つうか、なんでお前がここにいんのよ！
   Or rather, why are you here?!
2. 宿題で時間がないつってんのに、みきちゃんとデートしにいったと聞いたよ。
   Although he's saying he doesn't have time due to homework, I heard he went on a date with Miki-chan.
3. 明日は試験だぞ。つっても、勉強はしてないだろうな。
   Yo, tomorrow's the test. Even if I say that, you probably didn't study anyway, huh?
4. だから、違うんだつうの！
   Like I said, you're wrong!

If you want even more emphasis, you can even add a small 「つ」. This usually means you are really at the brink of your patience.

- だから、違うんだっつうの！
  Like I said, you're wrong!

Using 「ってば」 and 「ったら」 to show exasperation

Vocabulary

1. もう - already
2. 行く 【い・く】 (u-verb) - to go
3. あなた - you
4. いつも - always
5. 忘れる 【わす・れる】 (ru-verb) - to forget

「ってば」 and 「ったら」 is yet another type of abbreviation for 「という」 similar to 「って」 as discussed in the defining and describing section. In this case, it's an abbreviation of the conditional form of 「という」, which is 「といえば」 and 「といったら」. By using this abbreviation, you are essentially saying something along the lines of, "If I told you once, I told you a million times!" You can use this expression when you tired of repeating yourself or when you are exasperated with somebody for not listening to you.

Examples

1. もう行くってば！
   I told you I'm going already!
2. あなたったら、いつも忘れるんだから。
   You're always forgetting.

Using 「なんか」 just about everywhere

Vocabulary

1. 何 【なに／なん】 - what
2. 食べる 【たべ・る】 (ru-verb) - to eat
3. 今日 【きょう】 - today
4. 忙しい 【いそが・しい】 (i-adj) - busy
5. 風呂 【ふ・ろ】 - bath
6. 超 【ちょう】 - super
7. 気持ち 【き・も・ち】 - feeling
8. いい (i-adj) - good
9. お母さん 【お・かあ・さん】 - mother (polite)
10. 明日 【あした】 - tomorrow
11. 戻る 【もど・る】 (u-verb) - to return
12. 私 【わたし】 - me; myself; I
13. こと - event, matter
14. 本当 【ほん・とう】 - real
15. 好き 【す・き】 (na-adj) - likable; desirable

By now, you're probably aware that 「何」 can be either read as 「なに」 or 「なん」 depending on what comes after it such as 「何色」（なにいろ）versus 「何人」（なんにん）. In the case of 「何か」, while 「なにか」 is the correct reading, it is often contracted to just 「なんか」 in casual speech.

- なにか食べる？
  Eat something?
- なんか食べる？
  Eat something?

However, 「なんか」 also has a function similar to the word "like" in English. By "like", I'm not talking about the actual word but the kind that has no meaning and some people use just about anywhere in the sentence. Similarly, 「なんか」 can also be used as a filler without any actual meaning. For instance, take a look at the example below.

- 今日は、なんか忙しいみたいよ。
  I guess he's like busy today.

While 「なんか」 is a shorter version of 「なにか」, only 「なんか」 can be used in this way as a filler.

- 今日は、なにか忙しいみたいよ。

  （「なにか」 cannot be used as a filler word.）

Let's take a look at a few more examples.

Examples

1. なんかね。お風呂って超気持ちいいよね！
   Like, baths feel really good, huh?

2. お母さんが、なんか明日まで戻らないんだってよ。
Mom said she's not coming back until like tomorrow.

3. なんかさ。ボブは、私のことなんか本当に好きかな？
-Hey like, do you really think that Bob likes somebody like me?

Showing contempt for an action with 「～やがる」

Vocabulary

1. あんな - that sort of
2. 奴【やつ】 - guy (derogatory)
3. 負ける【ま・ける】 (ru-verb) - to lose
4. どう - how
5. する (exception) - to do
6. やる (u-verb) - to do
7. 気【き】 - mood; intent
8. さっさと - quickly
9. 来る【く・る】 (exception) - to come

「やがる」 is a verb suffix used to indicate hatred or contempt for the person doing the action. Unlike the rest of the slang covered here, this extremely strong language is **not** used in normal, everyday conversations. You will probably never hear this expression outside of movies, comic books, games, and the like. However, it is covered here so that you can understand when it is used in those mediums.

In order to use 「やがる」, you simply attach it to the stem of the verb. After that, 「やがる」 is conjugated just like a regular u-verb.

Examples

1. あんなやつに負けやがって。じゃ、どうすんだよ？
   Losing to a guy like that. Well, what are you going to do?
2. やる気か？だったらさっさと来やがれ！
   You want to fight? If so, then hurry up and come on!

Review and more sentence-ending particles

We are coming to the end of the fourth major section of the guide. Do you feel like your Japanese has improved? We've come to the point where we've learned enough conjugations to be able to start mixing them together in various useful combinations. Of course this can be a little difficult to do without some practice, which is the reason for this lesson. But first, since we've come to the end of yet another section, let's learn some more sentence-endings particles.

「な」 and 「さ」 sentence-ending particles

Vocabulary

1. あのう／あの - say; well; errr
2. うん - yes (casual)
3. この - this (abbr. of これの)
4. 間 【あいだ】 - space (between); time (between); period
5. ディズニーランド - Disney Land
6. 行く 【い・く】 (u-verb) - to go
7. すごい (i-adj) - to a great extent
8. 込む 【こ・む】 (u-verb) - to become crowded
9. 何 【なに／なん】 - what
10. 出来る 【で・き・る】 (ru-verb) - to be able to do
11. 今 【いま】 - now
12. 図書館 【と・しょ・かん】 - library

260

13. 何で 【なん・で】 - why; how
14. 日本語 【に・ほん・ご】 - Japanese (language)
15. たくさん - a lot (amount)
16. 勉強 【べん・きょう】 - study
17. する (exception) - to do
18. まだ - yet
19. 全然 【ぜん・ぜん】 - not at all (when used with negative)
20. 分かる 【わ・かる】 (u-verb) - to understand
21. 大丈夫 【だい・じょう・ぶ】 (na-adj) - ok
22. なる (u-verb) - to become
23. いい (i-adj) - good
24. 今日 【きょう】 - today
25. 雨 【あめ】 - rain
26. 降る 【ふ・る】 (u-verb) - to precipitate
27. 大学 【だい・がく】 - college

After the 「よ」 and 「ね」, 「さ」 and 「な」 are the next most commonly used sentence-ending particles.

「さ」, which is basically a very casual form of 「よ」, is similar to the English "like" in that some people throw it in at the end of almost every single phrase. Of course, that doesn't mean it's necessarily a very sophisticated manner of speech but just like using "like" all the time, I cannot deny that it is an easy habit to fall into. In that sense, due to its over-use, it has almost lost any specific meaning. You may overhear a conversation like the following:

A：あのさ・・・ A: Hey... B：うん。 B: Yeah. A：この間さ・・・ A: This one time... B：うん。 B: Yeah. A：ディズニーランドに行ったんだけどさ、なんかさ、すごい込んでて・・・ A: I went to Disney Land and it was really crowded... B：うん B: Uh huh. A：何もできなくてさ・・・ A: Couldn't do anything, you know... And it goes on like this, sometimes the other person might break in to say something related to the topic.

You can use 「な」 in place of 「ね」 when it sounds too soft and reserved for what you want to say or for the audience you are speaking to. Its rough sound generally applies to the male gender but is not necessarily restricted to only males.

Example 1

洋介: 今、図書館に行くんだよな。 Yousuke: You are going to the library now huh? (seeking explanation) 智子: うん、なんで？ Tomoko: Yeah, why?

Example 2

ボブ：日本語は、たくさん勉強したけどな。まだ全然わからない。 Bob: I studied Japanese a lot, right? But, I still don't get it at all. アリス：大丈夫よ。きっとわかるようになるからさ。 Alice: No problem. You'll become able to understand for sure, you know? ボブ：ならいいけどな。 Bob: If so, it would be good.

The 「な」 sentence-ending particle is often used with the question marker 「か」 to indicate that the speaker is considering something.

1. 今日は雨が降るかな? I wonder if it'll rain today.
2. いい大学に行けるかな? I wonder if I can go to a good college.

「かい」 and 「だい」 sentence-ending particles

Vocabulary

1. おい - hey
2. どこ - where
3. 行く 【い・く】 (u-verb) - to go

4. 呼ぶ 【よ・ぶ】 (u-verb) - to call

5. いい (i-adj) - good

6. 一体 【いったい】 - forms an emphatic question (e.g. "why on earth?")

7. 何時 【なん・じ】 - what time

8. 帰る 【かえ・る】 (u-verb) - to go home

9. つもり - intention, plan

10. 俺 【おれ】 - me; myself; I (masculine)

11. 土曜日 【ど・よう・び】 - Saturday

12. 映画 【えい・が】 - movie

13. 見る 【み・る】 (ru-verb) - to see

14. 一緒 【いっ・しょ】 - together

「かい」 and 「だい」 are strongly masculine sentence endings for asking questions. 「かい」 is used for yes/no questions while 「だい」 is used for open-ended questions.

Examples

1. おい、どこに行くんだい? Hey, where are (you) going?

2. さきちゃんって呼んでもいいかい? Can (I) call you Saki-chan?

3. 一体何時に帰ってくるつもりだったんだい? What time were (you) planning on coming home exactly?

4. 俺は土曜日、映画を見に行くけど、一緒に行くかい? I'm going to see a movie Saturday, go together?

Gender-specific sentence-ending particles

These sentence-ending particles are primarily used just to emphasize something and doesn't really have a meaning per se. However, they can make your statements sound much stronger and/or very gender-specific. Using 「わ」 is just like 「よ」 except it will make you sound very feminine (this is a different sound from the 「わ」 used in Kansai dialect). 「かしら」 is also a very feminine version of 「かな」, which we just went over. 「ぞ」 and 「ぜ」 are identical to 「よ」 except that it makes you sound "cool" and manly, or at least, that is the intent. These examples may not be very helpful without actually hearing what they sound like.

Vocabulary

1. もう - already
2. 時間 【じ・かん】 - time
3. ある (u-verb) - to exist (inanimate)
4. おい - hey
5. 行く 【い・く】 (u-verb) - to go
6. これ - this
7. 終わり 【お・わり】 - end
8. いい (i-adj) - good
9. 大学 【だい・がく】 - college
10. 入る 【はい・る】 (u-verb) - to enter

1. もう時間がないわ。 There is no more time.
2. おい、行くぞ! Hey, we're going!
3. これで、もう終わりだぜ。 With this, it's over already.
4. いい大学に入れるかしら? I wonder if I can enter a good college.

That's a wrap!

Vocabulary

1. 加賀 【か・が】 - Kaga (last name)
2. 先生 【せん・せい】 - teacher
3. ちょっと - a little

4. 質問 【しつ・もん】 - question
5. 聞く 【き・く】 (u-verb) - to ask; to listen
6. いい (i-adj) - good
7. はい - yes (polite)
8. 日本語 【に・ほん・ご】 - Japanese (language)
9. 何 【なに／なん】 - what
10. 言う 【い・う】 (u-verb) - to say
11. そう - (things are) that way
12. 大体 【だい・たい】 - mostly
13. こんにちは - good day
14. 思う 【おも・う】 (u-verb) - to think
15. ただし - however
16. 書く 【か・く】 (u-verb) - to write
17. 時 【とき】 - time
18. 他 【ほか】 - other
19. 表現 【ひょう・げん】 - expression
20. ある (u-verb) - to exist (inanimate)
21. これ - this
22. 覚える 【おぼ・える】 (ru-verb) - to memorize
23. 朝 【あさ】 - morning
24. おはよう - good morning
25. でも - but
26. 上 【うえ】 - above
27. 人 【ひと】 - person
28. おはようございます - good morning (polite)
29. 分かる 【わ・かる】 (u-verb) - to understand
30. 間違える 【ま・ちが・える】 (ru-verb) - to make a mistake
31. 勉強 【べん・きょう】 - study
32. なる (u-verb) - to become
33. 洋介 【よう・すけ】 - Yousuke (first name)
34. あのう／あの - say; well; errr
35. 英語 【えい・ご】 - English (language)
36. 教える 【おし・える】 (ru-verb) - to teach; to inform
37. もらう (u-verb) - to receive

38. もし - if by any chance
39. 時間 【じ・かん】 - time
40. うん - yes (casual)
41. アメリカ - America
42. 留学 【りゅう・がく】 - study abroad
43. する (exception) - to do
44. 去年 【きょ・ねん】 - last year
45. 行く 【い・く】 (u-verb) - to go
46. お金 【お・かね】 - money
47. ある (u-verb) - to exist (inanimate)
48. いつ - when
49. 欲しい 【ほ・しい】 (i-adj) - wanted; desirable
50. 来週 【らい・しゅう】 - next week
51. 木曜日 【もく・よう・び】 - Thursday
52. ありがとう - thank you
53. 怠ける 【なま・ける】 (ru-verb) - to neglect, to be lazy about
54. 来る 【く・る】 (exception) - to come
55. そんな - that sort of
56. こと - event, matter

We learned quite a lot of things in this section. Let's try to put it all together by seeing how different kinds of conjugations are used in different combinations. This is of course by no means an exhaustive list but merely an illustration of how we can use what we learned in various combinations to create a lot of useful expressions.

Example 1

アリス：加賀先生、ちょっと質問を聞いてもいいですか？
加賀先生：はい、いいですよ。
アリス：「Hello」を日本語で何と言えばいいですか。

何と言えば = quoted sub-clause + if conditional of 言う

加賀先生：　そうね。大体、「こんにちは」と言うと思いますよ。ただし、書く時は「こんにちわ」じゃなくて、「こんにちは」と書かなくてはなりません。

「と言うと思います」 = quoted sub-clause + quoted sub-clause

「じゃなくて」 = negative sequence of states

アリス：そうですか。他に何かいい表現はありますか。

加賀先生：これも覚えといてね。朝は、「おはよう」と言うの。でも、上の人には「おはようございます」と言ってください。

「覚えといて」 - 覚える + abbreviated form of 〜ておく + casual 〜てください with ください dropped.

アリス：はい、分かりました。間違えないようにします。いい勉強になりました！

Literal translation of Example 1

Alice: Kaga-sensei, is it ok to ask you a question? Kaga-sensei: Yes, it's ok. Alice: If you say what for "hello" in Japanese, is it ok? Kaga-sensei: Well, mostly, I think people say "konnichiwa". Only, when you write it, you must write "konnichiha" and not "konnichiwa". Alice: Is that so? Are there any other good expressions? Kaga-sensei: Please memorize this too (in preparation for the future). In the morning, everybody says, "ohayou". But, please say, "ohayou-gozaimasu" to a higher person. Alice: Yes, I understood. I'll do in the manner of not making mistake. It became good study!

Interpretative translation of Example 1

Alice: Kaga-sensei, is it ok to ask you a question? Kaga-sensei: Sure. Alice: How do you say "Hello" in Japanese? Kaga-sensei: Well, most of the time, I think people say "konnichiwa". Only, when you write it, you must write "konnichiha" and not "konnichiwa". Alice:

Is that so? Are there any other good expressions? Kaga-sensei: You should know this too. In the morning, everybody says, "ohayou". But, please say, "ohayou-gozaimasu" to a higher person. Alice: Ok, I got it. I'll try not to make that mistake. That was very informative!

Example 2

洋介: お！アリスだ。あのね、質問を聞いてもいい？ アリス: 何?

洋介: ちょっと英語を教えてもらいたいんだけどさ、もし時間があれば、教えてくれない？「教えてもらいたい」= receiving favor + to want（たい）

アリス: え？英語を勉強するの？

洋介: うん、アメリカで留学してみたいなと思ってね。去年も行こうとしたけど、お金がなくて・・・「してみたいなと思って」= to try something out（〜てみる）+ want to（たい）+ な sentence-ending particle + quoted subquote + te-form of 思う「行こうとした」= volitional of 行く + to attempt（とする）

アリス: そうなの？いいよ。いつ教えてほしいの？ 洋介: いつでもいいよ。 アリス: じゃ、来週の木曜日からはどう？ 洋介: うん、いいよ。ありがとう！

アリス: 勉強を怠けたり、来なかったり、しないでね。「怠けたり来なかったりしないで」= List of actions（〜たりする）+ negative request of する.

洋介: そんなことしないよ！

Literal translation of Example 2

Yousuke: Oh! It's Alice. Hey, is it ok to ask a question? Alice: What? Yousuke: I want to receive the favor of you teaching English and if, by any chance, you have time, will you give the favor of teaching? Alice: Huh? You are going to study English? Yousuke: Yeah, I was thinking that I want to try studying abroad in America. I tried to make motion toward going last year too but, without money... Alice: Is that so? It's good. When do you want me to teach you? Yousuke: Anytime is good. Alice: Then what about from next week Thursday? Yousuke: Yeah, ok. Thanks! Alice: Don't do things like shirk on your studies or not come, ok? Yousuke: I won't do anything like that!

Interpretative translation of Example 2

Yousuke: Oh! It's Alice. Hey, can I ask you a question? Alice: What up? Yousuke: I want to learn English so if you have time, can you teach me? Alice: Huh? You're going to study English? Yousuke: Yeah, I was thinking about studying abroad in America. I tried going last year too but I didn't have the money. Alice: Really? No problem. When do you want me to teach you? Yousuke: Anytime is fine. Alice: What about from next week Thursday then? Yousuke: OK, thanks! Alice: You're not going to shirk on your studies or not come or anything right? Yousuke: I won't do anything like that!

Special Expressions

I have decided to call this next section "Special Expressions" only because with the exception of the first few lessons, most of the grammar here applies to more specific areas than the grammar we have covered so far. These special expressions, while individually not vital, are, as a collection, necessary for regular everyday conversations. We are slowly entering the stage where we've built the toolbox and we now need to acquire the little tools that will make the toolbox complete. Now that we covered most of the base, it is time to look at all the little itty gritty bits. You are welcome to skip around the lessons, however; the examples will assume that you have gone over all previous sections.

Causative and Passive Verbs

We will now learn the last two major types of verb conjugations: causative and passive forms. These two verb conjugations are traditionally covered together because of the notorious causative-passive combination. We will now go over what all these things are and how they are used.

Causative Verbs

Vocabulary

1. あげる (ru-verb) - to give; to raise
2. くれる (ru-verb) - to give
3. 全部 【ぜん・ぶ】 - everything
4. 食べる 【た・べる】 (ru-verb) - to eat
5. 着る 【き・る】 (ru-verb) - to wear
6. 信じる 【しん・じる】 (ru-verb) - to believe
7. 寝る 【ね・る】 (ru-verb) - to sleep
8. 起きる 【お・きる】 (ru-verb) - to wake; to occur
9. 出る 【で・る】 (ru-verb) - to come out
10. 掛ける 【か・ける】 (ru-verb) - to hang
11. 捨てる 【す・てる】 (ru-verb) - to throw away
12. 調べる 【しら・べる】 (ru-verb) - to investigate
13. 話す 【はな・す】 (u-verb) - to speak
14. 聞く 【き・く】 (u-verb) - to ask; to listen
15. 泳ぐ 【およ・ぐ】 (u-verb) - to swim
16. 遊ぶ 【あそ・ぶ】 (u-verb) - to play

17. 待つ 【ま・つ】 (u-verb) - to wait
18. 飲む 【の・む】 (u-verb) - to drink
19. 直る 【なお・る】 (u-verb) - to be fixed
20. 死ぬ 【し・ぬ】 (u-verb) - to die
21. 買う 【か・う】 (u-verb) - to buy
22. する (exception) - to do
23. 来る 【く・る】 (exception) - to come
24. 先生 【せん・せい】 - teacher
25. 学生 【がく・せい】 - student
26. 宿題 【しゅく・だい】 - homework
27. たくさん - a lot (amount)
28. 質問 【しつ・もん】 - question
29. 今日 【きょう】 - today
30. 仕事 【し・ごと】 - job
31. 休む 【やす・む】 (u-verb) - to rest
32. その - abbreviation of 「それの」
33. 部長 【ぶ・ちょう】 - section manager
34. いい (i-adj) - good
35. 長時間 【ちょう・じ・かん】 - long period of time
36. 働く 【はたら・く】 (u-verb) - to work
37. トイレ - bathroom; toilet
38. 行く 【い・く】 (u-verb) - to go

Verbs conjugated into the causative form are used to indicate an action that someone makes happen. Like Captain Picard so succinctly puts it, the causative verb means to "make it so". This verb is usually used in the context of making somebody do something. The really confusing thing about the causative verb is that it can also mean to *let* someone do something. Or maybe this is a different type of verb with the exact same conjugation rules. Whichever the case may be, a verb in the causative form can mean either making or letting someone do something. The only good news is that when the causative form is used with 「あげる」 and 「くれる」, it almost always means to "let someone do". Once you get used to it, surprisingly, it becomes quite clear which meaning is being used when.

1. 全部食べさせた。
   Made/Let (someone) eat it all.
2. 全部食べさせてくれた。
   Let (someone) eat it all.

Causative Conjugation Rules
Here are the conjugation rules for the causative form.
All causative verbs become ru-verbs.

- **For ru-verbs:** Replace the last 「る」 with 「させる」.
- **For u-verbs:** Change the last character as you would for negative verbs but attach 「せる」 instead of 「ない」.
- **Exception Verbs:**
  1. 「する」 becomes 「させる」
  2. 「くる」 becomes 「こさせる」.

Plain	Causative	Plain	Causative	Positive	Causative
食べる	食べさせる	話す	話させる	する	させる
着る	着させる	聞く	聞かせる	くる	こさせる
信じる	信じさせる	泳ぐ	泳がせる		
寝る	寝させる	遊ぶ	遊ばせる		
起きる	起きさせる	待つ	待たせる		
出る	出させる	飲む	飲ませる		
掛ける	掛けさせる	直る	直らせる		
捨てる	捨てさせる	死ぬ	死なせる		
調べる	調べさせる	買う	買わせる		

Examples

Here are some examples using the causative verb. Context will usually tell you which is being meant, but for our purposes we will assume that when the verb is used with 「あげる」 and 「くれる」（ください） it means "to <u>let</u> someone do" while it means, "to <u>make</u> someone do" when used without it.

1. 先生が学生に宿題をたくさんさせた。
   Teacher made students do lots of homework.

2. 先生が質問をたくさん聞かせてくれた。
Teacher let (someone) ask lots of questions.

3. 今日は仕事を休ませてください。
Please let me rest from work today. (Please let me take the day off today.)

4. その部長は、よく長時間働かせる。
That manager often makes (people) work long hours.

When asking for permission to let someone do something, it is more common to use the 「〜てもいい」 grammar.

1. トイレに行かせてくれますか。
Can you let me go to the bathroom? (Sounds like a prisoner, even in English)

2. トイレに行ってもいいですか。
Is it ok to go to the bathroom? (No problem here)

A Shorter Alternative

Vocabulary

1. 食べる 【た・べる】 (ru-verb) - to eat
2. 行く 【い・く】 (u-verb) - to go
3. する (exception) - to do
4. 来る 【く・る】 (exception) - to come
5. 同じ 【おな・じ】 - same
6. こと - event, matter
7. 何回 【なん・かい】 - how many times
8. 言う 【い・う】 (u-verb) - to say
9. お腹 【お・なか】 - stomach
10. 空く 【あ・く】 (u-verb) - to become empty
11. 何 【なに／なん】 - what
12. くれる (ru-verb) - to give

There is a shorter version of the causative conjugation, which I will go over for completeness. However, since this version is mostly used in very rough slang, you are free to skip this section until you've had time to get used to the regular form. Also, textbooks usually don't cover this version of the causative verb.

The key difference in this version is that all verbs become an u-verbs with a 「す」 ending. Therefore, the resulting verb would conjugate just like any other u-verb ending in 「す」 such as 「話す」 or 「指す」. The first part of the conjugation is the same as the original causative form. However, for ru-verbs, instead of attaching 「させる」, you attach 「さす」 and for u-verbs, you attach 「す」 instead of 「せる」. As a result, all the verbs become an u-verb ending in 「す」.

Shortened Causative Form

- This form is rarely used so you may just want to stick with the more traditional version of the causative form.
  - **For ru-verbs:** Replace the last 「る」 with 「さす」.
    Example
    食べる → 食べさす
  - **For u-verbs:** Change the last character as you would for negative verbs but attach 「す」 instead of 「ない」.
    Example
    行く → 行か → 行かす
  - **Exception Verbs:**
    1. 「する」 becomes 「さす」
    2. 「くる」 becomes 「こさす」

Examples

1. 同じことを何回も言わすな！
Don't make me say the same thing again and again!
2. お腹空いているんだから、なんか食べさしてくれよ。
I'm hungry so let me eat something.

Passive Verbs

Vocabulary

1. 食べる　【た・べる】　(ru-verb) - to eat
2. 着る　【き・る】　(ru-verb) - to wear
3. 信じる　【しん・じる】　(ru-verb) - to believe
4. 寝る　【ね・る】　(ru-verb) - to sleep
5. 起きる　【お・きる】　(ru-verb) - to wake; to occur
6. 出る　【で・る】　(ru-verb) - to come out
7. 掛ける　【か・ける】　(ru-verb) - to hang
8. 捨てる　【す・てる】　(ru-verb) - to throw away
9. 調べる　【しら・べる】　(ru-verb) - to investigate
10. 話す　【はな・す】　(u-verb) - to speak
11. 聞く　【き・く】　(u-verb) - to ask; to listen
12. 泳ぐ　【およ・ぐ】　(u-verb) - to swim
13. 遊ぶ　【あそ・ぶ】　(u-verb) - to play
14. 待つ　【ま・つ】　(u-verb) - to wait
15. 飲む　【の・む】　(u-verb) - to drink
16. 直る　【なお・る】　(u-verb) - to be fixed
17. 死ぬ　【し・ぬ】　(u-verb) - to die
18. 買う　【か・う】　(u-verb) - to buy
19. する　(exception) - to do
20. 来る　【く・る】　(exception) - to come

21. ポリッジ - porridge
22. 誰【だれ】 - who
23. 皆【みんな】 - everybody
24. 変【へん】 (na-adj) - strange
25. 言う【い・う】 (u-verb) - to say
26. 光【ひかり】 - light
27. 速い【はや・い】 (i-adj) - fast
28. 超える【こ・える】 (ru-verb) - to exceed
29. 不可能【ふ・か・のう】 - impossible
30. 思う【おも・う】 (u-verb) - to think
31. この - this (abbr. of これの)
32. 教科書【きょう・か・しょ】 - textbook
33. 多い【おお・い】 (i-adj) - numerous
34. 人【ひと】 - person
35. 読む【よ・む】 (u-verb) - to read
36. 外国人【がい・こく・じん】 - foreigner
37. 質問【しつ・もん】 - question
38. 答える【こた・える】 (ru-verb) - to answer
39. パッケージ - package
40. あらゆる - all
41. 含む【ふく・む】 (u-verb) - to include

Passive verbs are verbs that are done to the (passive) subject. Unlike English style of writing which discourages the use of the passive form, passive verbs in Japanese are often used in essays and articles.

Passive Conjugation Rules
All passive verbs become ru-verbs.

- **For ru-verbs:** Replace the last 「る」 with 「られる」

- **For u-verbs:** Change the last character as you would for negative verbs but attach 「れる」 instead of 「ない」.
- **Exception Verbs:**
  1. 「する」 becomes 「される」
  2. 「くる」 becomes 「こられる」

Plain	Passive	Plain	Passive	Positive	Passive
食べる	食べられる	話す	話される	する	される
着る	着られる	聞く	聞かれる	くる	こられる
信じる	信じられる	泳ぐ	泳がれる		
寝る	寝られる	遊ぶ	遊ばれる		
起きる	起きられる	待つ	待たれる		
出る	出られる	飲む	飲まれる		
掛ける	掛けられる	直る	直られる		
捨てる	捨てられる	死ぬ	死なれる		
調べる	調べられる	買う	買われる		

Examples

1. ポリッジが誰かに食べられた！
The porridge was eaten by somebody!

2. みんなに変だと言われます。
I am told by everybody that (I'm) strange.

3. 光の速さを超えるのは、不可能だと思われる。
Exceeding the speed of light is thought to be impossible.

4. この教科書は多くの人に読まれている。
This textbook is being read by a large number of people.

5. 外国人に質問を聞かれたが、答えられなかった。
I was asked a question by a foreigner but I couldn't answer.

6. このパッケージには、あらゆるものが含まれている。
Everything is included in this package.

Using passive form to show politeness

Vocabulary

1. どう - how
2. する (exception) - to do
3. 領収証 【りょう・しゅう・しょう】 - receipt
4. 明日 【あした】 - tomorrow
5. 会議 【かい・ぎ】 - meeting
6. 行く 【い・く】 (u-verb) - to go

While we will go over various types of grammar that express a politeness level above the normal -masu/-desu forms in the next lesson, it is useful to know that using passive form is another more polite way to express an action. In Japanese, a sentence is usually more polite when it is less direct. For example, it is more polite to refer to someone by his or her name and not by the direct pronoun "you". It is also more polite to ask a negative question than a positive one. (For example, 「しますか？」 vs. 「しませんか？」) In a similar sense, using the passive form makes the sentence less direct because the subject does not directly perform the action. This makes it sound more polite. Here is the same sentence in increasing degrees of politeness.

1. どうする? - What will you do? (lit: How do?)
2. どうしますか? - Regular polite.
3. どうされますか? - Passive polite.
4. どうなさいますか? - Honorific (to be covered next lesson)
5. どうなさいますでしょうか? - Honorific + a lesser degree of certainty.

Notice how the same sentence grows longer and longer as you get more and more indirect.

Examples

1. 領収証はどうされますか？
   What about your receipt? (lit: How will you do receipt?)
2. 明日の会議に行かれるんですか？
   Are you going to tomorrow's meeting?

Causative-Passive Forms

Vocabulary

1. 食べる 【た・べる】 (ru-verb) - to eat
2. 行く 【い・く】 (u-verb) - to go
3. 朝ご飯 【あさ・ご・はん】 - breakfast

4. 日本 【に・ほん】 - Japan
5. お酒 【お・さけ】 - alcohol
6. 飲む 【の・む】 (u-verb) - to drink
7. こと - event, matter
8. 多い 【おお・い】 (i-adj) - numerous
9. あいつ - that guy (derogatory)
10. ～時間 【～じ・かん】 - counter for span of hour(s)
11. 待つ 【ま・つ】 (u-verb) - to wait
12. 親 【おや】 - parent
13. 宿題 【しゅく・だい】 - homework
14. する (exception) - to do

The causative-passive form is simply the combination of causative and passive conjugations to mean that the action of making someone do something was done to that person. This would effectively translate into, "[someone] is made to do [something]". The important thing to remember is the order of conjugation. The verb is first conjugated to the causative and then passive, never the other way around.

Causative-Passive Conjugation Form
The causative-passive verb is formed by first conjugating to the causative form and then by conjugating the result to the passive form.
Examples

1. 食べる → 食べさせる → 食べさせられる
2. 行く → 行かせる → 行かせられる

Examples

1. 朝ご飯は食べたくなかったのに、食べさせられた。
   Despite not wanting to eat breakfast, I was made to eat it.

2. 日本では、お酒を飲ませられることが多い。
   In Japan, the event of being made to drink is numerous.

3. あいつに二時間も待たせられた。
   I was made to wait 2 hours by that guy.

4. 親に毎日宿題をさせられる。
   I am made to do homework everyday by my parent(s).

A Shorter Alternative

Vocabulary

1. 行く 【い・く】 (u-verb) - to go
2. 立つ 【た・つ】 (u-verb) - to stand
3. 食べる 【た・べる】 (ru-verb) - to eat
4. 話す 【はな・す】 (u-verb) - to speak
5. 学生 【がく・せい】 - student
6. 廊下 【ろう・か】 - hall, corridor
7. 日本 【に・ほん】 - Japan
8. お酒 【お・さけ】 - alcohol
9. 飲む 【の・む】 (u-verb) - to drink
10. こと - event, matter
11. 多い 【おお・い】 (i-adj) - numerous
12. あいつ - that guy (derogatory)
13. ~時間 【~じ・かん】 - counter for span of hour(s)
14. 待つ 【ま・つ】 (u-verb) - to wait

Going along with the shorter causative alternative, you can also use the same conjugation for the causative-passive form. I won't cover it in too much detail because the usefulness of this form is rather limited just like the shorter causative form itself. The idea is to simply used the shortened causative form instead of using the regular causative conjugation. The rest is the same as before.

Shortened causative-passive form examples
First conjugate to the shortened causative form. Then conjugate to the passive form.
Examples

1. 行く → 行か → 行かす → 行かされる
2. 立つ → 立た → 立たす → 立たされる

This form cannot be used in cases where the shorter causative form ends in 「さす」, in other words, you can't have a 「さされる」 ending.

Verbs that cannot be used in this form
Examples of verbs you *can't* use in this form.

1. 食べる → 食べさす → 食べさされる
2. 話す → 話さす → 話さされる

Examples

1. 学生が廊下に立たされた。
   The student was made to stand in the hall.

283

2. 日本では、お酒を飲まされることが多い。
In Japan, the event of <u>being made to drink</u> is numerous.

3. あいつに二時間も待たされた。
I <u>was made to wait</u> 2 hours by that guy.

Honorific and Humble Forms

Japanese can be roughly separated into three levels of politeness: casual, polite, and honorific/humble. So far, we have already gone over the polite forms using 「〜です」 and 「〜ます」. We will now cover the next level of politeness using honorific and humble forms. You will often hear this type of language in any customer/consumer type situations such as fast food counters, restaurants, etc. For now, the first thing to remember is that the speaker always considers himself/herself to be at the lowest level. So any actions performed by oneself are in humble form while actions performed by anyone else seen from the view of the speaker uses the honorific form.

Set Expressions

Vocabulary

1. する (exception) - to do
2. なさる - to do (honorific)
3. 致す 【いた・す】 (u-verb) - to do (humble)
4. 行く 【い・く】 (u-verb) - to go
5. いらっしゃる - to be; to go; to come (honorific)
6. おいでになる - to be; to go; to come (honorific)
7. 参る 【まい・る】 (u-verb) - to go; to come (humble)
8. いる (ru-verb) - to exist (animate)
9. おる (ru-verb) - to exist (animate) (humble)
10. 見る 【み・る】 (ru-verb) - to see

11. ご覧になる 【ご・らん・になる】 - to see (honorific)
12. 拝見する 【はい・けん・する】 - to see (humble)
13. 聞く 【き・く】 (u-verb) - to ask; to listen
14. 伺う 【うかが・う】 (u-verb) - to ask; to listen (humble)
15. 言う 【い・う】 (u-verb) - to say
16. おっしゃる - to say (honorific)
17. 申す 【もう・す】 (u-verb) - to say (humble)
18. 申し上げる 【もう・し・あ・げる】 (u-verb) - to say (humble)
19. あげる (ru-verb) - to give; to raise
20. 差し上げる 【さ・し・あ・げる】 (ru-verb) - to give; to raise (humble)
21. くれる (ru-verb) - to give
22. 下さる 【くだ・さる】 - to give (honorific)
23. もらう (u-verb) - to receive
24. いただく (u-verb) - to receive; to eat; to drink (humble)
25. 食べる 【た・べる】 (ru-verb) - to eat
26. 召し上がる 【め・し・あ・がる】 (u-verb) - to eat; to drink (honorific)
27. 飲む 【の・む】 (u-verb) - to drink
28. 知る 【し・る】 (u-verb) - to know
29. ご存じ 【ご・ぞん・じ】 - knowing (honorific)
30. 存じる 【ぞん・じる】 (ru-verb) - to know (humble)
31. ござる - to be (formal)
32. もう - already
33. 仕事 【し・ごと】 - job
34. 何 【なに／なん】 - what
35. 推薦状 【すい・せん・じょう】 - letter of recommendation
36. 書く 【か・く】 (u-verb) - to write
37. どちら - which way
38. 今日 【きょう】 - today
39. 私 【わたし】 - me; myself; I
40. レポート - report
41. 失礼 【しつ・れい】 - discourtesy

The difficult part of learning honorific and humble language is that there are a number of words that have separate verbs for honorific and humble forms. Anything that does not have its own special expression fall under the general rules of humble and honorific conjugations that we will cover next.

Honorific and Humble Verbs

Plain	Honorific	Humble
する	なさる	致す
行く	いらっしゃる／ おいでになる	参る
来る	いらっしゃる／ おいでになる	参る
いる	いらっしゃる／ おいでになる	おる
見る	ご覧になる	拝見する
聞く	-	伺う
言う	おっしゃる	申す／申し 上げる
あげる	-	差し上げる
くれる	下さる	-
もらう	-	いただく
食べ	召し上がる	いただく

る		
飲む	召し上がる	いただく
知っている	ご存知（です）	存じる

Honorific verbs with special conjugations

A number of these verbs do not follow the normal masu-conjugation rules and they include: 「なさる」、「いらっしゃる」、「おっしゃる」、「下さる」、and 「ござる」 (which we will soon cover). For all masu-form tenses of these verbs, instead of the 「る」 becoming a 「り」 as it does with normal u-verbs, it instead becomes an 「い」. All other conjugations besides the masu-form do not change from regular u-verbs.

ます-conjugations

Plain	ます-form	Past ます-form	Negative ます-form	Past-negative ます-form
なさる	なさい ます	なさい ました	なさいま せん	なさいませ んでした
いらっ しゃる	いらっ しゃい ます	いらっ しゃい ました	いらっしゃ いません	いらっしゃい ませんでした
おっ しゃる	おっしゃ います	おっしゃ いました	おっしゃ いません	おっしゃいま せんでした
下さる	下さい ます	下さい ました	下さいま せん	下さいませ んでした
ござる	ござい ます	ござい ました	ございま せん	ございませ んでした

Examples of honorific form

We can now begin to see that 「ください」 is just a special conjugation of 「下さる」 which is the honorific version of 「くれる」. Let's look at some actual examples. Since these examples are all questions directed directly to someone (second person), they all use the honorific form.

1. アリスさん、もう召し上がりましたか。 Alice-san, did (you) eat already?
2. 仕事で何をなさっているんですか。 What are you doing at work?

3. 推薦状を書いてくださるんですか。 You're going to give me the favor of writing a recommendation letter?
4. どちらからいらっしゃいましたか。 Where did you come from?
5. 今日は、どちらへいらっしゃいますか。 Where are you going today?

Examples of humble form

The following examples are all actions done by the speaker so they all use the humble form.

1. 私はキムと申します。 As for me, (people) say Kim. (I am called Kim.)
2. 私が書いたレポートを見ていただけますか。 Will I be able to receive the favor of getting my report looked at?
3. 失礼致します。 Excuse me. (lit: I am doing a discourtesy.)

Other substitutions

Vocabulary

1. こちら - this way
2. 私 【わたし】 - me, myself, I
3. 部屋 【へ・や】 - room
4. ござる - to be (formal)
5. お手洗い 【お・て・あら・い】 - bathroom
6. この - this (abbr. of これの)
7. ビル - building
8. ～階 【～かい】 - counter for story/floor
9. いい (i-adj) - good
10. よろしい (i-adj) - good (formal)
11. 悪い 【わる・い】 (i-adj) - bad

12. すいません - sorry (polite)

13. ごめん - sorry (casual)

14. ごめんなさい - sorry (polite)

15. すみません - sorry (polite)

16. 申し訳ありません 【もう・し・わけ・ありません】 - sorry (formal)

17. 言い訳 【い・い・わけ】 - excuse

18. 恐れ入ります 【おそ・れ・い・ります】 - sorry (formal)

19. 恐縮です 【きょう・しゅく・です】 - sorry (formal)

20. ～様 【～さま】 - honorific name suffix

21. ～さん - polite name suffix

22. お客様 【お・きゃく・さま】 - customer (formal)

23. 神様 【かみ・さま】 - god (formal)

In addition to these set expressions, there are some words that also have more polite counterparts. Probably the most important is the politer version of 「ある」, which is 「ござる」. This verb can be used for both inanimate and animate objects. It is neither honorific nor humble but it is a step above 「ある」 in politeness. However, unless you want to sound like a samurai, 「ござる」 is always used in the polite form: 「ございます」.

By extension, the politer version of 「です」 is 「でございます」. This is essentially the masu-form conjugation of 「でござる」, which comes from 「である」 literally meaning, "to exist as" (to be covered much later).

Examples

1. こちらは、私の部屋です。 Over here is my room.

2. こちらは、私の部屋でございます。 This way is my room.

1. お手洗いはこのビルの二階にあります。 The bathroom is on the second floor of this building.

2. お手洗いはこのビルの二階にございます。 The bathroom is on the second floor of this building.

Other examples include 「いい」, which is more formally expressed as 「よろしい」. There are also six different ways to say, "I'm sorry" (not counting 「悪いね」 or slight inflection changes like 「すいません」).

Successively politer expressions for apologizing:

1. ごめん。
2. ごめんなさい。
3. すみません。
4. 申し訳ありません。 (申し訳 is the humble form of 言い訳)
5. 恐れ入ります。
6. 恐縮です。

In addition, the politest suffix for names is 「様」, one level above 「さん」. You won't be using this suffix too often in actual speech even if you speak to that person in honorific/humble speech. However, expect to use it when writing letters even to people you are somewhat familiar with. Also, service people such as cashiers or waitresses/waiters will normally refer to the customer as 「お客様」. Of course, royalty and deities are always accompanied by 「様」 such as 「神様」.

Honorific and Humble Conjugations

Vocabulary

1. お酒 【お・さけ】 - alcohol
2. お茶 【お・ちゃ】 - tea
3. お金 【お・かね】 - money
4. 音読み 【おん・よ・み】 - Chinese reading

5. 意見 【い・けん】 - opinion
6. ご飯 【ご・はん】 - rice; meal
7. 訓読み 【くん・よ・み】 - Japanese reading
8. 仕事 【し・ごと】 - job
9. お好み焼き 【お・この・み・や・き】 - okonomiyaki (Japanese-style pancake)
10. お土産 【お・みやげ】 - souvenir
11. 返事 【へん・じ】 - reply
12. 先生 【せん・せい】 - teacher
13. 見える 【み・える】 (ru-verb) - to be visible
14. なる (u-verb) - to become
15. もう - already
16. 帰る 【かえ・る】 (u-verb) - to go home
17. 店内 【てん・ない】 - store interior
18. 召し上がる 【め・し・あ・がる】 (ru-verb) - to eat; to drink (honorific)
19. 二重敬語 【に・じゅう・けい・ご】 - redundant honorific
20. 下さる 【くだ・さる】 - to give (honorific)
21. 少々 【しょう・しょう】 - just a minute; small quantity;
22. 待つ 【ま・つ】 (u-verb) - to wait
23. こちら - this way
24. ご覧下さい 【ご・らん・くだ・さい】 - please look (honorific)
25. 閉まる 【し・まる】 (u-verb) - to close
26. ドア - door
27. 注意 【ちゅう・い】 - caution
28. よろしい (i-adj) - good (formal)
29. 願う 【ねが・う】 (u-verb) - to wish; to request
30. する (exception) - to do
31. 聞く 【き・く】 (u-verb) - to ask; to listen
32. こと - event, matter
33. ある (u-verb) - to exist (inanimate)
34. すみません - sorry (polite)
35. 千円 【せん・えん】 - 1,000 yen
36. 預かる 【あず・かる】 - to look after; to hold on to;

37. 致す 【いた・す】 (u-verb) - to do (humble)

For all other verbs without set expressions, there are conjugation rules to change them into honorific and humble forms. They both involve a common practice of attaching a polite prefix 「御」. In Japanese, there is an practice of attaching an honorific prefix 「御」 to certain (not all) nouns to show politeness. In fact, some words like 「お酒」、「お茶」、or 「お金」 come with this prefix so often that it's become practically the word itself. In general, 「御」 is written in hiragana as either 「ご」 for words read as 音読み (e.g. ご意見、ご飯) or 「お」 for words read as 訓読み (e.g. お金、お仕事). In fact, you may have been using this prefix already without realizing it like 「お好み焼き」 or 「お土産」. There are some exceptions to this rule such as 「お返事」. Luckily since 「御」 is rarely written in kanji, identifying the exceptions should not really be a problem.

Honorific Form

The honorific form of verbs *that are not among the set honorific expressions given above* can be formed in two different ways.

Honorific Conjugation 1: お + stem + に + なる

This kind of makes sense if you think of it as a person becoming the honorific state of a verb. All subsequent conjugations follow the normal rules of conjugating the u-verb 「なる」. To be honest, this type of sentence formulation is rarely used.

- 先生はお見えになりますか。 Have you seen the teacher?

Honorific Conjugation 2: お + stem + です

1. もうお帰りですか。 You're going home already?

2. 店内でお召し上がりですか。 Will you be dining in?

Service people want to be extra polite so they will often use this type of "double honorific" conjugation or 二重敬語 (in this case, the honorific 「召し上がる」 combined with the honorific conjugation). Whether it's necessary or grammatically proper is another story.

Using 「ください」 with honorifics

You can also use 「下さい」 with a honorific verb by replacing 「になる」 with 「ください」. This is useful for when you want to ask somebody to do something but still use a honorific verb. Yet another often-used expression.

- 少々お待ちください。 - Please wait a moment.

Similarly, with 「ご覧になる」, you simply replace 「になる」 with 「ください」.

- こちらにご覧下さい。 Please look this way.

This works for other nouns as well. For example, riding the trains...

- 閉まるドアにご注意下さい。 Please be careful of the closing doors.

Humble Form

Humble verbs are formed in the following fashion.

Humble Conjugation: お + stem + する

You've probably already heard the first example many times before but now you know exactly where it comes from.

1. よろしくお願いします。 I properly make request.
2. 先生、お聞きしたいことがありますが。 Teacher, there's something I want to ask you.
3. すみません、お待たせしました。 Sorry, I made you wait (causative form).
4. 千円からお預かりいたします。 We'll be holding on [from?] your 1000 yen.

You'll hear something like example 4 when, for example, you need to get change after paying 1000 yen. Again, the 二重敬語 where 「する」 has been converted to the humble 「致す」 form when it's already in the お+stem+する humble form. Some Japanese people complain that this makes no sense and that 「から」 should really be 「を」.

Making honorific requests

Vocabulary

1. 下さる 【くだ・さる】 - to give (honorific)
2. いらっしゃる - to be; to go; to come (honorific)
3. なさる - to do (honorific)
4. おっしゃる - to say (honorific)
5. する (exception) - to do
6. いらっしゃいませ - please come in (formal)
7. いらっしゃい - please come in
8. ありがとうございました - thank you (polite)
9. また - again
10. 越す 【こ・す】 - to go over
11. どうぞ - please
12. ゆっくり - slowly

We learned how to make polite requests using 「〜ください」 in a previous section and we just looked at how to use honorific verbs with requests as well. However, there is yet another way to make requests using honorific verbs. This grammar only applies to the honorific verbs with special 「〜ます」 conjugations that we just covered. This includes 「下さる」、「いらっしゃる」、「なさる」、and 「おっしゃる」.　I've never actually seen this used with 「おっしゃる」, but it is grammatically possible.

Making requests for honorific actions

- Conjugate the honorific verb to the special masu-conjugation and replace the last 「す」 with 「せ」 Examples
  1. 下さる → 下さいます → 下さいませ
  2. いらっしゃる → いらっしゃいます → いらっしゃいませ

- An abbreviated and less formal version of this is to simply remove the 「ます」 after conjugating to the special masu-form Examples
  1. 下さる → 下さいます → 下さい
  2. いらっしゃる → いらっしゃいます → いらっしゃい

Now you finally know where grammar such as 「しなさい」 and 「してください」 actually came from. Let's look at a few quick examples.

Examples

You'll probably hear this one a million times every time you enter some kind of store in Japan.

- いらっしゃいませ。 Please come in!

However, a middle-aged sushi chef will probably use the abbreviated version.

- いらっしゃい！ Please come in!

Some more examples...

1. ありがとうございました。またお越しくださいませ。 Thank you very much. Please come again.
2. どうぞ、ごゆっくりなさいませ。 Please take your time and relax.

Unintended Actions

This is the first of many useful tools that will become essential in your day-to-day conversations. We will now learn how to express an action that has taken place unintentionally often with unsatisfactory results. This is primarily done by the verb 「しまう」. Let's look at an example.

Vocabulary

1. 康介 【こう・すけ】 - Kousuke (first name)
2. 宿題 【しゅく・だい】 - homework
3. やる (u-verb) - to do
4. しまう (u-verb) - to do something by accident; to finish completely

康介: 宿題をやった？ Kousuke: Did you do homework? アリス：し<u>まった</u>! Alice: Oh no! (I screwed up!)

Using 「しまう」 with other verbs

Vocabulary

1. しまう (u-verb) - to do something by accident; to finish completely
2. その - that (abbr. of それの)
3. ケーキ - cake
4. 全部 【ぜん・ぶ】 - everything
5. 食べる 【た・べる】 (ru-verb) - to eat
6. 毎日 【まい・にち】 - everyday
7. キロ - kilo
8. 太る 【ふと・る】 (u-verb) - to become fatter
9. ちゃんと - properly
10. 痩せる 【や・せる】 (ru-verb) - to become thin
11. 結局 【けっ・きょく】 - eventually
12. 嫌 【いや】 (na-adj) disagreeable; unpleasant
13. こと - event, matter
14. する (exception) - to do
15. ごめん - sorry
16. 待つ 【ま・つ】 (u-verb) - to wait
17. 金魚 【きん・ぎょ】 - goldfish
18. もう - already
19. 死ぬ 【し・ぬ】 (u-verb) - to die

When 「しまう」 is used in this sense, it is normal to attach it to the te-form of another verb to express an action that is done or happened unintentionally. As is common with this type of grammar, the tense is decided by the tense of 「しまう」.

1. そのケーキを全部食べてしまった。 Oops, I ate that whole cake.
2. 毎日ケーキを食べて、２キロ太ってしまいました。 I ate cake everyday and I (unintentionally) gained two kilograms.
3. ちゃんと食べないと、痩せてしまいますよ。 If you don't eat properly, you'll (unintentionally) lose weight you know.
4. 結局、嫌なことをさせてしまった。 In the end, I (unintentionally) made [someone] do something distasteful.
5. ごめん、待たせてしまって！ Sorry about (unintentionally) making you wait!
6. 金魚がもう死んでしまった。 The goldfish died already (oops).

Using the casual version of 「～てしまう」

Vocabulary

1. しまう (u-verb) - to do something by accident; to finish completely
2. 金魚 【きん・ぎょ】 - goldfish
3. もう - already
4. 死ぬ 【し・ぬ】 (u-verb) - to die
5. 帰る 【かえ・る】 (u-verb) - to go home
6. いい (i-adj) - good
7. 皆 【みんな】 - everybody
8. どっか - somewhere　(abbr. of どこか)
9. 行く 【い・く】 (u-verb) - to go
10. そろそろ - gradually; soon
11. 遅い 【おそ・い】 (i-adj) - late
12. なる (u-verb) - to become
13. また - again
14. 遅刻 【ち・こく】 - tardiness
15. する (exception) - to do
16. ごめん - sorry

17. つい - just (now); unintentionally
18. お前 【お・まえ】 - you (casual)
19. 呼ぶ 【よ・ぶ】 (u-verb) - to call

In casual speech, the 「～てしまう」 is often substituted by 「～ちゃう」 while 「～でしまう」 is substituted by 「じゃう」. Both 「～ちゃう」 and 「～じゃう」 conjugate just like regular u-verbs.

1. 金魚がもう死んじゃった。 The goldfish died already.
2. もう帰っちゃっていい？ Is it ok if I went home already?
3. みんな、どっか行っちゃったよ。 Everybody went off somewhere.
4. そろそろ遅くなっちゃうよ。 It'll gradually become late, you know.

There is yet another very colloquial version of 「～てしまう」 and 「～でしまう」 where it is replaced by 「～ちまう」 and 「～じまう」 respectively. Unlike the cuter 「～ちゃう」 and 「～じゃう」 slang, this version conjures an image of rough and coarse middle-aged man.

1. また遅刻しちまったよ。 Darn, I'm late again.
2. ごめん、ついお前を呼んじまった。 Sorry, I just ended up calling you unconsciously.

Another meaning of 「しまう」

Vocabulary

1. しまう (u-verb) - to do something by accident; to finish completely
2. 宿題 【しゅく・だい】 - homework
3. やる (u-verb) - to do

You may have noticed that 「しまう」 has another definition meaning "to finish something completely". You may want to consider this a totally separate verb from the 「しまう」 we have covered so far. Occasionally but not usually, 「しまう」 will have this meaning rather than the unintended action.

- 宿題をやってしまいなさい。 Finish your homework completely.

Special Expressions with Generic Nouns

We've already learned how to use generic nouns in order to modify nouns. Now we will go over some special expression used with generic nouns.

Using 「こと」 to say whether something has happened

Vocabulary

1. こと - event, matter
2. ある (u-verb) - to exist (inanimate)
3. 徹夜 【てつ・や】 - staying up all night
4. 宿題 【しゅく・だい】 - homework
5. する (exception) - to do
6. 一人 【ひとり】 - 1 person; alone
7. 行く 【い・く】 (u-verb) - to go
8. パリ - Paris
9. お寿司 【お・す・し】 - sushi
10. 食べる 【たべ・る】 (ru-verb) - to eat
11. 日本 【に・ほん】 - Japan
12. 映画 【えい・が】 - movie

13. 観る 【み・る】 (ru-verb) - to watch
14. ヨーロッパ - Europe
15. いい (i-adj) - good
16. そう - (things are) that way
17. 言う 【い・う】 (u-verb) - to say
18. 見る 【み・る】 (ru-verb) - to see
19. ～度 【～ど】 - counter for number of times

When you combine 「こと」, the generic word for an event with 「ある」, you can talk about whether an event exists or not.

Examples

1. 徹夜して、宿題することはある。
   There are times when I do homework while staying up all night.

2. 一人で行くことはありません。
   I never go by myself.

Using the past tense of the verb with 「こと」, you can talk about whether an event has ever taken place. This is essentially the only way you can say "have done" in Japanese so this is a very useful expression. You need to use this grammar any time you want to talk about whether someone has ever done something.

Examples

1. パリに行ったことはありますか。
   Have you ever gone to Paris?

2. お寿司を食べたことがある。
   I've had sushi before.

3. 日本の映画を観たことないの？
   You've never seen a Japanese movie?

4. ヨーロッパに行ったことがあったらいいな。
   It would be nice if I ever go to Europe.

5. そういうのを<u>見</u>たことがなかった<u>。</u>
   I had never seen anything like that.

6. 一度<u>行</u>ったこと<u>も</u>ないんです。
   I've never gone, not even once.

Using 「ところ」 as an abstract place

Vocabulary

1. 所 【ところ】 - place
2. 早い 【はや・い】 (i-adj) - fast; early
3. 来る 【く・る】 (exception) - to come
4. 映画 【えい・が】 - movie
5. 今 【いま】 - now
6. ちょうど - just right; exactly
7. いい - good
8. 彼 【かれ】 - he; boyfriend
9. 優しい 【やさ・しい】 (i-adj) - gentle; kind
10. ある (u-verb) - to exist (inanimate)
11. 授業 【じゅ・ぎょう】 - class
12. 終わる 【お・わる】 (u-verb) - to end
13. これ - this
14. 行く 【い・く】 (u-verb) - to go

「ところ」 （所） is usually used to indicate a generic physical location. However, it can also hold a much broader meaning ranging from a characteristic to a place in time.

Examples

1. 早くきて。映画は今ちょうどいい<u>ところ</u>だよ。
   Come quickly. We're at the good part of the movie.

2. 彼は優しいところもあるよ。
His personality has some gentle parts too.

3. 今は授業が終ったところです。
Class has ended just now.

4. これから行くところでした。
I was just about to go from now.

Using 「もの」 as a casual feminine way to emphasize

Vocabulary

1. 物 【もの】 - object
2. どうして - why
3. 来る 【く・る】 (exception) - to come
4. 授業 【じゅ・ぎょう】 - class
5. ある (u-verb) - to exist (inanimate)

The generic object noun 「もの」 can be used as a casual and feminine way of emphasizing something. This is identical to the explanatory feminine emphasis expressed by the 「の」 particle. Just like the explanatory 「の」 particle, the 「の」 is often changed into 「ん」 resulting in 「もん」. Using 「もん」 sounds very feminine and a little cheeky (in a cute way).

Examples

- どうしてこなかったの？
Why didn't (you) come?

1. 授業があったの。
(I) had class. [feminine explanatory]

2. 授業があったもの。
   (I) had class. [feminine explanatory]
3. 授業があったもん。
   (I) had class, so there. [feminine explanatory]

Various degrees of certainty

In general, Japanese people don't assert themselves of something unless they are absolutely sure that it is correct. This accounts for the incredibly frequent use of 「〜と思う」 and the various grammatical expressions used to express specific levels of certainty. We will go over these expressions starting from the less certain to the most certain.

Using 「かもしれない」 to express uncertainty

Vocabulary

1. 多分 【た・ぶん】 - perhaps; probably
2. 映画 【えい・が】 - movie
3. 観る 【み・る】 (ru-verb) - to watch
4. 彼 【かれ】 - he; boyfriend
5. 学生 【がく・せい】 - student
6. それ - that
7. 面白い 【おも・し・ろい】 (i-adj) - interesting
8. 先生 【せん・せい】 - teacher
9. 退屈 【たい・くつ】 - boredom
10. 食堂 【しょく・どう】 - cafeteria
11. 行く 【い・く】 (u-verb) - to go
12. 雨 【あめ】 - rain
13. 試合 【し・あい】 - match, game
14. 中止 【ちゅう・し】 - cancellation

15. なる (u-verb) - to become
16. この - this　(abbr. of これの）
17. 映画 【えい・が】 - movie
18. ~回 【～かい】 - counter for number of times
19. こと - event, matter
20. ある (u-verb) - to exist (inanimate)
21. あそこ - over there
22. 代々木公園 【よ・よ・ぎ・こう・えん】 - Yoyogi park
23. もう - already
24. 逃げる 【に・げる】 (ru-verb) - to escape; to run away

「かもしれない」 is used to mean "maybe" or "possibly" and is less certain than the word 「多分」. It attaches to the end of a complete clause. For noun and na-adjective clauses, the declarative 「だ」 must be removed. It can also be written in kanji as 「かも知れない」 and you can treat it the same as a negative ru-verb (there is no positive equivalent) so the masu-form would become 「かもしれません」. In casual speech, it can be abbreviated to just 「かも」. There is also a very masculine version 「かもしれん」, which is simply a different type of negative verb.

Expressing uncertainty with 「かもしれない」

- Simply attach 「かもしれない」 or 「かも知れない」 to the clause
  Examples
  1. 映画を観たかもしれない
  2. 彼は学生かもしれない
  3. それは面白いかもしれない

- Noun and na-adjective clauses must **not** use the declarative 「だ」

Examples
  1. 先生だかもしれない → 先生かもしれない
  2. 退屈だかもしれない → 退屈かもしれない
- It can be abbreviated to just 「かも」 in casual speech
  Example
  1. 面白いかもしれない → 面白いかも

Examples

1. スミスさんは食堂に行ったかもしれません。
   Smith-san may have gone to the cafeteria.
2. 雨で試合は中止になるかもしれないね。
   The game may become canceled by rain, huh?
3. この映画は一回観たことあるかも！
   I might have already seen this movie once.
4. あそこが代々木公園かもしれない。
   That might be Yoyogi park over there.
5. もう逃げられないかもしれんぞ。
   Might not be able to escape anymore, you know.

Using 「でしょう」 to express a fair amount of certainty (polite)

Vocabulary

1. 多分 【た・ぶん】 - perhaps; probably
2. 明日 【あした】 - tomorrow
3. 雨 【あめ】 - rain
4. 学生 【がく・せい】 - student

308

5. これ - this
6. どこ - where
7. 行く 【い・く】 (u-verb) - to go
8. 休む 【やす・む】 (u-verb) - to rest
9. いただく (u-verb) - to receive; to eat; to drink (humble)

「でしょう」 is used to express a level of some certainty and is close in meaning to 「多分」. Just like 「〜です／〜ます」, it must come at the end of a complete sentence. It does not have any other conjugations. You can also replace 「〜ですか」 with 「〜でしょうか」 to make the question sound slightly more polite and less assuming by adding a slight level of uncertainty.

Examples

1. 明日も雨でしょう。
   Probably rain tomorrow too.

2. 学生さんでしょうか。
   Are (you) student?

3. これからどこへ行くんでしょうか？
   Where (are you) going from here?

If you want to sound really, really polite, you can even add 「〜でしょうか」 to the end of a 「〜ます」 ending.

- 休ませていただけますでしょうか。 - May I receive the favor of resting, possibly?

Using 「でしょう」 and 「だろう」 to express strong amount of certainty (casual)

Vocabulary

309

1. 遅刻 【ち・こく】 - tardiness
2. する (exception) - to do
3. 時間 【じ・かん】 - time
4. ある (u-verb) - to exist (inanimate)
5. 言う 【い・う】 (u-verb) - to say
6. これ - this
7. 食べる 【た・べる】 (ru-verb) - to eat
8. 行く 【い・く】 (u-verb) - to go
9. 掃除 【そう・じ】 - cleaning
10. 手伝う 【て・つだ・う】 (u-verb) - to help, to assist
11. くれる (ru-verb) - to give
12. そう - (things are) that way
13. どこ - where
14. もう - already
15. 寝る 【ね・る】 (ru-verb) - to sleep
16. 家 【1) うち; 2) いえ】 - 1) one's own home; 2) house
17. 帰る 【かえ・る】 (u-verb) - to go home

The casual equivalent of 「でしょう」 is surprisingly enough 「でしょう」. However, when you are speaking in a polite manner, the 「でしょう」 is enunciated flatly while in casual speech, it has a rising intonation and can be shortened to 「でしょ」. In addition, since people tend to be more assertive in casual situations, the casual version has a much stronger flavor often sounding more like, "See, I told you so!"

Example 1

A: あっ！遅刻しちゃう！
A: Ah! We're going to be late!

B: だから、時間がないって言ったでしょう！
B: That's why I told you there was no time!

310

Example 2

A：これから食べに行くんでしょ。
A: You're going to eat from now aren't you?

B：だったら？
B: So what if I am?

Example 3

A：掃除、手伝ってくれるでしょう。
A: You're going to help me clean, right?

B：え？そうなの？
B: Huh? Is that so?

「だろう」 means essentially the same thing as 「でしょう」
except that it sounds more masculine and is used mostly by males.

Example 4

A：アリスはどこだ？
A: Where is Alice?

B：もう寝ているだろう。
B: Probably sleeping already.

Example 5

A：もう家に帰るんだろう。
A: You're going home already, right?

B：そうよ。
B: That's right.

Expressing Amounts

This lesson will cover various expressions used to express various *degrees* of amounts. For example, sentences like, "I <u>only</u> ate one", "That was <u>all</u> that was left", "There's <u>just</u> old people here", or "I ate <u>too much</u>" all indicate whether there's a lot or little of something. Most of these expressions are made with particles and not as separate words as you see in English.

Indicating that's all there is using 「だけ」

Vocabulary

1. りんご - apple
2. これ - this
3. それ - that
4. 食べる 【たべ・る】 (ru-verb) - to eat
5. この - this (abbr. of これの)
6. 歌 【うた】 - song
7. 歌う 【うた・う】 (u-verb) - to sing
8. その - that (abbr. of それの)
9. 人 【ひと】 - person
10. 好き 【す・き】 (na-adj) - likable; desirable
11. 販売機 【はん・ばい・き】 - vending machine
12. 五百円玉 【ご・ひゃく・えん・だま】 - 500 yen coin
13. 小林 【こ・ばやし】 - Kobayashi (last name)
14. 返事 【へん・じ】 - reply
15. 来る 【く・る】 (exception) - to come
16. 準備 【じゅん・び】 - preparations
17. 終わる 【お・わる】 (u-verb) - to end
18. ここ - here
19. 名前 【な・まえ】 - name

20. 書く 【か・く】 (u-verb) - to write

21. いい (i-adj) - good

The particle 「だけ」 is used to express that that's all there is. Just like the other particles we have already learned, it is directly attached to the end of whichever word that it applies to.

Examples

1. りんごだけ。
   Just apple(s) (and nothing else).
2. これとそれだけ。
   Just that and this (and nothing else).

When one of the major particles are also applied to a word, these particles must come after 「だけ」. In fact, the ordering of multiple particles usually start from the most specific to the most general.

1. それだけは、食べないでください。
   Just don't eat that. (Anything else is assumed to be OK).
2. この歌だけを歌わなかった。
   Didn't sing just this song.
3. その人だけが好きだったんだ。
   That person was the only person I liked.

The same goes for double particles. Again 「だけ」 must come first.

- この販売機だけでは、五百円玉が使えない。
  Cannot use 500 yen coin in just this vending machine.

With minor particles such as 「から」 or 「まで」, it is difficult to tell which should come first. When in doubt, try googling to see the level of popularity of each combination. It turns out that 「からだけ」 is almost twice as popular as 「だけから」 with a hit number of 90,000 vs. 50,000.

- 小林さんからだけは、返事が来なかった。
  A reply has not come from only Kobayashi-san.

Unlike some particles, you can directly attach 「だけ」 to verbs as well.

1. 準備が終わったから、これからは食べるだけだ。
   Since the preparations are done, from here we just have to eat.
2. ここに名前を書くだけでいいですか？
   Is it ok to just write [my] name here?

Using 「のみ」 as a formal version of 「だけ」

Vocabulary

1. この - this　(abbr. of これの）
2. 乗車券 【じょう・しゃ・けん】 - passenger ticket
3. 発売 【はつ・ばい】 - sale
4. 当日 【とう・じつ】 - that very day
5. 有効 【ゆう・こう】 - effective
6. アンケート - survey
7. 対象 【たい・しょう】 - target
8. 大学生 【だい・がく・せい】 - college student

A particle that is essentially identical both grammatically and in meaning to 「だけ」 is 「のみ」. However, unlike 「だけ」, which is used in regular conversations, 「のみ」 is usually only used in a written context. It is often used for explaining policies, in manuals, and other things of that nature. This grammar really belongs in the advanced section since formal language has a different flavor and tone from what we have seen so far. However, it is covered here because it is essentially identical to 「だけ」. Just googling for 「のみ」 will quickly show the difference in the type of language that is used with 「のみ」 as opposed to 「だけ」.

1. この乗車券は発売当日のみ有効です。
   This boarding ticket is <u>only</u> valid on the date on which it was purchased.
2. アンケート対象は大学生のみです。
   The targets of this survey are <u>only</u> college students.

Indication that there's nothing else using 「しか」

Vocabulary

1. これ - this
2. ある (u-verb) - to exist (inanimate)
3. 見る 【み・る】 (ru-verb) - to see
4. 今日 【きょう】 - today
5. 忙しい 【いそが・しい】 (i-adj) - busy
6. 朝ご飯 【あさ・ご・はん】 - breakfast
7. 食べる 【た・べる】 (ru-verb) - to eat
8. 全部 【ぜん・ぶ】 - everything
9. 買う 【か・う】 (u-verb) - to buy
10. ううん - no (casual)
11. 何【なに】 - what
12. もらう - to receive
13. 頑張る 【がん・ば・る】 (u-verb) - to try one's best
14. こう - (things are) this way
15. なる (u-verb) - to become
16. 逃げる 【に・げる】 (ru-verb) - to escape; to run away
17. もう - already
18. 腐る 【くさ・る】 (u-verb) - to rot; to spoil

19. 捨てる 【す・てる】 (ru-verb) - to throw away

I carefully phrased the title of this section to show that 「しか」 must be used to indicate the **lack** of everything else. In other words, the rest of the sentence must always be negative.

- これしかない。
  There's nothing but this.

The following is incorrect.

- これしかある。

  (Should be using 「だけ」 instead)

As you can see, 「しか」 has an embedded negative meaning while 「だけ」 doesn't have any particular nuance.

1. これだけ見る。
   See just this.
2. これだけ見ない。
   Don't see just this.
3. これしか見ない。
   Don't see anything else but this.

Examples

- 今日は忙しくて、朝ご飯しか食べられなかった。
  Today was busy and couldn't eat anything but breakfast.

Notice that unlike 「だけ」, it is necessary to finish off the sentence.

- 全部買うの？
  You're buying everything?

1. ううん、これだけ。
   Nah, just this.
2. ううん、これしか買わない
   Nah, won't buy anything else but this.
3. ~~ううん、これしか。~~
   (Wrong, the sentence must explicitly indicate the negative.)

While the major particles always come last, it turns out that 「しか」 must come after 「から」 and 「まで」. A google search of 「からしか」 beats 「しかから」 by an overwhelming 60,000 to 600.

- アリスからしか何ももらってない。
  I didn't receive anything except from Alice.

You can also use this grammar with verbs.

1. これから頑張るしかない！
   There's nothing to do but try our best!
2. こうなったら、逃げるしかない。
   There no choice but to run away once it turns out like this.
3. もう腐っているから、捨てるしかないよ。
   It's rotten already so there's nothing to do but throw it out.

「っきゃ」, an alternative to 「しか」

Vocabulary

1. これ - this
2. 買う 【か・う】 (u-verb) - to buy
3. ある (u-verb) - to exist (inanimate)
4. こう - (things are) this way
5. なる (u-verb) - to become
6. もう - already
7. やる (u-verb) - to do

「っきゃ」 is another version of 「しか」 that means essentially the same thing and works exactly the same way. Just substitute 「しか」 with 「っきゃ」 and you're good to go. This version is a bit stronger than 「しか」 in emphasis but it's not used nearly as often so I wouldn't worry about it too much. I briefly cover it here just in case you do run into this expression.

Examples

1. これは買う<u>っきゃ</u>ない！
   There's nothing but to buy this!
2. こうなったら、もうやる<u>っきゃ</u>ない！
   If things turn out like this, there nothing to do but to just do it!

Expressing the opposite of 「だけ」 with 「ばかり」

Vocabulary

1. 何 【なに／なん】 - what
2. おばさん - middle-aged lady
3. 嫌 【いや】 (na-adj) disagreeable; unpleasant
4. 崇 【たかし】 - Takashi (first name)
5. ~君 【～くん】 - name suffix
6. 漫画 【まん・が】 - comic book
7. 読む 【よ・む】 (u-verb) - to read
8. かっこ悪い 【かっこ・わる・い】 (i-adj) - unattractive; uncool
9. 彼 【かれ】 - he; boyfriend
10. 麻雀 【マー・ジャン】 - mahjong
11. 直美 【なお・み】 - Naomi (first name)
12. 遊ぶ 【あそ・ぶ】 (u-verb) - to play
13. 最近 【さい・きん】 - recent; lately

14. 仕事 【し・ごと】 - job

「ばかり」 is used to express the condition where there's so much of something to the point where there's nothing else. Notice this is fundamentally different from 「しか」 which expresses a **lack** of everything else but the item in question. In more casual situations, 「ばかり」 is usually pronounced 「ばっかり」 or just 「ばっか」. For example, let's say you went to a party to find, much to your dismay, the whole room filled with middle-aged women. You might say the following.

- 何だよ！おばさんばっかりじゃないか？
  What the? Isn't it nothing but obasan?

Or perhaps a little more girly:

- いやだ。おばさんばっかり。
  Eww. It's nothing but obasan.

Examples

- 崇君は漫画ばっかり読んでてさ。かっこ悪い。
  Takashi-kun is reading nothing but comic books... He's so uncool.

It is quite common in casual speech to end midsentence like this. Notice 「読んでて」 is the te-form of 「読んでいる」 with the 「い」 dropped. We assume that the conclusion will come somewhere later in the story.

1. 彼は麻雀ばかりです。
   He's nothing but mahjong. (He does nothing but play mahjong.)
2. 直美ちゃんと遊ぶばっかりでしょう！
   You're hanging out with Naomi-chan all the time, aren't you!

319

3. 最近は仕事ばっかだよ。
Lately, it's nothing but work.

Saying there's too much of something using 「すぎる」

Vocabulary

1. 過ぎる 【す・ぎる】 (ru-verb) - to exceed; to pass
2. 食べる 【た・べる】 (ru-verb) - to eat
3. 飲む 【の・む】 (u-verb) - to drink
4. 太る 【ふと・る】 (u-verb) - to become fatter
5. 静か 【しず・か】 (na-adj) - quiet
6. 大きい 【おお・きい】 (i-adj) - big
7. 面白い 【おも・しろ・い】 (i-adj) - interesting
8. もったいない (i-adj) - wasteful
9. 情けない 【なさ・けない】 (i-adj) - pitiable
10. 危ない 【あぶ・ない】 (i-adj) - dangerous
11. 少ない 【すく・ない】 (i-adj) - few
12. 佐藤 【さ・とう】 - Satou (last name)
13. 料理 【りょう・り】 - cooking; cuisine; dish
14. 上手 【じょう・ず】 (na-adj) - skillful
15. また - again
16. お酒 【お・さけ】 - alcohol
17. 気 【き】 - mood; intent
18. つける - to attach
19. 気をつける - (expression) to be careful
20. トランク - trunk
21. 入る 【はい・る】 (u-verb) - to enter
22. 罠 【わな】 - trap
23. 時間 【じ・かん】 - time
24. 足りる 【た・りる】 (ru-verb) - to be sufficient
25. 何【なに】 - what

26. 出来る 【で・き・る】 (ru-verb) - to be able to do
27. 彼 【かれ】 - he; boyfriend
28. 彼女 【かの・じょ】 - she; girlfriend
29. 昨晩 【さく・ばん】 - last night
30. こと - event, matter
31. 全然 【ぜん・ぜん】 - not at all (when used with negative)
32. 覚える 【おぼ・える】 (ru-verb) - to memorize
33. それ - that

「すぎる」 is a regular ru-verb written 「過ぎる」 meaning, "to exceed". When 「すぎる」 is attached to the end of other verbs and adjectives, it means that it is too much or that it has exceeded the normal levels. For verbs, you must directly attach 「すぎる」 to the stem of the verb. For example, 「食べすぎる」 means "to eat too much" and 「飲みすぎる」 means "to drink too much". For adjectives, you just attach it to the end after you remove the last 「い」 from the i-adjectives (as usual). One more rule is that for both negative verbs and adjectives, one must remove the 「い」 from 「ない」 and replace with 「さ」 before attaching 「すぎる」. There is no tense (past or non-past) associated with this grammar. Since 「すぎる」 is a regular ru-verb, this grammar always results in a regular ru-verb.

Using 「すぎる」 to indicate there's too much of something

- **For verbs:** First change the verb to the *stem* and attach 「すぎる」.
  Examples
     1. 食べる → 食べすぎる
     2. 太る → 太り → 太りすぎる

- **For na-adjectives:** Attach 「すぎる」. For i-adjectives, remove the last 「い」 first before attaching 「すぎる」.
  Examples
  1. 静か → 静かすぎる
  2. 大き~~い~~ → 大きすぎる

- **For negative verbs and adjectives:** Replace the last 「い」 from 「ない」 with 「さ」 and then attach 「すぎる」
  Examples
  1. 食べな~~い~~ → 食べなさ → 食べなさすぎる
  2. 面白くな~~い~~ → 面白くなさ → 面白くなさすぎる

- I-adjectives that end in 「ない」 which incorporate the negative 「無い」 such as 「もったいない」（勿体<u>無</u>い）or 「情けない」（情け<u>無</u>い） follow the third rule.
  Examples
  1. もったいな~~い~~ → もったいなさ → もったいなさすぎる
  2. 情けな~~い~~ → 情けなさ → 情けなさすぎる

  Most regular i-adjectives such as 「危ない」 or 「少ない」 follow the regular rule (rule 2).
-
  Examples
  1. 危な~~い~~ → 危なすぎる
  2. 少な~~い~~ → 少なすぎる

Examples

1. 佐藤さんは料理が上手で、また食べ過ぎました。
   Satou-san is good at cooking and I ate too much again.

2. お酒を飲みすぎないように気をつけてね。
Be careful to not drink too much, ok?

3. 大きすぎるからトランクに入らないぞ。
It won't fit in the trunk cause it's too big, man.

4. 静かすぎる。罠かもしれないよ。
It's too quiet. It might be a trap, you know.

5. 時間が足りなさすぎて、何もできなかった。
Due to too much of a lack of time, I couldn't do anything.

6. 彼には、彼女がもったいなさすぎるよ。
She is totally wasted on him (too good for him).

It is also common to change 「すぎる」 into its stem and use it as a noun.

A: 昨晩のこと、全然覚えてないな。
A: Man, I don't remember anything about last night.

B: それは飲みすぎだよ。
B: That's drinking too much.

Adding the 「も」 particle to express excessive amounts

Vocabulary

1. 昨日【きのう】- yesterday
2. 電話 【でん・わ】- phone
3. ~回 【~かい】- counter for number of times
4. する (exception) - to do
5. 試験 【し・けん】- exam
6. ため - for the sake/benefit of
7. ~時間 【~じ・かん】- counter for span of hour(s)
8. 勉強 【べん・きょう】- study

323

9. 今年 【こ・とし】 - this year
10. キロ - kilo
11. 太る 【ふと・る】 (u-verb) - to become fatter

When the 「も」 particle comes after some type of amount, it means that the amount indicated is way too much. For instance, let's look at the next example.

- 昨日、電話三回もしたよ！
  I called you like three times yesterday!

Notice that the 「も」 particle is attached to the amount "three times". This sentence implies that the speaker called even three times and still the person didn't pick up the phone. We understand this to mean that three times are a lot of times to call someone.

1. 試験のために三時間も勉強した。
   I studied three whole hours for the exam.
2. 今年、十キロも太っちゃった！
   I gained 10 whole kilograms this year!

Using 「ほど」 to express the extent of something

Vocabulary

1. 程 【ほど】 - degree, extent
2. 今日 【きょう】 - today
3. 天気 【てん・き】 - weather
4. それ - that
5. 暑い 【あつ・い】 (i-adj) - hot
6. 寝る 【ね・る】 (ru-verb) - to sleep
7. 時間 【じ・かん】 - time

8. ある (u-verb) - to exist (inanimate)
9. 忙しい 【いそが・しい】 (i-adj) - busy
10. 韓国 【かん・こく】 - Korea
11. 料理 【りょう・り】 - cooking; cuisine; dish
12. 食べる 【たべ・る】 (ru-verb) - to eat
13. おいしい (i-adj) - tasty
14. なる (u-verb) - to become
15. 歩く 【ある・く】 (u-verb) - to walk
16. 迷う 【まよ・う】 (u-verb) - to get lost
17. 勉強 【べん・きょう】 - study
18. 頭 【あたま】 - head
19. いい (i-adj) - good
20. ハードディスク - hard disk
21. 容量 【よう・りょう】 - capacity
22. 大きい 【おお・きい】 (i-adj) - big
23. もっと - more
24. たくさん - a lot (amount)
25. 曲 【きょく】 - tune
26. 保存 【ほ・ぞん】 - save
27. 出来る 【で・き・る】 (ru-verb) - to be able to do
28. 航空券 【こう・くう・けん】 - plane ticket
29. 安い 【やす・い】 (i-adj) - cheap
30. 限る 【かぎ・る】 (u-verb) - to limit
31. 文章 【ぶん・しょう】 - sentence; writing
32. 短い 【みじか・い】 (i-adj) - short
33. 簡単 【かん・たん】 (na-adj) - simple
34. 良い 【よ・い】 (i-adj) - good

The noun 「ほど」 （程） is attached to a word in a sentence to express the extent of something. It can modify nouns as well as verbs as seen in the next example.

1. 今日の天気はそれほど暑くない。
   Today's weather is not hot to that extent.

325

2. 寝る時間がないほど忙しい。
Busy to the extent that there's no time to sleep.

When you use this with conditionals, you can express something that translates into English as, "The more you [verb], the more..." The grammar is always formed in the following sequence:

[conditional of verb] followed immediately by [same verb+ ほど]

- 韓国料理は食べれば食べるほど、おいしくなる。
About Korean food, the more you eat the tastier it becomes.

The literal translation is, "About Korean food, if you eat, to the extent that you eat, it becomes tasty." which essentially means the same thing. The example uses the 「ば」 conditional form, but the 「たら」 conditional will work as well. Since this is a general statement, the contextual 「なら」 conditional will never work. The decided 「と」 conditional won't work very well here either since it may not always be true depending on the extent of the action.

1. 歩いたら歩くほど、迷ってしまった。
The more I walked, the more I got lost.
2. 勉強をすればするほど、頭がよくなるよ。
The more you study, the more you will become smarter.

You can also use this grammar with i-adjectives by using the 「ば」 conditional.

1. iPodは、ハードディスクの容量が大きければ大きいほどもっとたくさんの曲が保存できます。
About iPod, the larger the hard disk capacity, the more songs you can save.
2. 航空券は安ければ安いほどいいとは限らない。
It's not necessarily the case that the cheaper the ticket, the better it is.

For na-adjectives, since you can't use the 「ば」 conditional you have to resort to the 「なら」 conditional. Because it sounds strange to use the 「なら」 conditional in this fashion, you will hardly ever see this grammar used with na-adjectives. Since 「ほど」 is treated as a noun, make sure you don't forget to use 「な」 to attach the noun to the na-adjective.

- 文章は、短ければ短いほど、簡単なら簡単なほどよいです。
  The shorter and simpler the sentences, the better it is.

Using 「〜さ」 with adjectives to indicate an amount

Vocabulary

1. 高い 【たか・い】 (i-adj) - high; tall; expensive
2. 低い 【ひく・い】 (i-adj) - short
3. 穏やか 【おだ・やか】 (na-adj) - calm, peaceful
4. この - this (abbr. of これの)
5. ビル - building
6. 何 【なに／なん】 - what
7. 犬 【いぬ】 - dog
8. 聴覚 【ちょう・かく】 - sense of hearing
9. 敏感 【びん・かん】 (na-adj) - sensitive
10. 人間 【にん・げん】 - human
11. 比べる 【くら・べる】 (ru-verb) - to compare
12. はるか - far more
13. 上 【うえ】 - above

We will now learn how to add 「さ」 to adjectives to indicate an amount of that adjective. For example, we can attach 「さ」 to the adjective for "high" in order to get "height". Instead of looking at the height, we can even attach 「さ」 to the adjective for "low" to focus on the amount of lowness as opposed to the amount of highness. In fact, there is nothing to stop us from using this with any adjective to indicate an amount of that adjective. The result becomes a regular noun indicating the amount of that adjective.

Adding 「～さ」 to adjectives to indicate an amount

- **For i-adjectives**: First remove the trailing 「い」 from the i-adjective and then attach 「さ」
  1. 高い → 高さ
  2. 低い → 低さ
- **For na-adjectives**: Just attach 「さ」 to the end of the na-adjective
  Example
  1. 穏やか → 穏やかさ

The result becomes a regular noun.

Examples

1. このビルの高さは何ですか？
   What is the height of this building?
2. 犬の聴覚の敏感さを人間と比べると、はるかに上だ。
   If you compare the level of sensitivity of hearing of dogs to humans, it is far above.

Similarity or hearsay

In Japanese there are many different ways to express likeness or similarity depending on appearance, behavior, or outcome. When learning these expressions for the first time, it is difficult to understand what the differences are between them because they all translate to the same thing in English. This lesson is designed to study the differences between these expressions so that you can start to get a sense of which is appropriate for what you want to say.

Expressing similarity with よう（様）

Vocabulary

1. ここ - here
2. 誰【だれ】 - who
3. いる (ru-verb) - to exist (animate)
4. 映画【えい・が】 - movie
5. 観る【み・る】(ru-verb) - to watch
6. 学生【がく・せい】 - student
7. 静か【しず・か】(na-adj) - quiet
8. あの - that (over there)（abbr. of あれの）
9. 人【ひと】 - person
10. 見る【み・る】(ru-verb) - to see
11. 気【き】 - mood; intent
12. する (exception) - to do
13. 彼【かれ】 - he; boyfriend
14. 雰囲気【ふん・い・き】 - atmosphere; mood
15. ちょっと - a little
16. 怒る【おこ・る】(u-verb) - to get angry
17. 聞こえる【き・こえる】(ru-verb) - to be audible
18. 何【なに／なん】 - what
19. 起こる【おこ・る】(u-verb) - to happen
20. 言う【い・う】(u-verb) - to say

We've already briefly gone over 「よう」 and learned that 「よう」 means an appearance or manner. We can use this definition to say that something has an appearance or manner of a certain state. This word can be used in many ways to express similarity. The simplest example is by directly modifying the relative clause. When the sentence ends in 「よう」, you must explicitly express the state-of-being by adding 「だ」, 「です」, or 「でございます」.

1. ここには、誰もいないようだ。
   Looks like no one is here.
2. 映画を観たようです。
   Looks like (he) watched the movie.

When directly modifying nouns or na-adjectives, you must use the 「の」 particle for nouns or attach 「な」 to na-adjectives.

1. 学生のようだ。
   Looks like it's a student.
2. ここは静かなようだ。
   Looks like it's quiet.

Notice that example 1 does not say that the person looks *like a student*. Rather, the declarative 「だ」 states that the person appears to *be a student*. On a side note, you can't say 「おいしいようだ」 to say that something looks tasty. This is like saying, "This dish apparently is tasty," which can actually be kind of rude.

You can also use it as a na-adjective to describe something that appears to be something else.

1. あの人を見たような気がした。
   Had a feeling like I saw that person before.
2. 彼は学生のような雰囲気ですね。
   He has a student-like atmosphere.

Finally, we can attach the target particle to say things like, "I heard it like that" or "I said it like...".

1. ちょっと怒ったように聞こえた。
   Was able to hear it like (she) was a little mad.
2. 何も起こらなかったように言った。
   Said (it) like nothing happened.

Using 「みたい」 to say something looks like something else

Vocabulary

1. 見る 【み・る】 (ru-verb) - to see
2. 犬 【いぬ】 - dog
3. もう - already
4. 売り切れ 【う・り・き・れ】 - sold out
5. 制服 【せい・ふく】 - uniform
6. 着る 【き・る】 (ru-verb) - to wear
7. 姿 【すがた】 - figure
8. 学生 【がく・せい】 - student
9. この - this (abbr. of これの)
10. ピザ - pizza
11. お好み焼き 【お・この・み・や・き】 - okonomiyaki
    (Japanese-style pancake)
12. 見える 【み・える】 (ru-verb) - to be visible

Another way to express similarity which is considered more casual is by using 「みたい」. Do not confuse this with the 「たい」 conjugation of 「見る」. The main difference is that this 「みたい」 can be attached directly to nouns, adjectives, and verbs just like particles which i-adjectives like 「～たい」 obviously can't do.

Using 「みたい」 to say something looks like something else

Attach 「みたい」 to the noun that bears the resemblance. 「みたい」 conjugates like a noun or na-adjective and not an i-adjective.

Conjugation Example with 「犬」

	Positive	**Negative**
Non-Past	犬みたい looks like a dog	犬じゃないみたい doesn't look like a dog
Past	犬だったみたい looked like a dog	犬じゃなかったみたい didn't look like a dog

Examples

1. もう売り切れみたい。
   Looks like it's sold out already.

2. 制服を着ている姿をみると、学生みたいです。
   Looking at the uniform-wearing figure, (person) looks like a

student.

The implied meaning here is the person wearing the uniform is not really a student because he/she only *looks* like a student. This is different from example 3 from the previous 「よう」 section which implied that the person appears to be (but might not be) a student. Again, we also can't say 「おいしいみたい」 to say that something looks tasty because it implies that, in actuality, the food might not be so good.

Don't forget that 「みたい」 does not conjugate like the 「〜たい」 form or i-adjectives.

- このピザはお好み焼きみた~~くない~~?

  (みたい conjugates like a na-adjective.)

- このピザはお好み焼きみたいじゃない?
  Doesn't this pizza looks like okonomiyaki?

「みたい」 is a grammar used mostly for conversational Japanese. Do not use it in essays, articles, or anything that needs to sound authoritative. You can use 「よう」 instead in the following fashion.

1. もう売り切れのようだ。
   It appears that it is sold-out already.
2. このピザはお好み焼きのように見える。
   This pizza looks like okonomiyaki.

Guessing at an outcome using 「〜そう」

Vocabulary

1. いい (i-adj) - good
2. バランス - balance

3. 崩れる 【くず・れる】 (ru-verb) - to collapse; to crumble
4. 一瞬 【いっ・しゅん】 - an instant
5. 倒れる 【たお・れる】 (ru-verb) - to collapse; to fall
6. この - this (abbr. of これの)
7. 辺り 【あた・り】 - vicinity
8. ある (u-verb) - to exist (inanimate)
9. 漬物 【つけ・もの】 - pickled vegetable
10. おいしい (i-adj) - tasty
11. これ - this
12. 結構 【けっ・こう】 - fairly, reasonably
13. やはり／やっぱり - as I thought
14. 高い 【たか・い】 (i-adj) - high; tall; expensive
15. お前 【お・まえ】 - you (casual)
16. 金髪 【きん・ぱつ】 - blond hair
17. 女 【おんな】 - woman; girl
18. 好き 【す・き】 (na-adj) - likable; desirable
19. もう - already
20. ～時 【～じ】 - counter for hours
21. なる (u-verb) - to become
22. 来る 【く・る】 (exception) - to come
23. ただ - free of charge; only
24. 試合 【し・あい】 - match, game
25. その - that (abbr. of それの)
26. 人 【ひと】 - person
27. 学生 【がく・せい】 - student
28. かわいい (i-adj) - cute
29. かわいそう (i-adj) - pitiable
30. 犬 【いぬ】 - dog

The problem with English is that the expression, "seems like" has too many meanings. It can mean similarity in appearance, similarity in behavior or even that current evidence points to a likely outcome. We will now learn how to say the third meaning: how to indicate a likely outcome given the situation.

Just like the grammar we have learned so far in this lesson, we can use this grammar by simply attaching 「そう」 to the end of verbs, and adjectives. However, there are four important different cases. Actually, I just noticed this but the conjugation rules are exactly the same as the 「～すぎる」 grammar we learned in the last section. The only difference is that for the adjective 「いい」, you need to change it to 「よさ」 before attaching 「そう」 to create 「よさそう」.

Rules for conjugation

1. Verbs must be changed to the *stem*.
2. The 「い」 in i-adjectives must be dropped except for 「いい」.
3. 「いい」 must first be conjugated to 「よさ」.
4. For all negatives, the 「い」 must be replaced with 「さ」.
5. This grammar does not work with plain nouns.

---

1. Verb must be changed to the stem.

For ru-verbs, remove the 「る」

- バランスが崩れて、一瞬倒れそうだった。
  Losing my balance, I seemed likely to fall for a moment.

For u-verbs, change the / u / vowel sound to an / i / vowel sound

- この辺りにありそうだけどな。
  It seems likely that it would be around here but...

2. The 「い」 in i-adjectives must be dropped.

In the next example, the 「い」 has been dropped from 「おいしい」.

- この漬物はおいしそう！
  I bet this pickled vegetable is tasty! (This pickled vegetable looks good!)

Exception: The only exception to this rule is the adjective 「いい」. When using this grammar with 「いい」, you must first change it to 「よさ」.

- これも結構よさそうだけど、やっぱり高いよね。
  This one also seems to be good but, as expected, it's expensive, huh?

Nothing needs to be done for na-adjectives.

- お前なら、金髪の女が好きそうだな。
  Knowing you, I bet you like blond-haired girls.

3. For all negatives, the 「い」 must be replaced with 「さ」.

The negative of 「来る」 is 「こない」 so when used with 「～そう」, it becomes 「こなさそう」.

1. もう10時になったから、来なさそうだね。
   Since it already became 10:00, it's likely that (person) won't come.
2. これはただの試合じゃなさそうだ。
   This isn't likely to be an ordinary match.

Identical to the 「〜すぎる」 grammar, i-adjectives that are derived from the negative 「〜ない」
like 「もったいない」 or 「情けない」 also follow this rule as well (which would be 「もったいなさそう」 and 「情けなさそう」 in this case).

4. This grammar does not work with plain nouns.

- その人は学生~~そう~~。

There are other grammar we have already covered that can be used to indicate that something is likely to be something else.

1. その人は学生でしょう。
   That person is probably student.
2. その人は学生だろう。
   That person is probably student.

Be careful never to use 「かわいい」 with this grammar. 「かわいそう」 is a completely different word used when you feel sorry for something or someone. 「かわいい」 means, "to look cute" already so you never need to use any of the grammar in this lesson to say something looks cute.

1. この犬はかわいそう。
   Oh, this poor dog.
2. この犬はかわいい。
   This dog is cute.

Expressing hearsay using 「〜そうだ」

Vocabulary

1. 明日 【あした】 - tomorrow
2. 雨 【あめ】 - rain
3. 降る 【ふ・る】 (u-verb) - to precipitate
4. 毎日 【まい・にち】 - everyday
5. 会う 【あ・う】 (u-verb) - to meet
6. 行く 【い・く】 (u-verb) - to go
7. 彼 【かれ】 - he; boyfriend
8. 高校生 【こう・こう・せい】 - high school student
9. 今日 【きょう】 - today
10. 田中 【た・なか】 - Tanaka (last name)
11. 来る 【く・る】 (exception) - to come

The reason that there are so many annoying rules to using 「～そう」 is to distinguish it from this next grammar we will learn. This is a useful grammar for talking about things you heard that doesn't necessary have anything to do with how you yourself, think or feel. Unlike the last grammar we learned, you can simply attach 「そうだ」 to verbs and i-adjectives. For na-adjectives and nouns, you must indicate the state-of-being by adding 「だ」 to the noun/na-adjective. Also, notice that 「そう」 itself must always end in 「だ」、 「です」、 or 「でございます」. These differences are what distinguishes this grammar from the one we learned in the last section. There are no tenses for this grammar.

1. 明日、雨が降るそうだ。
   I hear that it's going to rain tomorrow.
2. 毎日会いに行ったそうです。
   I heard he went to meet everyday.

Don't forget to add 「だ」 for nouns or na-adjectives.

• 彼は、高校生だそうです。
  I hear that he is a high school student.

When starting the sentence with this grammar, you also need to add 「だ」 just like you do with 「だから」

A：今日、田中さんはこないの？
A: Is Tanaka-san not coming today?

B：だそうです。
B: So I hear.

Expressing hearsay or behavior using 「〜らしい」

Vocabulary

1. 今日 【きょう】 - today
2. 田中 【た・なか】 - Tanaka (last name)
3. 来る 【く・る】 (exception) - to come
4. あの - that (over there) (abbr. of あれの)
5. 人 【ひと】 - person
6. 何 【なん】 - what
7. 美由紀 【み・ゆ・き】 - Miyuki (first name)
8. 友達 【とも・だち】 - friend
9. 子 【こ】 - child
10. 子供 【こ・ども】 - child
11. 大人 【おとな】 - adult
12. する (exception) - to do
13. つもり - intention, plan
14. 大騒ぎ 【おお・さわ・ぎ】 - big commotion

「らしい」 can be directly attached to nouns, adjectives, or verbs to show that things appear to be a certain way due to what you've heard. This is different from 「〜そうだ」 because 「〜そうだ」 indicates something you heard about specifically while 「らしい」

339

means things seem to be a certain way based on some things you heard about the subject. 「らしい」 conjugates like a normal i-adjective.

Example 1

A：今日、田中さんはこないの？
A: Is Tanaka-san not coming today?

B：こないらしい。
B: Seems like it (based on what I heard).

Example 2

A：あの人は何なの？
A: What is that person over there?

B：美由紀さんの友達らしいですよ。
B: Seems to be Miyuki-san's friend (based on what I heard).

Another way to use 「らしい」 is to indicate that a person seems to be a certain thing due to his behavior.

1. あの子は子供らしくない。
   That child does not act like a child.
2. 大人らしくするつもりだったのに、大騒ぎしてしまった。
   Despite the fact that I planned to act like an adult, I ended up making a big ruckus.

「っぽい」: Slang expression of similarity

Vocabulary

1. あの - that (over there) (abbr. of あれの)
2. 人 【ひと】 - person
3. 韓国人 【かん・こく・じん】 - Korean person
4. 皆 【みんな】 - everybody
5. もう - already
6. 全部 【ぜん・ぶ】 - everything
7. 食べる 【た・べる】 (ru-verb) - to eat
8. 恭子 【きょう・こ】 - Kyouko (first name)
9. 全然 【ぜん・ぜん】 - not at all (when used with negative)
10. 女 【おんな】 - woman; girl

A really casual way to express similarity is to attach 「っぽい」 to the word that reflects the resemblance. Because this is a very casual expression, you can use it as a casual version for all the different types of expression for similarity covered above.

「っぽい」 conjugates just like an i-adjective, as seen by example 3 below.

1. あの人はちょっと韓国人っぽいよね。
   That person looks a little like Korean person, huh?

2. みんなで、もう全部食べてしまったっぽいよ。
   It appears that everybody ate everything already.

3. 恭子は全然女っぽくないね。
   Kyouko is not womanly at all, huh?

Using 「方」 and 「よる」

If you were wondering how to make comparison in Japanese, well wonder no more. We will learn how to use 「方」 and 「より」 to make comparisons between two things. We will also learn other uses of 「方」 and 「よる」 along the way.

Using 「方」 for comparisons

Vocabulary

1. 方 【(1) ほう；2) かた】 - 1) direction; side; 2) person; way of doing
2. ご飯 【ご・はん】 - rice; meal
3. おいしい (i-adj) - tasty
4. 鈴木 【すず・き】 - Suzuki (last name)
5. 若い 【わか・い】 (i-adj) - young
6. 学生 【がく・せい】 - student
7. いい (i-adj) - good
8. 赤ちゃん 【あか・ちゃん】 - baby
9. 静か 【しず・か】 (na-adj) - quiet
10. 好き 【す・き】 (na-adj) - likable; desirable
11. ゆっくり - slowly
12. 食べる 【た・べる】 (ru-verb) - to eat
13. 健康 【けん・こう】 - health
14. こちら - this way
15. 行く 【い・く】 (u-verb) - to go
16. 早い 【はや・い】 (i-adj) - fast; early
17. 怖い 【こわ・い】 (i-adj) - scary
18. 映画 【えい・が】 - movie
19. 観る 【み・る】 (ru-verb) - to watch
20. そんな - that sort of
21. 飲む 【の・む】 (u-verb) - to drink

The noun 「方」 is read as 「ほう」 when it is used to mean a direction or orientation. As an aside, it can also be read as 「かた」 when it is used as a politer version of 「人」.

When we use 「方」 to mean direction, we can use it for comparison by saying one way of things is better, worse, etc., than the other way. Grammatically, it works just like any other regular nouns.

Examples

Use it with nouns by utilizing the 「の」 particle.

1. ご飯の方がおいしい
   Rice is tastier. (lit: The way of rice is tasty.)
2. 鈴木さんの方が若い。
   Suzuki-san is younger. (lit: The way of Suzuki is young.)

Grammatically, it's no different from a regular noun.

1. 学生じゃない方がいいよ。
   It's better to not be a student. (lit: The way of not being student is good.)
2. 赤ちゃんは、静かな方が好き。
   Like quiet babies more. (lit: About babies, the quiet way is desirable.)

For non-negative verbs, you can also use the past tense to add more certainty and confidence, particularly when making suggestions.

1. ゆっくり食べた方が健康にいいよ。
   It's better for your health to eat slowly.
2. こちらから行った方が早かった。
   It was faster to go from this way.

The same thing does <u>not</u> apply for negative verbs.

- 怖い映画は観ない方がいいよ。
  It's better not to watch scary movie(s).

The negative verb is only in the past tense when the comparison is of something that happened in the past.

- そんなに飲まなかった方がよかった。
  It was better not to have drunk that much.

Using 「より」 for comparisons

Vocabulary

1. 方 【1) ほう; 2) かた】 - 1) direction; side; 2) person; way of doing
2. 花 【はな】 - flower
3. 団子 【だん・ご】 - dango (dumpling)
4. ご飯 【ご・はん】 - rice; meal
5. パン - bread
6. おいしい (i-adj) - tasty
7. 若い 【わか・い】 (i-adj) - young
8. 鈴木 【すず・き】 - Suzuki (last name)
9. 毎日 【まい・にち】 - everyday
10. 仕事 【し・ごと】 - job
11. 嫌 【いや】 (na-adj) disagreeable; unpleasant
12. ある (u-verb) - to exist (inanimate)
13. まし - not as bad
14. ゆっくり - slowly
15. 食べる 【た・べる】 (ru-verb) - to eat
16. 早い 【はや・い】 (i-adj) - fast; early
17. いい (i-adj) - good

You can think of 「より」 as being the opposite of 「方」. It means, "rather than" or "as opposed to". It attaches directly to the back of any word. It is usually used in conjunction with 「方」 to say something like, "This way is better as opposed to that way."

Examples

1. 花より団子。
   Dango rather than flowers. (This is a very famous saying.)
2. ご飯の方が、パンよりおいしい。
   Rice tastes better than bread. (lit: The rice way is tasty as opposed to bread.)
3. キムさんより鈴木さんの方が若い。
   Suzuki-san is younger than Kim-san. (lit: The way of Suzuki is young as opposed to Kim-san.)

For those curious about the meaning of the proverb, dango is a sweet doughy treat usually sold at festivals. The proverb is saying that people prefer this treat to watching the flowers, referring to the 「花見」 event where people go out to see the cherry blossoms (and get smashed). The deeper meaning of the proverb, like all good proverbs, depends on how you apply it.

Of course, there is no rule that 「より」 must be used with 「方」. The other way of things can be gleaned from context.

鈴木：毎日仕事に行くのが嫌だ。
Suzuki: I don't like going to work everyday.

スミス：仕事がないよりましだよ。
Smith: It's not as bad as opposed to not having a job.

Words associated with 「より」 do not need any tense. Notice in the following sentence that 「食べる」 in front of 「より」 is present tense even though 「食べる」 in front of 「方」 is past tense.

- ゆっくり食べた方が早く食べるよりいい。
  It is better to eat slowly as opposed to eating quickly.

Using 「より」 as a superlative

Vocabulary

1. 誰 【だれ】 - who
2. 何【なに】 - what
3. どこ - where
4. 商品 【しょう・ひん】 - product
5. 品質 【ひん・しつ】 - quality of a good
6. 大切 【たい・せつ】 (na-adj) - important
7. する (exception) - to do
8. この - this (abbr. of これの)
9. 仕事 【し・ごと】 - job
10. 早い 【はや・い】 (i-adj) - fast; early
11. 出来る 【で・き・る】 (ru-verb) - to be able to do

You can also use 「より」 with question words such as 「誰」、「何」、or 「どこ」 to make a superlative by comparing with everything or everybody else. In this case, though not required, it is common to include the 「も」 particle.

Examples

1. 商品の品質を何より大切にしています。
We place value in product's quality over anything else.
2. この仕事は誰よりも早くできます。
Can do this job more quickly than anyone else.

Using 「方」 to express a way to do something

Vocabulary

1. 方 【1) ほう; 2) かた】 - 1) direction; side; 2) person; way of doing
2. 行く 【い・く】 (u-verb) - to go
3. 食べる 【た・べる】 (ru-verb) - to eat
4. 新宿 【しん・じゅく】 - Shinjuku
5. 分かる 【わ・かる】 (u-verb) - to understand
6. そう - (things are) that way
7. 言う 【い・う】 (u-verb) - to say
8. 体 【からだ】 - body
9. いい (i-adj) - good
10. 漢字 【かん・じ】 - Kanji
11. 書く 【か・く】 (u-verb) - to write
12. 教える 【おし・える】 (ru-verb) - to teach; to inform
13. くれる (ru-verb) - to give
14. パソコン - computer, PC
15. 使う 【つか・う】 (u-verb) - to use
16. 皆 【みんな】 - everybody
17. 知る 【し・る】 (u-verb) - to know

You can also attach 「方」 to the stem of verbs to express a way to do that verb. In this usage, 「方」 is read as 「かた」 and the result becomes a noun. For example, 「行き方」 (いきかた) means, "the way to go" or 「食べ方」 (たべかた) means, "the way to eat". This expression is probably what you want to use when you want to ask how to do something.

Examples

1. 新宿の行き方は分かりますか。
   Do you know the way to go to Shinjuku?

2. そういう食べ方は体によくないよ。
   Eating in that way is not good for your body.

3. 漢字の書き方を教えてくれますか？
   Can you teach me the way of writing kanji?

4. パソコンの使い方は、みんな知っているでしょう。
   Probably everybody knows the way to use PC's.

When verbs are transformed to this form, the result becomes a noun clause. Sometimes, this requires a change of particles. For instance, while 「行く」 usually involves a target (the 「に」 or 「へ」 particle), since 「行き方」 is a noun clause, example 1 becomes 「新宿の行き方」 instead of the familiar 「新宿に行く」.

Using 「によって」 to express dependency

Vocabulary

1. 人 【ひと】 - person
2. 話 【はなし】 - story
3. 違う 【ちが・う】 (u-verb) - to be different
4. 季節 【き・せつ】 - season
5. 果物 【くだ・もの】 - fruit
6. おいしい (i-adj) - tasty
7. なる (u-verb) - to become
8. まずい (i-adj) - unpleasant
9. 和子 【かず・こ】 - Kazuko (first name)
10. 今日 【きょう】 - today
11. 飲む 【の・む】 (u-verb) - to drink
12. 行く 【い・く】 (u-verb) - to go
13. 大樹 【だい・き】 - Daiki (first name)
14. それ - that
15. 裕子 【ゆう・こ】 - Yuuko (first name)

When you want to say, "depending on [X]", you can do this in Japanese by simply attaching 「によって」 to [X].

Examples

1. 人によって話が違う。
   The story is different depending on the person.
2. 季節によって果物はおいしくなったり、まずくなったりする。
   Fruit becomes tasty or nasty depending on the season.

This is simply the te-form of 「よる」 as seen by the following simple exchange.

和子: 今日は飲みに行こうか？
Kazuko: Shall we go drinking today?

大樹: それは、裕子によるね。
Daiki: That depends on Yuuko.

Indicating a source of information using 「によると」

Vocabulary

1. 天気 【てん・き】 - weather
2. 予報 【よ・ほう】 - forecast
3. 今日 【きょう】 - today
4. 雨 【あめ】 - rain
5. 友達 【とも・だち】 - friend
6. 話 【はなし】 - story
7. 朋子 【とも・こ】 - Tomoko (first name)
8. やっと - finally
9. ボーイフレンド - boyfriend
10. 見つける 【み・つける】 (ru-verb) - to find

Another expression using 「よる」 is by using it with the target and the decided conditional 「と」 to indicate a source of information. In

English, this would translate to "according to [X]" where 「によると」 is attached to [X].

Examples

1. 天気予報によると、今日は雨だそうだ。
   According to the weather forecast, I hear today is rain.
2. 友達の話によると、朋子はやっとボーイフレンドを見つけたらしい。
   According to a friend's story, it appears that Tomoko finally found a boyfriend.

Actions that are easy or hard to do

Vocabulary

1. 食べる 【た・べる】 (ru-verb) - to eat
2. しゃべる (u-verb) - to talk
3. この - this   (abbr. of これの)
4. 字 【じ】 - character; hand-writing
5. 読む 【よ・む】 (u-verb) - to read
6. カクテル - cocktail
7. ビール - beer
8. 飲む 【の・む】 (u-verb) - to drink
9. 部屋 【へ・や】 - room
10. 暗い 【くら・い】 (i-adj) - dark
11. 見る 【み・る】 (ru-verb) - to see
12. 難しい 【むずか・しい】 (i-adj) - difficult
13. 易しい 【やさ・しい】 (i-adj) - easy
14. 簡単 【かん・たん】 (na-adj) - simple
15. 容易 【よう・い】 (na-adj) - simple
16. その - that   (abbr. of それの)
17. 肉 【にく】 - meat

This is a short easy lesson on how to transform verbs into adjectives describing whether that action is easy or difficult to do. Basically, it consists of changing the verb into the stem and adding 「やすい」 for easy and 「にくい」 for hard. The result then becomes a regular i-adjective. Pretty easy, huh?

Using 「〜やすい、〜にくい」 to describe easy and difficult actions

To describe an action as being easy, change the verb to the stem and add 「やすい」. To describe an action as being difficult, attach 「にくい」 to the stem.
Examples

1. 食べる → 食べやすい
2. しゃべる → しゃべり → しゃべりにくい

The result becomes a regular i-adjective.

	Positive	Negative
Non-Past	食べにくい	食べにくくない
Past	食べにくかった	食べにくくなかった

Examples

1. この字は読みにくい
   This hand-writing is hard to read.
2. カクテルはビールより飲みやすい。
   Cocktails are easier to drink than beer.
3. 部屋が暗かったので、見にくかった。
   Since the room was dark, it was hard to see.

As an aside: Be careful with 「見にくい」 because 「醜い」 is a rarely used adjective meaning, "ugly". I wonder if it's just coincidence that "difficult to see" and "ugly" sound exactly the same?

Of course, you can always use some other grammatical structure that we have already learned to express the same thing using appropriate adjectives such as 「難しい」、「易しい」、「簡単」、「容易」、etc. The following two sentences are essentially identical in meaning.

1. その肉は食べにくい。
   That meat is hard to eat.
2. その肉を食べるのは難しい。
   The thing of eating that meat is difficult.

Variations of 「〜にくい」 with 「〜がたい」 and 「〜づらい」

Vocabulary

1. 彼 【かれ】 - he; boyfriend
2. 忘れる 【わす・れる】 (ru-verb) - to forget
3. 思い出 【おも・い・で】 - memories

4. 大切 【たい・せつ】 (na-adj) - important
5. する (exception) - to do
6. とても - very
7. 信じる 【しん・じる】 (ru-verb) - to believe
8. 話 【はなし】 - story
9. 本当 【ほん・とう】 - real
10. 起こる 【おこ・る】 (u-verb) - to happen
11. 辛い 【1) から・い; 2) つら・い】 (i-adj) - 1) spicy; 2) painful
12. 日本語 【に・ほん・ご】 - Japanese (language)
13. 読む 【よ・む】 (u-verb) - to read
14. 待ち合わせ 【ま・ち・あわ・せ】 - meeting arrangement
15. 分かる 【わ・かる】 (u-verb) - to understand
16. 場所 【ば・しょ】 - location

The kanji for 「にくい」 actually comes from 「難い」 which can also be read as 「かたい」. As a result, you can also add a voiced version 「〜がたい」 as a verb suffix to express the same thing as 「にくい」.「にくい」 is more common for speaking while 「がたい」 is more suited for the written medium. 「にくい」 tends to be used for physical actions while 「がたい」 is usually reserved for less physical actions that don't actually require movement. However, there seems to be no hard rule on which is more appropriate for a given verb so I suggest searching for both versions in google to ascertain the popularity of a given combination. You should also always write the suffix in hiragana to prevent ambiguities in the reading.

Examples

1. 彼との忘れがたい思い出を大切にしている。
   I am treating importantly the hard to forget memories of and with him.

2. とても信じがたい話だが、本当に起こったらしい。
   It's a very difficult to believe story but it seems (from hearsay)

that it really happened.

Yet another, more coarse variation of stem + 「にくい」 is to use 「づらい」 instead which is a slightly transformed version of 「辛い」（つらい）. This is not to be confused with the same 「辛い」（からい）, which means spicy!

Examples

1. 日本語は読みづらいな。
   Man, Japanese is hard to read.
2. 待ち合わせは、分かりづらい場所にしないでね。
   Please don't pick a difficult to understand location for the meeting arrangement.

More negative verbs

We already learned the most common type of negative verbs; the ones that end in 「ない」. However, there are couple more different types of negatives verbs. The ones you will find most useful are the first two, which expresses an action that was done without having done another action. The others are fairly obscure or useful only for very casual expressions. However, you *will* run into them if you learn Japanese for a fair amount of time.

Doing something without doing something else

Vocabulary

1. 食べる 【た・べる】 (ru-verb) - to eat
2. 寝る 【ね・る】 (ru-verb) - to sleep

3. 何 【なに／なん】 - what
4. 歯 【は】 - tooth
5. 磨く 【みが・く】 (u-verb) - to brush; to polish
6. 学校 【がっ・こう】 - school
7. 行く 【い・く】 (u-verb) - to go
8. 宿題 【しゅく・だい】 - homework
9. する (exception) - to do
10. 授業 【じゅ・ぎょう】 - class
11. 止める 【や・める】 (ru-verb) - to stop
12. 方 【1) ほう; 2) かた】 - 1) direction; side; 2) person; way of doing
13. いい (i-adj) - good
14. 先生 【せん・せい】 - teacher
15. 相談 【そう・だん】 - consultation
16. この - this (abbr. of これの)
17. 取る 【と・る】 (u-verb) - to take
18. こと - event, matter
19. 出来る 【で・き・る】 (ru-verb) - to be able to do
20. 彼 【かれ】 - he; boyfriend
21. 言う 【い・う】 (u-verb) - to say
22. 帰る 【かえ・る】 (u-verb) - to go home
23. そんな - that sort of
24. お酒 【お・さけ】 - alcohol
25. 飲む 【の・む】 (u-verb) - to drink
26. 当然 【とう・ぜん】 - naturally
27. 酔っ払う 【よ・っ・ぱ・らう】 (u-verb) - to get drunk
28. 勉強 【べん・きょう】 - study
29. 東大 【とう・だい】 - Tokyo University (abbr. for 「東京大学」)
30. 入る 【はい・る】 (u-verb) - to enter
31. 思う 【おも・う】 (u-verb) - to think

Way back when, we learned how to express a sequence of actions and this worked fine for both positive and negative verbs. For instance, the sentence "I didn't eat, and then I went to sleep" would become 「食べなくて寝た。」 However, this sentence sounds a bit strange because eating doesn't have much to do with sleeping. What we probably *really* want to say is that we went to sleep *without* eating. To express this, we need to use a more generalized form of the negative request we covered at the very end of the giving and receiving lesson. In other words, instead of substituting the last

「い」 with 「くて」, we need only append 「で」 instead.

Doing something without doing something else

To indicate an action that was done *without* doing another action, add 「で」 to the negative of the action that was <u>not</u> done.
Example

食べる → 食べない → 食べないで

Examples

1. 何も食べないで寝ました。
   Went to sleep without eating anything.

2. 歯を磨かないで、学校に行っちゃいました。
   Went to school without brushing teeth (by accident).

3. 宿題をしないで、授業に行くのは、やめた方がいいよ。
   It's better to stop going to class without doing homework.

4. 先生と相談しないで、この授業を取ることは出来ない。
   You cannot take this class without consulting with teacher.

Hopefully not too difficult. Another way to express the exact same thing is to replace the last 「ない」 part with 「ず」. However, the two exception verbs 「する」 and 「くる」 become 「せず」 and 「こず」 respectively. It is also common to see this grammar combined with the target 「に」 particle. This version is more formal than 「ないで」 and is not used as much in regular conversations.

Doing something without doing something else

- Another way to indicate an action that was done without doing another action is to replace the 「ない」 part of the negative action that was not done with 「ず」.
  Examples
    1. 食べる → 食べない → 食べず
    2. 行く → 行かない → 行かず
- **Exceptions:**
    1. する → せず
    2. くる → こず

Examples

1. 彼は何も言わず、帰ってしまった。
   He went home without saying anything.
2. 何も食べずにそんなにお酒を飲むと当然酔っ払いますよ。
   Obviously, you're going to get drunk if you drink that much without eating anything.
3. 勉強せずに東大に入れると思わないな。
   I don't think you can get in Tokyo University without studying.

A casual masculine type of negative that ends in 「ん」

Vocabulary

1. する (exception) - to do
2. 来る 【く・る】 (exception) - to come
3. すまん - sorry (masculine)
4. すみません - sorry (polite)
5. 知る 【し・る】 (u-verb) - to know
6. 韓国人 【かん・こく・じん】 - Korean person
7. 結婚 【けっ・こん】 - marriage
8. なる (u-verb) - to become
9. そんな - that sort of
10. こと - event, matter
11. 皆 【みんな】 - everybody
12. 今日 【きょう】 - today
13. 行く 【い・く】 (u-verb) - to go

Finally, we cover another type of negative that is used mostly by older men. Since 「ない」 is so long and difficult to say (sarcasm), you can shorten it to just 「ん」. However, you can't directly modify other words in this form; in other words, you can't make it a modifying relative clause. In the same manner as before, 「する」 becomes 「せん」 and 「くる」 becomes 「こん」 though I've never heard or seen 「こん」 actually being used. If you have ever heard 「すまん」 and wondered what that meant, it's actually an example of this grammar. Notice that 「すみません」 is actually in polite negative form. Well, the plain form would be 「すまない」, right? That further transforms to just 「すまん」. The word brings up an image of おじさん but that may be just me. Anyway, it's a male expression.

A shorter way to say negative verbs

- A shorter way to say a negative verb is to use 「ん」 instead of 「ない」.
Example
知る → 知らない → 知らん
- Exceptions:
   1. する → せん
   2. くる → こん

Examples

1. すまん。
   Sorry.
2. 韓国人と結婚しなくてはならん！
   You must marry a Korean!
3. そんなことはさせん！
   I won't let you do such a thing!

You can even use this slang for past tense verbs by adding 「かった」.

- 皆、今日行くって、知らんかったよ。
   I didn't know everybody was going today.

A classical negative verb that ends in 「ぬ」

Vocabulary

1. する (exception) - to do
2. 来る 【く・る】 (exception) - to come
3. 知る 【し・る】 (u-verb) - to know
4. 韓国人 【かん・こく・じん】 - Korean person

5. 結婚 【けっ・こん】 - marriage
6. なる (u-verb) - to become
7. 模擬 【も・ぎ】 - mock
8. 試験 【し・けん】 - exam
9. 何回 【なん・かい】 - how many times
10. 失敗 【しっ・ぱい】 - failure
11. 実際 【じっ・さい】 - actual
12. 受ける 【う・ける】 (ru-verb) - to receive
13. 思う 【おも・う】 (u-verb) - to think
14. 結果 【けっ・か】 - result
15. 出る 【で・る】 (ru-verb) - to come out

There is yet another version of the negative verb conjugation and it uses 「ぬ」 instead of the 「ない」 that attaches to the end of the verb. While this version of the negative conjugation is old-fashioned and part of classical Japanese, you will still encounter it occasionally. In fact, I just saw this conjugation on a sign at the train station today, so it's not too uncommon.

For any verb, you can replace 「ない」 with 「ぬ」 to get to an old-fashion sounding version of the negative. Similar to the last section, 「する」 becomes 「せぬ」 and 「くる」 becomes 「こぬ」. You may hear this grammar being used from older people or your friends if they want to bring back ye olde days.

An old-fashioned way to say negative verbs

- An old-fashioned way to say a negative verb is to use 「ぬ」 instead of 「ない」.
  Example
  知る → 知らない → 知らぬ
- **Exceptions:**

Examples

1. 韓国人と結婚してはならぬ!
   You must not marry a Korean!
2. 模擬試験に何回も失敗して、実際に受けてみたら思わぬ結果が
   出た。
   After having failed mock examination any number of times, a
   result I wouldn't have thought came out when I actually tried
   taking the test.

Hypothesizing and Concluding

In this section, we're going to learn how to make hypotheses and
reach conclusions using: 「とする」 and 「わけ」 （訳）.

Coming to a conclusion with 「わけ」

Vocabulary

1. 訳 【わけ】 - meaning; reason; can be deduced
2. 直子 【なお・こ】 - Naoko (first name)
3. いくら - how much
4. 英語 【えい・ご】 - English (language)
5. 勉強 【べん・きょう】 - study
6. する (exception) - to do
7. うまい (i-adj) - skillful; delicious
8. なる (u-verb) - to become

9. つまり - in short
10. 語学 【ご・がく】 - language study
11. 能力 【のう・りょく】 - ability
12. ある (u-verb) - to exist (inanimate)
13. 言う 【い・う】 (u-verb) - to say
14. 失礼 【しつ・れい】 - discourtesy
15. 中国語 【ちゅう・ごく・ご】 - Chinese language
16. 読む 【よ・む】 (u-verb) - to read
17. 広子 【ひろ・こ】 - Hiroko (first name)
18. 家 【1) うち; 2) いえ】 - 1) one's own home; 2) house
19. 行く 【い・く】 (u-verb) - to go
20. こと - event, matter
21. 一郎 【いち・ろう】 - Ichirou (first name)
22. 微積分 【び・せき・ぶん】 - (differential and integral) calculus
23. 分かる 【わ・かる】 (u-verb) - to understand
24. ここ - here
25. 試験 【し・けん】 - exam
26. 合格 【ごう・かく】 - pass (as in an exam)
27. 今度 【こん・ど】 - this time; another time
28. 負ける 【ま・ける】 (ru-verb) - to lose
29. 来る 【く・る】 (exception) - to come
30. あきらめる (ru-verb) - to give up

The noun 「わけ」（訳）is a bit difficult to describe but it's defined as: "meaning; reason; can be deduced". You can see how this word is used in the following mini-dialogue.

Example 1

直子: いくら英語を勉強しても、うまくならないの。
Naoko: No matter how much I study, I don't become better at English.

ジム：つまり、語学には、能力がないという訳か。
Jim: So basically, it means that you don't have ability at language.

直子: 失礼ね。
Naoko: How rude.

As you can see, Jim is concluding from what Naoko said that she must not have any skills at learning languages. This is completely different from the explanatory 「の」, which is used to explain something that may or may not be obvious. 「わけ」 is instead used to draw conclusions that anyone might be able to arrive at given certain information.

A very useful application of this grammar is to combine it with 「ない」 to indicate that there is no reasonable conclusion. This allows some very useful expression like, "How in the world am I supposed to know that?"

- 中国語が読める<u>わけがない</u>。
  There's no way I can read Chinese. (lit: There is no reasoning for [me] to be able to read Chinese.)

Under the normal rules of grammar, we must have a particle for the noun 「わけ」 in order to use it with the verb but since this type of expression is used so often, the particle is often dropped to create just 「～わけない」.

Example 2

直子: 広子の家に行ったことある？
Naoko: Have you ever gone to Hiroko's house?

一郎: ある<u>わけない</u>でしょう。
Ichirou: There's no way I would have ever gone to her house, right?

Example 3

直子: 微積分は分かる？
Naoko: Do you understand (differential and integral) calculus?

一郎: 分かるわけないよ！
Ichirou: There's no way I would understand!

There is one thing to be careful of because 「わけない」 can also mean that something is very easy (lit: requires no explanation). You can easily tell when this meaning is intended however, because it is used in the same manner as an adjective.

- ここの試験に合格するのはわけない。
  It's easy to pass the tests here.

Finally, although not as common, 「わけ」 can also be used as a formal expression for saying that something must or must not be done at all costs. This is simply a stronger and more formal version of 「〜てはいけない」. This grammar is created by simply attaching 「わけにはいかない」. The 「は」 is the topic particle and is pronounced 「わ」. The reason 「いけない」 changes to 「いかない」 is probably related to intransitive and transitive verbs but I don't want to get too caught up in the logistics of it. Just take note that it's 「いかない」 in this case and not 「いけない」.

1. 今度は負けるわけにはいかない。
   This time, I must not lose at all costs.
2. ここまできて、あきらめるわけにはいかない。
   After coming this far, I must not give up.

Making hypotheses with 「とする」

Vocabulary

1. する (exception) - to do
2. 明日 【あした】 - tomorrow
3. 行く 【い・く】 (u-verb) - to go
4. 今 【いま】 - now
5. ~時 【~じ】 - counter for hours
6. 着く 【つ・く】 (u-verb) - to arrive
7. 思う 【おも・う】 (u-verb) - to think
8. 観客 【かん・きゃく】 - spectator
9. 参加 【さん・か】 - participation
10. もらう - to receive
11. 被害者 【ひ・がい・しゃ】 - victim
12. 非常 【ひ・じょう】 - extreme
13. 幸い 【さいわ・い】 (na-adj) - fortunate
14. 朝ご飯 【あさ・ご・はん】 - breakfast
15. 食べる 【た・べる】 (ru-verb) - to eat
16. もう - already
17. 昼 【ひる】 - afternoon
18. お腹 【お・なか】 - stomach
19. 空く 【す・く】 (u-verb) - to become empty

While this next grammar doesn't necessarily have anything directly related to the previous grammar, I thought it would fit nicely together. In a previous lesson, we learn how to combine the volitional form with 「とする」 to indicate an attempt to perform an action. We will now learn several other ways 「とする」 can be used. It may help to keep in mind that 「とする」 is really just a combination of the quotation particle 「と」 and the verb 「する」 meaning "to do".

Let's say you have a sentence: [verb]とする. This means literally that you are doing like "[verb]" (in quotes). As you can see, when used with the volitional, it becomes: "Doing like making motion to do [verb]". In other words, you are acting as if to make a motion to do [verb]. As we have already seen, this translates to "attempt to do [verb]". Let's see what happens when we use it on plain verbs.

Examples

- 明日に行く<u>とする</u>。
  Assume we go tomorrow.

The example above is considering what would happen supposing that they should decide to go tomorrow. You can see that the literal translation "do like we go tomorrow" still makes sense. However, in this situation, we are making a hypothesis unlike the grammar we have gone over before with the volitional form of the verb. Since we are considering a hypothesis, it is reasonable to assume that the conditional will be very handy here and indeed, you will often see sentences like the following:

- 今から行く<u>としたら</u>、9時に着くと思います。
  If we suppose that we go from now, I think we will arrive at 9:00.

As you can see, the verb 「する」 has been conjugated to the 「たら」 conditional form to consider what would happen *if* you assume a certain case. You can also change 「する」 to the te-form （して） and use it as a sequence of actions like so:

1. 観客<u>として</u>参加させてもらった。
   Received favor of allowing to participate as spectator.
2. 被害者<u>としては</u>、非常に幸いだった。
   As a victim, was extremely fortunate.
3. 朝ご飯を食べた<u>としても</u>、もう昼だからお腹が空いたでしょう。
   Even assuming that you ate breakfast, because it's already noon, you're probably hungry, right?

The same idea applies here as well. In example 1, you are doing like a "spectator" and doing like a "victim" in example 2 and finally, doing like you ate breakfast in example 3. So you can see why the same grammar applies for all these types of sentences because they all mean the same thing in Japanese (minus the use of additional particles and various conjugations of 「する」).

Time-specific actions

In this lesson, we will go over various ways to express actions that take place in a certain time-frame. In particular, we will learn how to say: 1) an action has just been completed, 2) an action is taken immediately after another action took place, 3) an action occurs while another action is ongoing, and 4) one continuously repeats an action.

Expressing what just happened with 「〜ばかり」

Vocabulary

1. 食べる 【たべ・る】 (ru-verb) - to eat
2. すみません - sorry (polite)
3. 今 【いま】 - now
4. お腹 【お・なか】 - stomach
5. いっぱい - full
6. キロ - kilo
7. 走る 【はし・る】 (u-verb) - to run
8. 凄い 【すご・い】 (i-adj) - to a great extent
9. 疲れる 【つか・れる】 (ru-verb) - to get tired
10. 家 【1) うち; 2) いえ】 - 1) one's own home; 2) house
11. 帰る 【かえ・る】 (u-verb) - to go home
12. 昼ご飯 【ひる・ご・はん】 - lunch
13. もう - already

14. 空く 【す・く】 (u-verb) - to become empty
15. まさか - no way, you can't mean to say
16. 起きる 【お・きる】 (ru-verb) - to wake; to occur

This is a very useful grammar that is used to indicate that one has just finished doing something. For instance, the first time I really wished I knew how to say something like this was when I wanted to politely decline an invitation to eat because I had just eaten. To do this, take the past tense of verb that you want to indicate as just being completed and add 「ばかり」. This is used with only the past tense of verbs and is not to be confused with the 「ばかり」 used with nouns to express amounts.

Just like the other type of 「ばかり」 we have covered before, in slang, you can hear people use 「ばっか」 instead of 「ばかり」.

Using 「ばかり」 for actions just completed

- To indicate that an action has ended just recently, take the past tense of the verb and add 「ばかり」. Example: 食べる → 食べた → 食べたばかり
- For casual speech, you can abbreviate 「ばかり」 to just 「ばっか」 Example: 食べたばかり → 食べたばっか

You can treat the result as you would with any noun.

Positive		Negative	
食べた ばかり （だ）	Just ate	食べた ばかり じゃ ない	Didn't just eat

Examples

1. すみません、今食べたばかりなので、お腹がいっぱいです。
   Sorry, but I'm full having just eaten.
2. 10キロを走ったばかりで、凄く疲れた。 I just ran 10 kilometers and am really tired.
3. 今、家に帰ったばかりです。 I got back home just now.

Here are some examples of the abbreviated version.

1. 昼ご飯を食べたばっかなのに、もうお腹が空いた。 Despite the fact that I just ate lunch, I'm hungry already.
2. まさか、今起きたばっかなの？ No way, did you wake up just now?

Express what occurred immediately after with 「とたん」

Vocabulary

1. 開ける 【あ・ける】 (ru-verb) - to open
2. 取る 【と・る】 (u-verb) - to take
3. 窓 【まど】 - window
4. 猫 【ねこ】 - cat
5. 跳ぶ 【と・ぶ】 (u-verb) - to jump
6. 映画 【えい・が】 - movie
7. 観る 【み・る】 (ru-verb) - to watch
8. トイレ - bathroom; toilet
9. 行く 【い・く】 (u-verb) - to go
10. 眠い 【ねむ・い】 (i-adj) - sleepy
11. なる (u-verb) - to become

Kind of as a supplement to 「ばかり」, we will cover one way to say something happened as soon as something else occurs. To use this grammar, add 「とたん」 to the past tense of the first action that happened. It is also common to add the 「に」 target particle to indicate that specific point in time.

Using 「とたん」 to describe what happened immediately after

Change the verb that happened first to the *past tense* and attach 「とたん」 or 「とたんに」. Examples

1. 開ける → 開けた → 開けたとたん （に）
2. 取る → 取った → 取ったとたん （に）

※Note: You can only use this grammar for things that happen outside your control.

Examples

1. 窓を<u>開けたとたんに</u>、猫が跳んでいった。 As soon as I opened window, cat jumped out.

For many more examples, check these <u>examples sentences</u> from our old trusty WWWJDIC.

An important thing to realize is that you can only use this grammar for things that occur immediately after something else and not for an action that you, yourself carry out. For instance, compare the following two sentences.

- 映画を観たとたんに、~~トイレに行きました~~。 (You carried out the action of going to the bathroom so this is not correct.)

- 映画を観たとたんに、<u>眠くなりました</u>。 (Since becoming sleepy is something that happened outside your control, this sentence is ok.)

Using 「ながら」 for two concurrent actions

Vocabulary

1. 走る 【はし・る】 (u-verb) - to run
2. テレビ - TV, television
3. 観る 【み・る】 (ru-verb) - to watch
4. 宿題 【しゅく・だい】 - homework
5. する (exception) - to do
6. 音楽 【おん・がく】 - music
7. 聴く 【き・く】 (u-verb) - to listen (e.g. to music);
8. 学校 【がっ・こう】 - school
9. 歩く 【ある・く】 (u-verb) - to walk

10. 好き 【す・き】 (na-adj) - likable
11. 相手 【あい・て】 - other party
12. 何 【なに／なん】 - what
13. 言う 【い・う】 (u-verb) - to say
14. 自分 【じ・ぶん】 - oneself
15. 気持ち 【き・も・ち】 - feeling
16. 分かる 【わ・かる】 (u-verb) - to understand
17. 欲しい 【ほ・しい】 (i-adj) - desirable
18. 単なる 【たん・なる】 - simply
19. わがまま (na-adj) - selfish
20. 思う 【おも・う】 (u-verb) - to think
21. ポップコーン - popcorn
22. 食べる 【た・べる】 (ru-verb) - to eat
23. 映画 【えい・が】 - movie
24. 口笛 【くち・ぶえ】 - whistle
25. 手紙 【て・がみ】 - letter
26. 書く 【か・く】 (u-verb) - to write

You can use 「ながら」 to express that one action is taking place in conjunction with another action. To use 「ながら」, you must change the first verb to the stem and append 「ながら」. Though probably rare, you can also attach 「ながら」 to the negative of the verb to express the negative. This grammar has no tense since it is determined by the second verb.

Using 「ながら」 for concurrent actions

- Change the first verb to the *stem* and append 「ながら」
  Example 走る → 走り → 走りながら
- For the negative, attach 「ながら」 Example 走る → 走ら
  ない → 走らないながら

Examples

1. テレビを観ながら、宿題をする。 Do homework while watching TV.
2. 音楽を聴きながら、学校へ歩くのが好き。 Like to walk to school while listening to music.
3. 相手に何も言わないながら、自分の気持ちをわかってほしいのは単なるわがままだと思わない？ Don't you think that wanting the other person to understand one's feelings while not saying anything is just simply selfishness?

Notice that the sentence ends with the main verb just like it always does. This means that the main action of the sentence is the verb that ends the clause. The 「ながら」 simply describes another action that is also taking place. For example, if we switched the verbs in the first example to say, 「宿題をしながら、テレビを観る。」, this changes the sentence to say, "Watch TV while doing homework." In other words, the main action, in this case, becomes watching TV and the action of doing homework is describing an action that is taking place at the same time.

The tense is controlled by the main verb so the verb used with 「ながら」 cannot have a tense.

1. ポップコーンを食べながら、映画を観る。 Watch movie while eating popcorn.
2. ポップコーンを食べながら、映画を観た。 Watched movie while eating popcorn.
3. 口笛をしながら、手紙を書いていた。 Was writing letter while whistling.

Using 「ながら」 with state-of-being

Vocabulary

1. 残念 【ざん・ねん】 (na-adj) - unfortunate
2. 貧乏 【びん・ぼう】 (na-adj) - poor
3. 仕事 【し・ごと】 - job
4. いっぱい - full
5. 入る 【はい・る】 (u-verb) - to enter
6. 今日 【きょう】 - today
7. 行く 【い・く】 (u-verb) - to go
8. なる (u-verb) - to become
9. 高級 【こう・きゅう】 (na-adj) - high class, high grade
10. バッグ - bag
11. 買う 【か・う】 (u-verb) - to buy
12. 彼 【かれ】 - he; boyfriend
13. 初心者 【しょ・しん・しゃ】 - beginner
14. 実力 【じつ・りょく】 - actual ability
15. プロ - pro
16. 同じ 【おな・じ】 - same

A more advanced use of 「ながら」 is to use it with the implied state-of-being. In other words, you can use it with nouns or adjectives to talk about what something is while something else. The implied state-of-being means that you must not use the declarative 「だ」, you just attach 「ながら」 to the noun or adjective. For example, a common way this grammar is used is to say, "While it's unfortunate, something something..." In Japanese, this would become 「残念ながら・・・」 You can also attach the inclusive 「も」 particle to 「ながら」 to get 「ながらも」. This changes the meaning from "while" to "<u>even</u> while".

Using 「ながら」 or 「ながらも」 with state-of-being

- To say [X] is something while something else, attach 「な
がら」 to [X] Example 残念 → 残念ながら
- To say [X] is something even while something else, attach
「ながらも」 to [X] Example 貧乏 → 貧乏ながらも

Examples

1. 仕事がいっぱい入って、残念ながら、今日は行けなくなりまし
た。 While it's unfortunate, a lot of work came in and it became
so that I can't go today.
2. 貧乏ながらも、高級なバッグを買っちゃったよ。 Even while
I'm poor, I ended up buying a high quality bag.
3. 彼は、初心者ながらも、実力はプロと同じだ。 Even while he
is a beginner, his actual skills are the same as a pro.

To repeat something with reckless abandon using 「まくる」

Vocabulary

1. やる (u-verb) - to do
2. ゲーム - game
3. はまる (u-verb) - to get hooked
4. 最近 【さい・きん】 - recent; lately
5. パソコン - computer, PC
6. 使う 【つか・う】 (u-verb) - to use
7. アメリカ - America
8. いる (ru-verb) - to exist (animate)
9. 時 【とき】 - time
10. コーラ - cola

11. 飲む 【の・む】 (u-verb) - to drink

The WWWJDIC very succinctly defines the definition of this verb as a "verb suffix to indicate reckless abandon to the activity". Unfortunately, it doesn't go on to tell you exactly how it's actually used. Actually, there's not much to explain. You take the stem of the verb and simply attach 「まくる」. However, since this is a continuing activity, it is an *enduring state* unless you're going to do it in the future. This is a very casual expression.

Using 「まくる」 for frequent actions

Change the first verb to the *stem* and append 「まくっている」. Example やる → やり → やりまくっている

You can use all the normal conjugations you would expect with any other verb.

	Positive	Negative
Non-Past	やりまくっている doing all the time	やりまくっていない don't do all the time
Past	やりまくっていた did all the time	やりまくっていなかった didn't do all the time

Examples

1. ゲームにはまっちゃって、最近パソコンを使いまくっているよ。 Having gotten hooked by games, I do nothing but use the computer lately.
2. アメリカにいた時はコーラを飲みまくっていた。 When I was in the US, I drank coke like all the time.

Expressing a lack of change

Up until now, we've mostly been talking about things that have happened or changed in the course of events. We will now learn some simple grammar to express a *lack* of change.

Using 「まま」 to express a lack of change

Vocabulary

1. この - this　(abbr. of これの)
2. 宜しい 【よろ・しい】 (i-adj) - good (formal)
3. 半分 【はん・ぶん】 - half
4. 食べる 【た・べる】 (ru-verb) - to eat
5. 捨てる 【す・てる】 (ru-verb) - to throw away
6. 駄目 【だめ】 - no good
7. いる (ru-verb) - to exist (animate)
8. 今日 【きょう】 - today
9. 悲しい 【かな・しい】 (i-adj) - sad
10. その - that　(abbr. of それの)
11. 格好 【かっ・こう】 - appearance
12. クラブ - club; nightclub
13. 入る 【はい・る】 (u-verb) - to enter

「まま」, not to be confused with the childish expression for "mother" （ママ）, is a grammatical phrase to express a lack of change in something. Grammatically, it is used just like a regular noun. You'll most likely hear this grammar at a convenience store when you buy a very small item. Since store clerks use super polite expressions and at lightning fast speeds, learning this one expression will help you out a bit in advance. (Of course, upon showing a lack of comprehension, the person usually repeats the exact same phrase... at the exact same speed.)

Examples

- このままで宜しいですか？
  Is it ok just like this?

In other words, the clerk wants to know if you'll take it just like that or whether you want it in a small bag. 「宜しい」, in case I haven't gone over it yet, is simply a very polite version of 「いい」. Notice that 「まま」 grammatically works just like a regular noun which means, as usual, that you can modify it with verb phrases or adjectives.

- 半分しか食べてないままで捨てちゃダメ！
  You can't throw it out leaving it in that half-eaten condition!

Ok, the translation is very loose, but the idea is that it's in an unchanged state of being half-eaten and you can't just throw that out.

Here's a good example I found googling around.
Hint: The 「いさせる」 is the causative form of 「いる」 meaning "let/make me exist".

- 今日だけは悲しいままでいさせてほしい。
  For only today, I want you to let me stay in this sad condition.

Finally, just in case, here's an example of direct noun modification.

- その格好のままでクラブに入れないよ。
  You can't get in the club in that getup (without changing it).

Using 「っぱなし」 to leave something the way it is

Vocabulary

1. 放す 【はな・す】 (u-verb) - to release; to set loose
2. くれる (ru-verb) - to give
3. ほったらかす (u-verb) - to neglect
4. テレビ - TV, television
5. 開ける 【あ・ける】 (ru-verb) - to open
6. 書く 【か・く】 (u-verb) - to write
7. つける (ru-verb) - to attach; to turn on
8. する (exception) - to do
9. 眠れる 【ねむ・れる】 (ru-verb) - to fall asleep
10. 人 【ひと】 - person
11. 結構 【けっ・こう】 - fairly, reasonably
12. いる (ru-verb) - to exist (animate)
13. 窓 【まど】 - window
14. 蚊 【か】 - mosquito
15. いっぱい - full
16. 入る 【はい・る】 (u-verb) - to enter
17. しまう (u-verb) - to do something by accident; to finish completely

The verb 「放す」 meaning "to set loose", can be used in various ways in regards to leaving something the way it is. For instance, a variation 「放っとく」 is used when you want to say "Leave me alone". For instance, you might use the command form of a request （くれる） and say, 「ほっといてくれ！」 (Leave me alone!). Yet another variant 「ほったらかす」 means "to neglect".

The grammar I would like to discuss here is the 「っぱなし」 suffix variant. You can attach this suffix to the stem of any verb to describe the act of doing something and leaving it that way without changing it. You can treat the combination like a regular noun.

Here's a link with more examples of this grammar. As you can see by the examples, this suffix carries a nuance that the thing left alone is due to oversight or neglect. Here are the (simple) conjugation rules for this grammar.

Using 「っぱなし」 to complete an action and leave it that way

Take the stem of the verb and attach 「っぱなし」.
Examples

1. 開ける → 開けっぱなし
2. 書く → 書き → 書きっぱなし

Examples

1. テレビをつけっぱなしにしなければ眠れない人は、結構いる。
   There exists a fair number of people who cannot sleep unless they turn on the TV and leave it that way.
2. 窓が開けっ放しだったので、蚊がいっぱい入ってしまった。
   The window was left wide open so a lot of mosquitoes got in.

Advanced Topics

Whew! We've come a long way from learning the basic phonetic alphabet to covering almost all the grammar you're going to need for daily conversations. But wait, we're not finished yet! In fact, things are going to get even more challenging and interesting because, especially toward the latter part of this section, we are going to learn grammar that only *might* come in handy. In my experience, the most useful things are easiest to learn as they come up again and again. However, in order to completely master a language, we also must work hard to conquer the bigger area of things that don't come up very often and yet every native Japanese speaker instinctively understands. Believe it or not, even the more obscure grammar *will* come up eventually leaving you wondering what it's supposed to mean. That's why *I* bothered to learn them at least.

Formal Expressions

What do you mean by formal expressions?

So far we have learned casual, polite, and honorific/humble types of languages. So what do I mean by formal expressions? I think we are all aware of the type of language I am talking about. We hear it in speeches, read it in reports, and see it on documentaries. While discussing good writing style is beyond the scope of this guide, we will go over some of the grammar that you will commonly find in this type of language. Which is not to say that it won't appear in regular everyday speech. (Because it does.)

Using 「である」 for formal state-of-being

Vocabulary

1. 我輩 【わが・はい】 - I; we
2. 猫 【ねこ】 - cat
3. 夏目 【なつ・め】 - Natsume (last name)

4. 漱石 【そう・せき】 - Souseki (first name)
5. お任せ 【お・まか・せ】 - leaving a decision to someone else
6. 表示 【ひょう・じ】 - display
7. 混合物 【こん・ごう・ぶつ】 - mixture, amalgam
8. 種類 【しゅ・るい】 - type, kind, category
9. 以上 【い・じょう】 - greater or equal
10. 純物質 【じゅん・ぶっ・しつ】 - pure material
11. 混じりあう 【ま・じりあう】 (u-verb) - to mix together
12. 物質 【ぶっ・しつ】 - pure material
13. 何 【なに／なん】 - what

We have already learned how to speak with your friends in casual speech, your superiors in polite speech, and your customers in honorific / humble speech. We've learned 「だ」、「です」、and 「でございます」 to express a state-of-being for these different levels of politeness. There is one more type of state-of-being that is primarily used to state facts in a neutral, official sounding manner - 「である」. Just like the others, you tack 「である」 on to the adjective or noun that represents the state.

Examples

- 吾輩は猫である

  I am a cat. (This is the title of a famous novel by 夏目漱石)

Since I'm too lazy to look up facts, let's trot on over to the Japanese version of Wikipedia and look at some random articles by clicking on 「おまかせ表示」.

- 混合物(こんごうぶつ, mixture)とは、2種類以上の純物質が混じりあっている物質である。(Wikipedia - 混合物, July 2004)
  An amalgam is a mixture of two or more pure materials.

To give you an idea of how changing the 「である」 changes the tone, I've included some fake content around that sentence.

1. 混合物は何?
   混合物は、2種類以上の純物質が混じりあっている物質だ。
2. 混合物は何ですか?
   混合物は、2種類以上の純物質が混じりあっている物質です。
3. 混合物は何でしょうか。
   混合物は、2種類以上の純物質が混じりあっている物質でございます。
4. 混合物とは?
   混合物は、2種類以上の純物質が混じりあっている物質である。

Negative of 「である」

Vocabulary

1. ある (u-verb) - to exist (inanimate)
2. それ - that
3. 不公平 【ふ・こう・へい】 - unfair
4. 言語 【げん・ご】 - language
5. 簡単 【かん・たん】 (na-adj) - simple
6. マスター - master
7. する (exception) - to do
8. こと - event, matter
9. 出来る 【で・き・る】 (ru-verb) - to be able to do
10. 学生 【がく・せい】 - student

Because the negative of 「ある」 is 「ない」, you might expect the opposite of 「である」 to be 「でない」. However, for some reason I'm not aware of, you need to insert the topic particle before 「ない」 to get 「ではない」.

Examples

1. それは**不公平**ではないでしょうか。
   Wouldn't you consider that to be unfair?
2. 言語は簡単にマスターできることではない。
   Language is not something that can be mastered easily.

Using 「である」 to sound official

Attach 「である」 to the verb or adjective that the state-of-being applies to.
Example: 学生 → 学生である
For the negative, attach 「ではない」 to the verb or adjective that the state-of-being applies to.
Example: 学生 → 学生ではない
For the past tense state-of-being, apply the regular past tenses of 「ある」

Complete conjugation chart for 「である」

Positive		Negative	
学生である	is student	学生ではない	is not student
学生であった	was student	学生ではなかった	was not student

Sequential relative clauses in formal language

Vocabulary

1. 花火 【はな・び】 - fireworks
2. 火薬 【か・やく】 - gunpowder
3. 金属 【きん・ぞく】 - metal
4. 粉末 【ふん・まつ】 - fine powder
5. 混ぜる 【ま・ぜる】 (ru-verb) - to mix
6. 物 【もの】 - object
7. 火 【ひ】 - flame, light
8. 付ける 【つ・ける】 (ru-verb) - to attach
9. 燃焼時 【ねん・しょう・じ】 - at time of combustion
10. 火花 【ひ・ばな】 - spark
11. 楽しむ 【たの・しむ】 (u-verb) - to enjoy
12. ため - for the sake/benefit of
13. 企業内 【き・ぎょう・ない】 - company-internal
14. 顧客 【こ・きゃく】 - customer, client
15. データ - data
16. 利用 【り・よう】 - usage
17. する (exception) - to do
18. 彼 【かれ】 - he; boyfriend
19. 行方 【ゆく・え】 - whereabouts
20. 調べる 【しら・べる】 (ru-verb) - to investigate
21. こと - event, matter
22. 出来る 【で・き・る】 (ru-verb) - to be able to do
23. 封筒 【ふう・とう】 - envelope
24. 写真 【しゃ・しん】 - photograph
25. 数枚 【すう・まい】 - several sheets (flat objects)
26. 入る 【はい・る】 (u-verb) - to enter
27. 手紙 【て・がみ】 - letter

28. 添える　【そ・える】 (ru-verb) - to garnish; to accompany (as a card does a gift)
29. この - this　(abbr. of これの）
30. ファイル - file
31. パスワード - password
32. 設定　【せっ・てい】 - setting
33. 開く　【ひら・く】 (u-verb) - to open
34. ~際　【～さい】 - on the occasion of
35. それ - that
36. 入力　【にゅう・りょく】 - input
37. 必要　【ひつ・よう】 - necessity
38. ある (u-verb) - to exist (inanimate)

In the Compound Sentence lesson, we learned how to use the te-form of verbs to express multiples sequential actions in one sentence. This practice, however, is used only in regular everyday speech. Formal speeches, narration, and written publications employ the verb stem instead of the te-form to describe sequential actions. Particularly, newspaper articles, in the interest of brevity, always prefer verb stems to the te-form.

Examples

1. 花火（はなび）は、火薬と金属の粉末を混ぜたものに火を付け、燃焼時の火花を楽しむためのもの。
   (Wikipedia - 花火, August 2004)
   Fireworks are for the enjoyment of sparks created from combustion created by lighting up a mixture of gunpowder and metal powder.
2. 企業内の顧客データを利用し、彼の行方を調べることが出来た。
   Was able to investigate his whereabouts using the company's internal customer data.

For the 「〜ている」 forms, the stem becomes 「〜てい」 but because that doesn't fit very well into the middle of a sentence, it is common to use the humble form of 「いる」 which you will remember is 「おる」. This is simply so you can employ 「おり」 to connect relative clauses instead of just 「い」. It has nothing to do with the humble aspect of 「おる」

1. 封筒には写真が数枚入っており、手紙が添えられていた。
   Several photos were inside the envelope, and a letter was attached.
2. このファイルにはパスワードが設定されており、開く際にはそれを入力する必要がある。
   A password has been set on this file, and it needs to entered when opening.

Things that should be a certain way

In this lesson, we'll learn how to express the way things are supposed depending on what we mean by "supposed". While the first two grammar points 「はず」 and 「べき」 come up often and are quite useful, you'll rarely ever encounter 「べく」 or 「べからず」. You can safely skip those lessons unless you are studying for the JLPT.

Using 「はず」 to describe an expectation

Vocabulary

1. ある (u-verb) - to exist (inanimate)
2. 日曜日 【にち・よう・び】 - Sunday
3. 可能 【か・のう】 (na-adj) - possible
4. おいしい (i-adj) - tasty
5. 帰る 【かえ・る】 (u-verb) - to go home

6. 彼【かれ】 - he; boyfriend
7. 漫画【まん・が】 - comic book
8. マニア - mania
9. これ - this
10. 〜ら - pluralizing suffix
11. もう - already
12. 全部【ぜん・ぶ】 - everything
13. 読む【よ・む】 (u-verb) - to read
14. この - this (abbr. of これの)
15. 料理【りょう・り】 - cooking; cuisine; dish
16. 焦げる【こ・げる】 (ru-verb) - to burn, to be burned
17. まずい (i-adj) - unpleasant
18. 色々【いろ・いろ】 (na-adj) - various
19. 予定【よ・てい】 - plans, arrangement
20. する (exception) - to do
21. 今年【こ・とし】 - this year
22. 楽しい【たの・しい】 (i-adj) - fun
23. クリスマス - Christmas
24. そう - (things are) that way
25. 簡単【かん・たん】 (na-adj) - simple
26. 直す【なお・す】 (u-verb) - to correct, to fix
27. 打合せ【うち・あわ・せ】 - meeting
28. 毎週【まい・しゅう】 - every week
29. 〜時【〜じ】 - counter for hours
30. 始まる【はじ・まる】 (u-verb) - to begin

The first grammar we will learn is 「はず」, which is used to express something that was or is supposed to be. You can treat 「はず」 just like a regular noun as it is usually attached to the adjective or verb that is supposed to be or supposed to happen.

The only thing to be careful about here is expressing an expectation of something *not* happening. To do this, you must use the negative existence verb 「ない」 to say that such an expectation does not exist. This might be in the form of 「〜はずがない」 or 「〜はずはない」 depending on which particle you want to use. The negative conjugation 「はずじゃない」 is really only used when you want to confirm in a positive sense such as 「〜はずじゃないか？」.

Using 「はず」 to describe an expectation

Use 「はず」 just like a regular noun to modify the expected thing
Examples

1. 日曜日のはず (noun)
2. 可能なはず (na-adjective)
3. おいしいはず (i-adjective)
4. 帰るはず (verb)

For the case where you expect the negative, use the 「ない」 verb for nonexistence

Example: 帰るはず → 帰るはずがない

Examples

1. 彼は漫画マニアだから、これらをもう全部読んだはずだよ。
   He has a mania for comic book(s) so I expect he read all these already.
2. この料理はおいしいはずだったが、焦げちゃって、まずくなった。
   This dish was expected to be tasty but it burned and became distasteful.

3. 色々予定してあるから、今年は楽しいクリスマスのはず。
   Because various things have been planned out, I expect a fun Christmas this year.

4. そう簡単に直せるはずがないよ。
   It's not supposed to be that easy to fix.

5. 打合せは毎週２時から始まるはずじゃないですか？
   This meeting is supposed to start every week at 2 o'clock, isn't it?

Here are <u>more examples</u> from the WWWJDIC. You may also want to check out the <u>jeKai entry</u>.

Using 「べき」 to describe actions one should do

Vocabulary

1. 絶対 【ぜっ・たい】 (na-adj) - absolutely, unconditionally
2. ある (u-verb) - to exist (inanimate)
3. 強い 【つよ・い】 (i-adj) - strong
4. 推奨 【すい・しょう】 - recommendation
5. する (exception) - to do
6. 擦る 【す・る】 (u-verb) - to rub
7. 行う 【おこな・う】 (u-verb) - to conduct, to carry out
8. 何 【なに／なん】 - what
9. 買う 【か・う】 (u-verb) - to buy
10. 前 【まえ】 - front; before
11. 本当 【ほん・とう】 - real
12. 必要 【ひつ・よう】 - necessity
13. どう - how
14. いい (i-adj) - good
15. 考える 【かんが・える】 (ru-verb) - to think
16. 例え 【たと・え】 - example

17. 国 【くに】 - country
18. 国民 【こく・みん】 - people, citizen
19. 騙す 【だま・す】 (u-verb) - to trick, to cheat, to deceive
20. 思う 【おも・う】 (u-verb) - to think
21. 預金者 【よ・きん・しゃ】 - depositor
22. 大手 【おお・て】 - large corporation
23. 銀行 【ぎん・こう】 - bank
24. 相手 【あい・て】 - other party
25. 取る 【と・る】 (u-verb) - to take
26. 訴訟 【そ・しょう】 - litigation, lawsuit
27. 起こす 【お・こす】 (u-verb) - to cause, to wake someone
28. ケース - case
29. 出る 【で・る】 (ru-verb) - to come out
30. 金融庁 【きん・ゆう・ちょう】 - Financial Services Agency
31. 被害者 【ひ・がい・しゃ】 - victim
32. 救済 【きゅう・さい】 - relief, aid
33. 優先 【ゆう・せん】 - preference, priority, precedence
34. 金融 【きん・ゆう】 - financing
35. 機関 【き・かん】 - institution
36. 犯罪 【はん・ざい】 - crime
37. 防止 【ぼう・し】 - prevention
38. 強化 【きょう・か】 - strengthen
39. 促す 【うなが・す】 (u-verb) - to urge
40. 判断 【はん・だん】 - judgement, decision
41. 朝日 【あさ・ひ】 - Asahi
42. 新聞 【しん・ぶん】 - newspaper

「べき」 is a verb suffix used to describe something that is supposed to be done. This suffix is commonly defined as "should", however, one must realize that it cannot be used to make suggestions like the sentence, "You should go to the doctor." If you use 「べき」, it sounds more like, "You are supposed to go to the doctor." 「べき」 has a much stronger tone and makes you sound like a know-it-all telling people what to do. For making suggestions, it is customary to use the comparison 「方がいい」 grammar instead. For this reason, this grammar is almost never used to directly tell someone what to do. It is usually used in reference to oneself where you can be as bossy as you want or in a neutral context where circumstances dictate what is proper and what is not. One such example would be a sentence like, "We are supposed to raise our kids properly with a good education."

Unlike the 「はず」 grammar, there is no expectation that something is going to happen. Rather, this grammar describes what one should do in a given circumstance. In Japanese, you might define it as meaning 「絶対ではないが、強く推奨されている」.

There is very little of grammatical interest. 「べき」 works just like a regular noun and so you can conjugate it as 「べきじゃない」、「べきだった」, and so on. The only thing to note here is that when you're using it with 「する」, the verb meaning "to do", you can optionally drop the 「る」 from 「するべき」 to produce 「すべき」. You can do this with this verb only and it does not apply for any other verbs even if the verb is written as 「する」 such as 「擦る」, the verb meaning "to rub".

Using 「べき」 for actions that should be done

Attach 「べき」 to the action that should be done
Examples

1. 行う → 行うべき
2. する → するべき

For the generic "to do " verb 「する」 only, you can remove the 「る」
Example: する＋べき → すべき

Examples

1. 何かを買う前に本当に必要かどうかをよく<u>考えるべき</u>だ。
Before buying something, one <u>should</u> think well on whether it's really necessary or not.

2. 例え国のためであっても、国民を<u>騙すべき</u>ではないと思う。
Even if it is, for example, for the country, I don't think the country's citizens <u>should</u> be deceived.

3. 預金者が大手銀行を相手取って訴訟を起こすケースも出ており、金融庁は被害者の救済を優先させて、金融機関に犯罪防止対策の強化を<u>促すべき</u>だと判断。（朝日新聞）
With cases coming out of depositors suing large banks, the Financial Services Agency decided it <u>should</u> prioritize relief for victims and urge banks to strengthen measures for crime prevention.

Using 「べく」 to describe what one tries to do

Vocabulary

1. 連用形 【れん・よう・けい】 - conjunctive form
2. 早い 【はや・い】 (i-adj) - fast; early
3. 帰る 【かえ・る】 (u-verb) - to go home
4. 準備 【じゅん・び】 - preparations
5. する (exception) - to do
6. 始める 【はじ・める】 (ru-verb) - to begin
7. 思う 【おも・う】 (u-verb) - to think
8. 出来る 【で・き・る】 (ru-verb) - to be able to do

9. 行う 【おこな・う】 (u-verb) - to conduct, to carry out
10. 試験 【し・けん】 - exam
11. 合格 【ごう・かく】 - pass (as in an exam)
12. 皆 【みんな】 - everybody
13. 一生懸命 【いっ・しょう・けん・めい】 - with utmost effort
14. 勉強 【べん・きょう】 - study
15. 今後 【こん・ご】 - from now on
16. お客様 【お・きゃく・さま】 - guest, customer
17. 対話 【たい・わ】 - interaction
18. 窓口 【まど・ぐち】 - teller window, counter; point of contact
19. より - more
20. 充実 【じゅう・じつ】 - fulfilled
21. 行く 【い・く】 (u-verb) - to go
22. 努力 【ど・りょく】 - effort
23. 参る 【まい・る】 (u-verb) - to go; to come (humble)

Grammatically, 「べく」 is really a conjunctive form （連用形） of 「べき」, similar to what the te-form does to connect another phrase. However, what needs mentioning here is that by changing it into a conjunctive and adding a predicate, the meaning of 「べく」 changes from the ordinary meaning of 「べき」. While 「べき」 describes a strong suggestion, changing it to 「べく」 allows you to describe what one did in order to carry out that suggestion. Take a look that the following examples to see how the meaning changes.

1. 早く帰るべき。
   Should go home early.
2. 早く帰るべく、準備をし始めた。
   In trying to go home early, started the preparations.

As we can see in this example, adding the 「準備をし始めた」 tells us what the subject did in order to carry out the action he/she was supposed to do.In this way we can define 「べく」 as meaning, "in order to" or "in an effort to". Similarly, 「べく」 might mean the

Japanese equivalent of 「しようと思って」 or 「できるように」.
This is a very seldom-used old-fashioned expression and is merely
presented here to completely cover all aspects of 「べき」.

Using 「べく」 for actions that are attempted to be done

Attach 「べく」 to the action that is attempted to be done
Examples

1. 行う → 行うべく
2. する → するべく

Same as 「べき」, you can remove the 「る」 for the generic
"to do " verb 「する」 only
Example: する＋べく → すべく

Examples

1. 試験に合格すべく、皆一生懸命に勉強している。
   Everybody is studying very hard <u>in an effort</u> to pass the exam.
2. 今後もお客様との対話の窓口として、より充実していくべく努
   力してまいります
   We are working from here <u>in an effort</u> to provide a enriched
   window for customer interaction.

Using 「べからず」 to describe things one must not do

Vocabulary

1. 未然形 【み・ぜん・けい】 - imperfective form
2. 行う 【おこな・う】 (u-verb) - to conduct, to carry out
3. する (exception) - to do
4. ゴミ - garbage
5. 捨てる 【す・てる】 (ru-verb) - to throw away
6. 安全 【あん・ぜん】 - safety
7. 措置 【そ・ち】 - measures
8. 忘れる 【わす・れる】 (ru-verb) - to forget

Moving on to yet another from of 「べき」 is 「べからず」. This is undoubtedly related to the 「ず」 negative ending we learned in a previous section. However, it seems to be a conjugation of an old 未然形 of 「べから」. I have no idea what that means and you don't have to either. The only thing we need to take away from this is that 「べからず」 expresses the opposite meaning of 「べき」 as an action that one must **not** do. I suppose the short and abrupt ending of the 「ず」 form makes this more useful for laying out rules. In fact, searching around on google comes up with a bunch of 「べし・べからず」 or "do's and don'ts". （べし is an older form of べき, which I doubt you'll ever need.)

Using 「べからず」 for actions that must **not** be done

Attach 「べからず」 to the action that must not be done
Examples

1. 行う → 行うべからず

2. する → するべからず

Same as 「べき」, you can remove the 「る」 for the generic "to do " verb 「する」 only
Example: する＋べからず → すべからず

Examples

1. ゴミ捨てるべからず。
   You <u>must not</u> throw away trash.
2. 安全措置を忘れるべからず。
   You <u>must not</u> forget the safety measures.

The minimum expectation

In this section, we'll learn various ways to express the minimum expectation. This grammar is not used as often as you might think as there are many situations where a simpler expression would sound more natural, but you should still become familiar with it.

Using 「（で）さえ」 to describe the minimum requirement

Vocabulary

1. 私 【わたし】 - me; myself; I
2. 子供 【こ・ども】 - child
3. 食べる 【た・べる】 (ru-verb) - to eat
4. 行く 【い・く】 (u-verb) - to go
5. 言う 【い・う】 (u-verb) - to say
6. 読む 【よ・む】 (u-verb) - to read
7. 宿題 【しゅく・だい】 - homework
8. 多い 【おお・い】 (i-adj) - numerous
9. トイレ - bathroom; toilet
10. 時間 【じ・かん】 - time

11. ある (u-verb) - to exist (inanimate)
12. お金 【お・かね】 - money
13. 何 【なに／なん】 - what
14. 出来る 【で・き・る】 (ru-verb) - to be able to do
15. お弁当 【お・べん・とう】 - box lunch
16. 買う 【か・う】 (u-verb) - to buy
17. あんた - you (slang)
18. 楽ちん 【らく・ちん】 (na-adj) - easy
19. ビタミン - vitamin
20. 健康 【けん・こう】 - health
21. 保証 【ほ・しょう】 - guarantee
22. する (exception) - to do
23. 自分 【じ・ぶん】 - oneself
24. 過ち 【あやま・ち】 - fault, error
25. 認める 【みと・める】 (ru-verb) - to recognize, to acknowledge
26. 問題 【もん・だい】 - problem
27. 解決 【かい・けつ】 - resolution
28. 教科書 【きょう・か・しょ】 - textbook
29. もっと - more
30. ちゃんと - properly
31. いる (ru-verb) - to exist (animate)
32. 合格 【ごう・かく】 - pass (as in an exam)
33. 一言 【ひと・こと】 - a few words
34. くれる (ru-verb) - to give
35. こんな - this sort of
36. こと - event, matter
37. なる (u-verb) - to become

In English, we might say, "not even close" to show that not even the minimum expectation has been met. In Japanese, we can express this by attaching 「さえ」 to the object or verb that miserably failed to reach what one would consider to be a bare minimum requirement. Conversely, you can also use the same grammar in a positive sense to express something is all you need.

Using 「（で）さえ」 to describe the minimum requirement

For nouns: Attach 「さえ」 or 「でさえ」 to the minimum requirement.
Examples

1. 私さえ - even me
2. 子供でさえ - even children

For verbs: Change the verb to the stem and attach 「さえ」.
For verbs in te-form, attach 「さえ」 to 「て／で」.
Examples

1. 食べる → 食べさえ
2. 行く → 行き → 行きさえ
3. 言ってくれる → 言ってさえくれる
4. 読んでいる → 読んでさえいる

Examples

1. 宿題が多すぎて、トイレに行く時間さえなかった。
   There was so much homework, I didn't even have time to go to the bathroom.
2. お金さえあれば、何でも出来るよ。
   The least you need is money and you can do anything.
3. お弁当を買うお金さえなかった。
   I didn't even have money to buy lunch.

For nouns <u>only</u>, you can add 「で」 and use 「でさえ」 instead of just 「さえ」. There are no grammatical differences but it does sound a bit more emphatic.

1. 私でさえ出来れば、あんたには楽ちんでしょう。
   If even I can do it, it should be a breeze for you.

You can also attach 「さえ」 to the stem of verbs to express a minimum action for a result. This is usually followed up immediately by 「する」 to show that the minimum action is done (or not). If the verb happens to be in a te-form, 「さえ」 can also be attached directly to the end of the 「て」 or 「で」 of the te-form.

1. ビタミンを食べさえすれば、健康が保証されますよ。
   If you just eat vitamins, your health will be guaranteed.
2. 自分の過ちを認めさえしなければ、問題は解決しないよ。
   The problem won't be solved if you don't even recognize your own mistake, you know.
3. 教科書をもっとちゃんと読んでさえいれば、合格できたのに。
   If only I had read the textbook more properly, I could have passed.
4. 一言言ってさえくれればこんなことにならなかった。
   If you only had said something things wouldn't have turned out like this.

「（で）すら」 - Older version of 「（で）さえ」

Vocabulary

1. 私 【わたし】 - me; myself; I
2. 子供 【こ・ども】 - child
3. この - this （abbr. of これの）

4. 天才 【てん・さい】 - genius
5. 分かる 【わ・かる】 (u-verb) - to understand
6. 緊張 【きん・ちょう】 - nervousness
7. する (exception) - to do
8. ちらっと - a peek
9. 見る 【み・る】 (ru-verb) - to see
10. こと - event, matter
11. 出来る 【で・き・る】 (ru-verb) - to be able to do
12. 人 【ひと】 - person
13. 漢字 【かん・じ】 - Kanji
14. 知る 【し・る】 (u-verb) - to know
15. 生徒 【せい・と】 - student
16. いる (ru-verb) - to exist (animate)

「（で）すら」 is a older variation of 「（で）さえ」 that is not as commonly used. It is essentially interchangeable with 「（で）さえ」 except that it is generally used only with nouns.

「（で）すら」 is used in the same way as 「（で）さえ」 for nouns

For nouns: Attach 「すら」 or 「ですら」 to the minimum requirement.
Examples

1. 私すら - Even me
2. 子供ですら - Even children

Examples

1. この天才の私<u>ですら</u>わからなかった。
   Even a genius such as myself couldn't solve it.
2. 私は緊張しすぎて、ちらっと見ること<u>すら</u>出来ませんでした。
   I was so nervous that I couldn't even take a quick peek.
3. 「人」の漢字<u>すら</u>知らない生徒は、いないでしょ！

   There are no students that don't even know the 「人」 Kanji!

「おろか」 - It's not even worth considering

Vocabulary

1. 愚か 【おろ・か】 (na-adj) - foolish
2. 漢字 【かん・じ】 - Kanji
3. ひらがな - Hiragana
4. 読む 【よ・む】 (u-verb) - to read
5. 結婚 【けっ・こん】 - marriage
6. 〜ヶ月 【〜か・げつ】 - counter for span of month(s)
7. 付き合う 【つ・き・あ・う】 (u-verb) - to go out with; to accompany
8. 結局 【けっ・きょく】 - eventually
9. 別れる 【わか・れる】 (ru-verb) - to separate; to break up
10. 大学 【だい・がく】 - college
11. 高校 【こう・こう】 - high school
12. 卒業 【そつ・ぎょう】 - graduate
13. する (exception) - to do

This grammar comes from the adjective 「愚か」 which means to be foolish or stupid. However, in this case, you're not making fun of something, rather by using 「おろか」, you can indicate that something is so ridiculous that it's not even worth considering. In English, we might say something like, "Are you kidding? I can't touch my knees much less do a full split!" In this example, the full split is so beyond the person's abilities that it would be foolish to even consider it.

Examples

1. 漢字はおろか、ひらがなさえ読めないよ！
   Forget about Kanji, I can't even read Hiragana!
2. 結婚はおろか、2ヶ月付き合って、結局別れてしまった。
   We eventually broke up after going out two months much less get married.
3. 大学はおろか、高校すら卒業しなかった。
   I didn't even graduate from high school much less college.

This grammar is rarely used and is primarily useful for JLPT level 1. The expression 「どころか」 is far more common and has a similar meaning. However, unlike 「おろか」 which is used as an adjective, 「どころか」 is attached directly to the noun, adjective, or verb.

1. 漢字どころか、ひらがなさえ読めないよ！
   Forget about Kanji, I can't even read Hiragana!

Showing signs of something

In this lesson, we'll learn various expressions involving how to describe people who are expressing themselves without words. For example, we'll learn how to say expressions in Japanese such as "They <u>acted</u> as if they were saying goodbye," "He <u>acted</u> disgusted," and "She <u>acts</u> like she wants to go."

Showing outward signs of an emotion using 「～がる」

Vocabulary

1. 嫌 【いや】 (na-adj) disagreeable; unpleasant
2. 怖い 【こわ・い】 (i-adj) - scary
3. 嬉しい 【うれ・しい】 (i-adj) - happy
4. 恥ずかしい 【は・ずかしい】 (i-adj) - embarrassing
5. 早い 【はや・い】 (i-adj) - fast; early
6. する (exception) - to do
7. 何 【なに／なん】 - what
8. いる (ru-verb) - to exist (animate)
9. 彼女 【かの・じょ】 - she; girlfriend
10. 朝 【あさ】 - morning
11. 起こす 【お・こす】 (u-verb) - to cause, to wake someone
12. タイプ - type
13. うち - referring to one's in-group, i.e. company, etc.
14. 子供 【こ・ども】 - child
15. プール - pool
16. 入る 【はい・る】 (u-verb) - to enter
17. 理由 【り・ゆう】 - reason
18. ある (u-verb) - to exist (inanimate)
19. 欲しい 【ほ・しい】 (i-adj) - desirable
20. カレー - curry
21. 食べる 【た・べる】 (ru-verb) - to eat
22. 家 【1) うち; 2) いえ】 - 1) one's own home; 2) house
23. 帰る 【かえ・る】 (u-verb) - to go home
24. すぐ - soon
25. パソコン - computer, PC
26. 使う 【つか・う】 (u-verb) - to use
27. 皆 【みんな】 - everybody
28. イタリア - Italy
29. 行く 【い・く】 (u-verb) - to go
30. 私 【わたし】 - me, myself, I
31. 予算 【よ・さん】 - budget

32. どう - how

33. とても - very

34. 怪しい 【あや・しい】 (i-adj) - suspicious; dubious; doubtful

35. 妻 【つま】 - wife

36. バッグ - bag

37. そんな - that sort of

38. もん - object (short for もの)

39. 買う 【か・う】 (u-verb) - to buy

40. 訳 【わけ】 - meaning; reason; can be deduced

41. 恥ずかしがり屋 【は・ずかしがり・や】 - one who easily feels or acts embarrassed

42. 寒がり屋 【さむ・がり・や】 - one who easily feels cold

43. 暑がり屋 【あつ・がり・や】 - one who easily feels hot

44. ミネソタ - Minnesota

45. 暮らす 【く・らす】 (u-verb) - to live

46. 辛い 【つら・い】 (i-adj) - harsh

The 「〜がる」 grammar is used when you want to make an observation about how someone is feeling. This is simply an observation based on some type of sign(s). Therefore, you would not use it for your own emotions since guessing about your own emotions is not necessary. This grammar can only be used with adjectives so you can use this grammar to say, "He is acting scared," but you cannot say "He acted surprised," because "to be surprised" is a verb in Japanese and not an adjective. This grammar is also commonly used with a certain set of adjectives related to emotions such as: 「嫌」、「怖い」、「嬉しい」、or 「恥ずかしい」.

Using 「〜がる」 for observing the emotions or feelings of others

For i-adjectives: Remove the last 「い」 from the i-adjective and then attach 「がる」
Example: 怖い → 怖がる
For na-adjectives: Attach 「がる」 to the end of the na-adjective
Example: 嫌 → 嫌がる

All adjectives that are conjugated with 「〜がる」 become an u-verb

	Positive	**Negative**
Non-Past	怖がる act scared	怖がらない not act scared
Past	怖がった acted scared	怖がらなかった didn't act scared

Examples

1. 早くきてよ！何を恥ずかしがっているの？
   Hurry up and come here. What are you acting all embarrassed for?

2. 彼女は朝早く起こされるのを嫌がるタイプです。
My girlfriend is the type to show dislike towards getting woken up early in the morning.
3. うちの子供はプールに入るのを理由もなく怖がる。
Our child acts afraid about entering a pool without any reason.

This grammar is also used to observe very frankly on what you think someone other than yourself wants. This involves the adjective 「欲しい」 for things one wants or the 「～たい」 conjugation for actions one wants to do, which is essentially a verb conjugated to an i-adjective. This type of grammar is more suited for things like narration in a story and is rarely used in this fashion for normal conversations because of its impersonal style of observation. For casual conversations, it is more common to use 「でしょう」 such as in, 「カレーを食べたいでしょう。」. For polite conversations, it is normal to not make any assumptions at all or to use the 「よね」 sentence ending such as in 「カレーを食べたいですか。」 or 「カレーを食べたいですよね。」

Examples

1. 家に帰ったら、すぐパソコンを使いたがる。
(He) soon acts like wanting to use computer as soon as (he) gets home.
2. みんなイタリアに行きたがってるんだけど、私の予算で行けるかどうかはとても怪しい。
Everybody is acting like they want to go to Italy but it's suspicious whether I can go or not going by my budget.
3. 妻はルイヴィトンのバッグを欲しがっているんだけど、そんなもん、買えるわけないでしょう！
My wife was showing signs of wanting a Louis Vuitton bag but there's no way I can buy something like that!

「〜がる」 is also used with 「屋」 to indicate a type of person that often feels a certain way such as 「恥ずかしがり屋」 (one who easily feels or acts embarrassed)、 「寒がり屋」 (one who easily feels cold)、 or 「暑がり屋」 (one who easily feels hot).

- 私は寒がり屋だから、ミネソタで暮らすのは辛かった。
  I'm the type who easily gets cold and so living in Minnesota was painful.

Using 「ばかり」 to act as if one might do something

Vocabulary

1. 言う 【い・う】 (u-verb) - to say
2. ボール - ball
3. 爆発 【ばく・はつ】 - explosion
4. する (exception) - to do
5. 膨らむ 【ふく・らむ】 (u-verb) - to expand; to swell
6. あんた - you (slang)
7. 関係 【かん・けい】 - relation, relationship
8. ある (u-verb) - to exist (inanimate)
9. 彼女 【かの・じょ】 - she; girlfriend
10. 彼 【かれ】 - he; boyfriend
11. 無視 【む・し】 - ignore
12. 昨日【きのう】 - yesterday
13. 喧嘩 【けん・か】 - quarrel
14. 何 【なに／なん】 - what
15. 平気 【へい・き】 (na-adj) - coolness; calmness
16. 顔 【かお】 - face

We just learned how to observe the emotions and feelings of other by using 「〜がる」 with adjectives. But what about verbs? Indeed,

409

there is a separate grammar used to express the fact that someone else looks like they are about to do something but actually does not. Similar to the 「〜がる」 grammar, this is usually not used in normal everyday conversations. I have seen it several times in books and novels but have yet to hear this grammar in a conversation.

For the regular non-past, non-negative verb, you must first conjugate the verb to the negative ending with 「ん」, which was covered here. Then, you just attach 「ばかり」 to the end of the verb. For all other conjugations, nothing else is necessary except to just add 「ばかり」 to the verb. The most common verb used with this grammar is 「言う」. It is also usually used with the 「に」 target particle attached to the end of 「ばかり」.

This grammar is completely different from the 「ばかり」 used to express amounts and the 「ばかり」 used to express the proximity of an action.

Using 「ばかり」 to indicate that one seems to want to do something

For present, non-negative: Conjugate the verb to the 「ん」 negative form and attach 「ばかり」
Example: 言う → 言わない → 言わん → 言わんばかり
For all other tenses: Attach 「ばかり」 to the end of the verb
Example: 言わなかった → 言わなかったばかり

Summary of basic conjugations

	Positive	Negative
Non-Past	言わんばかり as if to say	言わないばかり as if [she] doesn't say
Past	言ったばかり as if [she] said	言わなかったばかり as if [she] didn't say

Examples

1. ボールは爆発せんばかりに、膨らんでいた。
   The ball was expanding as if it was going to explode.
2. 「あんたとは関係ない」と言わんばかりに彼女は彼を無視していた。
   She ignored him as if to say, "You have nothing to do with this."
3. 昨日の喧嘩で何も言わなかったばかりに、平気な顔をしている。
   Has a calm face as if [he] didn't say anything during the fight yesterday.

411

Using 「めく」 to indicate an atmosphere of a state

Vocabulary

1. 謎 【なぞ】 - puzzle
2. 秘密 【ひ・みつ】 - secret
3. 皮肉 【ひ・にく】 - irony
4. 紅葉 【こう・よう】 - leaves changing color
5. 始まる 【はじ・まる】 (u-verb) - to begin
6. すっかり - completely
7. 秋 【あき】 - autumn
8. 空気 【くう・き】 - air; atmosphere
9. なる (u-verb) - to become
10. そんな - that sort of
11. 顔 【かお】 - face
12. する (exception) - to do
13. うまい (i-adj) - skillful; delicious
14. 説明 【せつ・めい】 - explanation
15. 出来る 【で・き・る】 (ru-verb) - to be able to do
16. いつも - always
17. 言う 【い・う】 (u-verb) - to say
18. ～方 【～かた】 - way of doing ~
19. 皆 【みんな】 - everybody
20. 嫌 【いや】 (na-adj) disagreeable; unpleasant

By now, you're probably thinking, "Ok, we've done adjectives and verbs. What about nouns?" As a matter of fact, there is a similar grammar that is used usually for nouns and na-adjectives. It is used to indicate that something is showing the signs of a certain state. Unlike the 「～がる」 grammar, there is no action that indicates anything; merely the atmosphere gives off the impression of the state. Just like the previous grammar we learned in this section, this grammar has a list of commonly used nouns such as 「謎」、「秘密」、or 「皮肉」. This grammar is used by simply attaching 「めく」 to the noun or na-adjective. The result then becomes a regular u-verb.

Using 「めく」 to indicate that one seems to want to do something

Attach 「めく」 to the noun or na-adjective. The result then becomes a regular u-verb.

Example: 謎 → 謎めく

Summary of basic conjugations

	Positive	Negative
Non-Past	謎めく puzzling atmosphere	*謎めかない not puzzling atmosphere
Past	謎めいた puzzled atmosphere	*謎めかなかった not puzzled atmosphere

---

*The negatives conjugations are theoretically possible but are not likely used. The most common usage is the past tense.

Examples

1. 紅葉が始まり、すっかり秋めいた空気になってきた。
   With the leaves starting to change color, the air came to become quite autumn like.

2. そんな謎めいた顔をされても、うまく説明できないよ。
   Even having that kind of puzzled look done to me, I can't explain it very well, you know.

3. いつも皮肉めいた言い方をしたら、みんなを嫌がらせるよ。
   You'll make everyone dislike you if you keep speaking with that ironic tone, you know.

For a whole slew of additional real world examples, check out the jeKai entry. It states that the grammar can be used for adverbs and other parts of speech but none of the numerous examples show this and even assuming it's possible, it's probably not practiced in reality.

Expressing non-feasibility

We learned how to express feasibility in the section on the potential form quite a while ways back. In this section, we'll learn some advanced and specialized ways to express certain types of feasibility or the lack thereof. Like much of the grammar in the Advanced Section, the grammar covered here is mostly used for written works and rarely used in regular speech.

Expressing the inability to not do using 「～ざるを得ない」

Vocabulary

1. 得る 【え・る】 (ru-verb) - to obtain
2. 意図 【い・と】 - intention; aim; design
3. する (exception) - to do

4. 来る 【く・る】 (exception) - to come
5. 食べる 【た・べる】 (ru-verb) - to eat
6. 行く 【い・く】 (u-verb) - to go
7. この - this (abbr. of これの)
8. テレビ - TV, television
9. これ - this
10. 以上 【い・じょう】 - greater or equal
11. 壊れる 【こわ・れる】 (ru-verb) - to break
12. 新しい 【あたら・しい】 (i-adj) - new
13. 買う 【か・う】 (u-verb) - to buy
14. ずっと - the whole time, all along
15. 我慢 【が・まん】 - tolerance; self-control
16. 状態 【じょう・たい】 - situation
17. 歯医者 【は・い・しゃ】 - dentist
18. 上司 【じょう・し】 - superior; boss
19. 話 【はなし】 - story
20. 聞く 【き・く】 (u-verb) - to ask; to listen
21. どうしても - by any means, no matter what
22. 海外 【かい・がい】 - overseas

This grammar is used when there's something that just can't be
helped and must be done. It is the negative version of the grammar
we previously covered for something that has to be done. It uses the
negative of the verb 「得る」 or "obtain", to roughly mean that "one
cannot obtain not doing of an action". This means that you can't not
do something even if you wanted to. As a result of the use of double
negatives, this grammar carries a slight suggestion that you really
don't want to do it, but you have to because it can't be helped.
Really, the negative connotation is the only difference between this
grammar and the grammar we covered in this "have to" section.
That, and the fact that this grammar is fancier and more advanced.

This grammar uses an archaic negative form of verbs that ends in
「～ざる」. It is really not used in modern Japanese with the

exception of this grammar and some expressions such as 「意図せ ざる」. The rules for conjugation are the same as the negative verbs, except this grammar attaches 「ざる」 instead. To reiterate, all you have to do is conjugate the verb to the negative form and then replace the 「ない」 with 「ざる」. The two exception verbs are 「する」 which becomes 「せざる」 and 「くる」 which becomes 「こざる」. Finally, all that's left to be done is to attach 「を得ない」 to the verb. It is also not uncommon to use Hiragana instead of the Kanji.

Using 「～ざるを得ない」 for actions that must be done

- To say that you can't not do something replace the 「な い」 part of the negative verb with 「ざる」, then attach 「を得ない」 to the end of the verb. Examples
  1. 食べる → 食べない → 食べざる → 食べざるを得ない
  2. 行く → 行かない → 行かざる → 行かざるを得ない
- **Exceptions:**
  1. する → せざる → せざるをえない
  2. くる → こざる → こざるをえない

Examples

1. このテレビがこれ以上壊れたら、新しいのを買わざるを得ない な。 If this TV breaks even more, there's no choice but to buy a new one.
2. ずっと我慢してきたが、この状態だと歯医者さんに行かざるを 得ない。 I tolerated it all this time but in this situation, I can't not go to the dentist.

416

3. 上司の話を聞くと、どうしても海外に出張をせざるを得ないよ
うです。 Hearing the story from the boss, it seems like I can't
not go on a business trip overseas no matter what.

Expressing the inability to stop doing something using 「やむを得ない」

Vocabulary

1. 止む 【や・む】 (u-verb) - to stop
2. 仕方 【し・かた】 - way, method
3. ある (u-verb) - to exist (inanimate)
4. しょうがない - it can't be helped, nothing can be done
5. 得る 【え・る】 (ru-verb) - to obtain
6. 事由 【じ・ゆう】 - reason; cause
7. 手続 【て・つづき】 - procedure, paperwork
8. 遅れる 【おく・れる】 (ru-verb) - to be late
9. 必ず 【かなら・ず】 - without exception, without fail
10. 連絡 【れん・らく】 - contact
11. この - this (abbr. of これの)
12. 仕事 【し・ごと】 - job
13. 厳しい 【きび・しい】 (i-adj) - strict
14. 最近 【さい・きん】 - recent; lately
15. 不景気 【ふ・けい・き】 - recession, depression
16. 新しい 【あたら・しい】 (i-adj) - new
17. 見つかる 【み・つかる】 (u-verb) - to be found
18. 状態 【じょう・たい】 - situation

This grammar is very similar to the one we just learned above
except that it uses the verb 「止む」 to say that one cannot obtain
the stopping of something. Remember that we normally can't just
attach the 「を」 direct object particle to verbs, so this is really a set
expression. Just like the previous grammar we learned, it is used to

417

describe something that one is forced to do due to some circumstances. The difference here is that this is a complete phrase, which can be used for a general situation that doesn't involve any specific action. In other words, you're not actually forced to *do* something; rather it describes a situation that cannot be helped. If you have already learned 「仕方がない」 or 「しょうがない」, this grammar means pretty much the same thing. The difference lies in whether you want to say, "Looks like we're stuck" vs "Due to circumstances beyond our control..."

Since this is a set expression, there are really no grammar points to discuss. You only need to take the phrase and use it as you would any regular relative clause.

Examples

1. やむを得ない事由により手続が遅れた場合、必ずご連絡下さい。 If the paperwork should be late due to uncontrollable circumstance, please make sure to contact us.
2. この仕事は厳しいかもしれませんが、最近の不景気では新しい仕事が見つからないのでやむを得ない状態です。 This job may be bad but because (I) can't find a new job due to the recent economic downturn, it's a situation where nothing can be done.

Expressing what cannot be done with 「〜かねる」

Vocabulary

1. かねる (ru-verb) - to be unable to; to find difficult (unpleasant, awkward, painful) to do;
2. 決める 【き・める】 (ru-verb) - to decide
3. する (exception) - to do

4. なる (u-verb) - to become
5. この - this　(abbr. of これの）
6. 場 【ば】 - place, spot
7. ちょっと - a little
8. また - again
9. 別途 【べっ・と】 - separate
10. 会議 【かい・ぎ】 - meeting
11. 設ける 【もう・ける】 (ru-verb) - to establish
12. 個人 【こ・じん】 - personal
13. 情報 【じょう・ほう】 - information
14. 漏洩 【ろう・えい】 - disclosure; leakage
15. 速やか 【すみ・やか】 (na-adj) - speedy; prompt
16. 対応 【たい・おう】 - dealing with; support
17. 願う 【ねが・う】 (u-verb) - to wish; to request
18. 致す 【いた・す】 (u-verb) - to do (humble)

The meaning and usage of 「かねる」 is covered pretty well in this jeKai entry with plenty of examples. While much of this is a repetition of what's written there, 「かねる」 is a ru-verb that is used as a suffix to other verbs to express a person's inability, reluctance, or refusal to do something

「かねる」 is often used in the negative as 「かねない」 to indicate that there is a possibility that the verb in question might happen. As the jeKai entry mentions, this is usually in reference to something bad, which you might express in English as, "there is a risk that..." or "there is a fear that..."

One important thing that the jeKai doesn't mention is how you would go about using this grammar. It's not difficult and you may have already guessed from the example sentences that all you need to do is just attach 「かねる」 or 「かねない」 to the stem of the verb.

Examples

1. この場ではちょっと決めかねますので、また別途会議を設けましょう。 Since making a decision here is impossible, let's set up a separate meeting again.
2. このままでは、個人情報が漏洩しかねないので、速やかに対応をお願い致します。 At this rate, there is a possibility that personal information might leak so I request that this be dealt with promptly.

Tendencies

In this lesson, we will go over various types of grammar that deal with tendencies. Like much of the Advanced Section, all the grammar in this lesson are used mostly in written works and are generally not used in conversational Japanese.

Saying something is prone to occur using 「〜がち」

Vocabulary

1. 見る 【み・る】 (ru-verb) - to see
2. なる (u-verb) - to become
3. 病気 【びょう・き】 - disease; sickness
4. 確定 【かく・てい】 - decision; settlement
5. 申告 【しん・こく】 - report; statement; filing a return
6. 確定申告 【かく・てい・しん・こく】 - final income tax return
7. 忘れる 【わす・れる】 (ru-verb) - to forget
8. 手続 【て・つづき】 - procedure, paperwork
9. 留守 【るす】 - being away from home
10. 家庭 【か・てい】 - household
11. 犬 【いぬ】 - dog
12. 猫 【ねこ】 - cat
13. 勧め 【すす・め】 - recommendation
14. 父親 【ちち・おや】 - father
15. 皆 【みんな】 - everybody
16. 心配 【しん・ぱい】 - worry; concern
17. する (exception) - to do

This is arguably the most useful grammar in this lesson in terms of practically. By that, I mean that it's the only grammar here that you might actually hear in a regular conversation though again, it is far more common in a written context.

With this grammar, you can say that something is likely to occur by simply attaching 「がち」 to the stem of the verb. While, 「がち」 is a suffix, it works in much same way as a noun or na-adjective. In other words, the result becomes a description of something as being likely. This means that we can do things like modifying nouns by attaching 「な」 and other things we're used to doing with na-adjectives. You can also say that something is prone to *be* something by attaching 「がち」 to the noun.

As the word "prone" suggest, 「がち」 is usually used for tendencies that are bad or undesirable.

Using 「〜がち」 as a description of an action prone to occur

- **For verbs:** Attach 「がち」 to the stem of the verb.
  Examples
  1. 見る → 見がち
  2. なる → なり → なりがち
- **For nouns:** Attach 「がち」 to the appropriate noun
  Example: 病気 → 病気がち

All adjectives that are conjugated with
「〜がち」 become a noun/na-adjective

	Positive	**Negative**
Non-Past	なりがち prone to become	なりがち じゃない is not prone to become
Past	なりがち だった was prone to become	なりがち じゃなかっ た was not prone to become

Examples

1. 確定申告は忘れがちな手続のひとつだ。
   Filing income taxes is one of those processes that one is prone to forget.

2. 留守がちなご家庭には、犬よりも、猫の方がおすすめです。
   For families that tend to be away from home, cats are recommended over dogs.

3. 父親は病気がちで、みんなが心配している。
Father is prone to illness and everybody is worried.

For more examples, check out the WWWJDIC examples.

Describing an ongoing occurrence using 「~つつ」

Vocabulary

1. テレビ - TV, television
2. 見る 【み・る】 (ru-verb) - to see
3. 寝る 【ね・る】 (ru-verb) - to sleep
4. 思う 【おも・う】 (u-verb) - to think
5. なる (u-verb) - to become
6. 二日酔い 【ふつ・か・よい】 - hangover
7. 痛む 【いた・む】 (u-verb) - to feel pain
8. 頭 【あたま】 - head
9. 押さえる 【おさ・える】 (ru-verb) - to hold something down; to grasp
10. トイレ - bathroom; toilet
11. 入る 【はい・る】 (u-verb) - to enter
12. 体 【からだ】 - body
13. いい (i-adj) - good
14. 最近 【さい・きん】 - recent; lately
15. 全然 【ぜん・ぜん】 - not at all (when used with negative)
16. 運動 【うん・どう】 - exercise
17. する (exception) - to do
18. 電気 【でん・き】 - electricity; (electric) light
19. 製品 【せい・ひん】 - manufactured goods, product
20. 発展 【はっ・てん】 - development; growth; advancement
21. つれる (ru-verb) - to lead
22. ハードディスク - hard disk

23. 容量 【よう・りょう】 - capacity
24. ますます - increasingly
25. 大きい 【おお・きい】 (i-adj) - big
26. ある (u-verb) - to exist (inanimate)
27. 今 【いま】 - now
28. 日本 【に・ほん】 - Japan
29. 終身 【しゅう・しん】 - lifetime
30. 雇用 【こ・よう】 - employment
31. 年功 【ねん・こう】 - long service
32. 序列 【じょ・れつ】 - order
33. 年功序列 【ねん・こう・じょ・れつ】 - seniority system
34. 言う 【い・う】 (u-verb) - to say
35. 慣行 【かん・こう】 - customary practice
36. 崩れる 【くず・れる】 (ru-verb) - to collapse; to crumble

「つつ」 is a verb modifier that can be attached to the stem of verbs to express an ongoing occurrence. Though the meaning stays essentially the same, there are essentially two ways to use this grammar. The first is almost identical to the 「〜ながら」 grammar. You can use 「つつ」 to describe an action that is taking place while another action is ongoing. However, there are several major differences between 「つつ」 and 「〜ながら」. First, the tone of 「つつ」 is very different from that of 「〜ながら」 and you would rarely, if ever, use it for regular everyday occurrences. To go along with this, 「つつ」 is more appropriate for more literary or abstract actions such as those involving emotions or thoughts. Second, 「〜ながら」 is used to describe an auxiliary action that takes place while the main action is going on. However, with 「つつ」, both actions have equal weight.

For example, it would sound very strange to say the following.

- テレビを見つつ、寝ちゃダメよ！
  (Sounds unnatural)

- テレビを見ながら、寝ちゃダメよ！
Don't watch TV while sleeping!

The second way to use this grammar is to express the existence of a continuing process by using 「ある」, the verb for existence. Everything is the same as before except that you attach 「ある」 to 「つつ」 to produce 「～つつある」. This is often used in magazine or newspaper articles to describe a certain trend or tide.

Using 「～つつ」 to describe a repetitive occurrence

- To describe an ongoing action, attach 「つつ」 to the stem of the verb.
Examples
    1. 見る → 見つつ
    2. 思う → 思い → 思いつつ
- To show the existence of a trend or tide, add 「ある」 to 「つつ」

    Example: なる → なり → なりつつ → なりつつある

Examples

1. 二日酔いで痛む頭を押さえつつ、トイレに入った。
Went into the bathroom while holding an aching head from a hangover.
2. 体によくないと思いつつ、最近は全然運動してない。
While thinking it's bad for body, haven't exercised at all recently.
3. 電気製品の発展につれて、ハードディスクの容量はますます大きくなりつつある。

Lead by the advancement of electronic products, hard disk drive capacities are becoming ever larger.

4. 今の日本では、終身雇用や年功序列という雇用慣行が崩れつつ
ある。

In today's Japan, hiring practices like life-time employment and age-based ranking are tending to break down.

For more examples, check out the WWWJDIC examples.

Describing a negative tendency using 「きらいがある」

Vocabulary

1. 嫌い 【きら・い】 (na-adj) - distasteful, hateful
2. 依存症 【い・ぞん・しょう】 - dependence; addiction
3. ある (u-verb) - to exist (inanimate)
4. 多い 【おお・い】 (i-adj) - numerous
5. 大学生 【だい・がく・せい】 - college student
6. 締切日 【しめ・きり・び】 - closing day; deadline
7. ぎりぎり - at the last moment; just barely
8. 宿題 【しゅく・だい】 - homework
9. やる (u-verb) - to do
10. コーディング - coding
11. 好き 【す・き】 (na-adj) - likable; desirable
12. 開発者 【かい・はつ・しゃ】 - developer
13. ちゃんと - properly
14. する (exception) - to do
15. ドキュメント - document
16. 作成 【さく・せい】 - creation
17. 十分 【じゅう・ぶん】 - sufficient, adequate
18. テスト - test
19. 怠る 【おこた・る】 (u-verb) - to shirk

「きらいがある」 is a fixed expression used to describe a bad tendency or habit. I suspect that 「きらい」 here *might* have something to do with the word for hateful: 「嫌い」. However, unlike 「嫌い」, which is a na-adjective, the 「きらい」 in this grammar functions as a noun. This is made plain by the fact that the 「が」 particle comes right after 「きらい」, which is not allowed for adjectives. The rest of the phrase is simply expressing the fact that the negative tendency exists.

Using 「きらいがある」 to describe a negative tendency

- The 「きらい」 in this grammar functions as a noun. 「ある」 is simply the existence verb for inanimate objects.
  Example: 依存症のきらいがある。

Examples

1. 多くの大学生は、締切日ぎりぎりまで、宿題をやらないきらいがある。
   A lot of college students have a bad tendency of not doing their homework until just barely it's due date.
2. コーディングが好きな開発者は、ちゃんとしたドキュメント作成と十分なテストを怠るきらいがある。
   Developers that like coding have a bad tendency to neglect proper documents and adequate testing.

Advanced Volitional

We learned in a previous lesson that the volitional form is used when one is set out to do something. In this section, we're going to cover some other ways in which the volitional form is used, most notably, the negative volitional form.

Negative Volitional

Vocabulary

1. 見る 【み・る】 (ru-verb) - to see
2. 行く 【い・く】 (u-verb) - to go
3. する (exception) - to do
4. 来る 【く・る】 (exception) - to come
5. なる (u-verb) - to become
6. 相手 【あい・て】 - other party
7. 剣 【けん】 - sword
8. 達人 【たつ・じん】 - master, expert
9. そう - (things are) that way
10. 簡単 【かん・たん】 (na-adj) - simple
11. 勝つ 【か・つ】 (u-verb) - to win
12. そんな - that sort of
13. 無茶 【む・ちゃ】 - unreasonable; excessive
14. 手段 【しゅ・だん】 - method
15. 認める 【みと・める】 (ru-verb) - to recognize, to acknowledge
16. その - that (abbr. of それの)
17. 時 【とき】 - time
18. 決して 【けっ・して】 - by no means; decidedly
19. 彼 【かれ】 - he; boyfriend
20. 会う 【あ・う】 (u-verb) - to meet
21. 心 【こころ】 - heart; mind
22. 決める 【き・める】 (ru-verb) - to decide
23. あの - that (over there) (abbr. of あれの)

24. 人 【ひと】 - person
25. ~度 【~ど】 - counter for number of times
26. 嘘 【うそ】 - lie
27. つく (u-verb) - to be attached
28. 誓う 【つか・う】 (u-verb) - to swear, to pledge
29. 明日 【あした】 - tomorrow
30. やめる (ru-verb) - to stop; to quit
31. 肉 【にく】 - meat
32. 食べる 【た・べる】 (ru-verb) - to eat

You may have seen the negative volitional form in a verb conjugation table and wondered, "What the heck is that used for?" Well the answer is not much, or to put it more accurately, there are various ways it can be used but almost all of them are extremely stiff and formal. In fact, it's so rare that I only found one explanation in English on the web or anywhere else. (I also found this one in Japanese.)

The negative volitional is used to express negative intention. This means that there is a will for something to **not** happen or that someone is set out to **not** do something. As a result, because one is trying not to do something, it's probably not going to happen. Essentially, it is a very stiff and formal version of 「でしょう」 and 「だろう」. While this form is practically never used in daily conversations, you might still hear it in movies, etc.

Verbs are conjugated to the negative volitional by simply attaching 「まい」 to the verb. Another alternative is to attach 「まい」 to the stem. The conjugation for the negative volitional is quite different from those we are used to because it is always the last conjugation to apply even for the masu-form. There is no way to conjugate 「まい」 to the masu-form, you simply attach 「まい」 to the masu-form conjugation.

Using 「まい」 to express a will to not do something

- **For ru-verbs:** Attach 「まい」 to the stem.
  Example: 見る → 見まい
- **For u-verbs:** Attach 「まい」 to the end of the verb
  Example: 行くまい
  Exceptions:
  1. する → するまい or しまい
  2. くる → くるまい
  This conjugation must always come last. For masu-form,
  attach 「まい」 to the masu-form verb.
  Example: なる → なり → なります → なりますまい

Examples

1. 相手は剣の達人だ。そう簡単には勝てまい。
   Your opponent is a master of the sword. I doubt you can win so
   easily.
2. そんな無茶な手段は認めますまい！

   I won't approve of such an unreasonable method!

We already learned that you could use the volitional form to say
"let's" and to express an attempt do something. But that doesn't
mean you can use the negative volitional to say "let's not" or "try not
to". The tone of this grammar is one of very strong determination to
not do something, as you can see in the following examples.

1. その時までは決して彼に会うまいと心に決めていた。
   Until that time, I had decided in my heart to not meet him by
   any means.

2. あの人は、二度と嘘を<u>つくまい</u>と誓ったのです。
That person had sworn to never lie again.

In order to express "let's not", you can use the verb, 「やめる」 with the regular volitional. In order to express an effort to not do something, you can use 「ようにする」 with the negative verb.

1. 明日に行くのを<u>やめよう</u>。
Let's not go tomorrow. (lit: Let's quit going tomorrow.)
2. 肉を食べない<u>ようにしている</u>。
Trying not to eat meat.

Using the volitional to express a lack of relation

Vocabulary

1. 食べる 【た・べる】 (ru-verb) - to eat
2. 行く 【い・く】 (u-verb) - to go
3. あいつ - that guy (derogatory)
4. 大学 【だい・がく】 - college
5. 入る 【はい・る】 (u-verb) - to enter
6. 俺 【おれ】 - me; myself; I (masculine)
7. 関係 【かん・けい】 - relation, relationship
8. ある (u-verb) - to exist (inanimate)
9. 時間 【じ・かん】 - time
10. 合う 【あ・う】 (u-verb) - to match
11. 間に合う 【ま・に・あ・う】 - to be in time
12. 最近 【さい・きん】 - recent; lately
13. ウィルス - virus
14. 強力 【きょう・りょく】 (na-adj) - powerful, strong
15. プログラム - program
16. 実行 【じっ・こう】 - execute

17. する (exception) - to do
18. ページ - page
19. 見る 【み・る】 (ru-verb) - to see
20. 感染 【かん・せん】 - infection

We will now learn a grammar that's actually practical for everyday use using the negative volitional grammar. Basically, we can use both volitional and negative volitional forms to say it doesn't matter whether something is going to happen or not. This is done by attaching 「が」 to both the volitional and the negative volitional form of the verb that doesn't matter.

Using the volitional to express a lack of relation

- Attach 「が」 to the volitional and negative volitional form of the verb.
  Examples
  1. 食べる → 食べよう、食べまい → 食べようが食べまいが
  2. 行く → 行こう、行くまい → 行こうが行くまいが

Examples

1. あいつが大学に入ろうが入るまいが、俺とは関係ないよ。
   Whether that guy is going to college or not, it has nothing to do with me.
2. 時間があろうがあるまいが、間に合わせるしかない。
   Whether there is time or not, there's nothing to do but make it on time.

3. 最近のウィルスは強力で、プログラムを<u>実行しようがしまい</u>が、ページを見るだけで感染するらしい。

The viruses lately have been strong and whether you run a program or not, I hear it will spread just by looking at the page.

Using 「であろう」 to express likelihood

Vocabulary

1. ある (u-verb) - to exist (inanimate)
2. 困難 【こん・なん】 (na-adj) - difficulty, distress
3. する (exception) - to do
4. 今後 【こん・ご】 - hereafter
5. ～年 【～ねん】 - counter for year
6. 人間 【にん・げん】 - human
7. 直面 【ちょく・めん】 - confrontation
8. 問題 【もん・だい】 - problem
9. 正面 【しょう・めん】 - front; facade
10. 向き合う 【む・き・あ・う】 (u-verb) - to face each other
11. 自ら 【みずか・ら】 - for one's self
12. 解決 【かい・けつ】 - resolution
13. はかる (u-verb) - to plan, to devise
14. その - that (abbr. of それの)
15. ノウハウ - know-how
16. 次 【つぎ】 - next
17. 産業 【さん・ぎょう】 - industry
18. なる (u-verb) - to become
19. シナリオ - scenario
20. 考える 【かんが・える】 (ru-verb) - to think
21. もちろん - of course
22. 生徒数 【せい・と・すう】 - number of students
23. 減少 【げん・しょう】 - decline, reduction
24. 現在 【げん・ざい】 - present time

25. 学科 【がっ・か】 - course of study
26. 新設 【しん・せつ】 - newly organized or established
27. 職業科 【しょく・ぎょう・か】 - occupational studies
28. 統廃合 【とう・はい・ごう】 - reorganization
29. 科内 【か・ない】 - within study course
30. コース - course
31. 改編 【かい・へん】 - reorganization
32. 時代 【じ・だい】 - period, era
33. 合う 【あ・う】 (u-verb) - to match
34. 変革 【へん・かく】 - reform
35. 求める 【もと・める】 (ru-verb) - to request; to seek

We already found out that the negative volitional can be used as kind of a formal version of 「でしょう」 and 「だろう」. You may wonder, how would you do the same thing for the volitional? The answer is to conjugate the verb 「ある」 from the formal state-of-being 「である」 to the volitional to produce 「であろう」. Remember 「でしょう」 can already be used as a polite form, so this form is even a step above that in formality. We'll see what kind of language uses this form in the examples.

Using 「であろう」 to express likelihood

- Attach 「であろう」 to the noun, adjective, or verb. Examples
    1. 困難 → 困難であろう
    2. する → するであろう

Examples

1. 今後50年、人間が直面するであろう問題に正面から向き合って、自ら解決をはかりつつ、そのノウハウが次の産業となるシナリオを考えたい。(from www.jkokuryo.com)
I would like to directly approach problems that humans have likely encounter the next 50 years and while devising solutions, take that knowledge and think about scenarios that will become the next industry.

2. もちろん、生徒数減少の現在、学科の新設は困難であろうが、職業科の統廃合や科内コースの改編などで時代に合わせた変革が求められているはずである。(from www1.normanet.ne.jp)
Of course, setting up new courses of study will likely be difficult with this period of decreasing student population but with reorganizations of occupational studies and courses within subjects, there is supposed to be demand for reform fit for this period.

Using 「かろう」 as volitional for 「い」 endings

Vocabulary

1. ある (u-verb) - to exist (inanimate)
2. 早い 【はや・い】 (i-adj) - fast; early
3. どんな - what kind of
4. 商品 【しょう・ひん】 - product
5. ネット - net
6. 販売 【はん・ばい】 - selling
7. 売上 【うり・あげ】 - amount sold, sales
8. 伸びる 【の・びる】 (ru-verb) - to extend, to lengthen
9. 言う 【い・う】 (u-verb) - to say
10. 物 【もの】 - object
11. 運動 【うん・どう】 - exercise
12. 始める 【はじ・める】 (ru-verb) - to begin

13. 遅い　【おそ・い】 (i-adj) - late
14. 健康　【けん・こう】 - health
15. いい (i-adj) - good
16. 変わる　【か・わる】 (u-verb) - to change
17. 休日　【きゅう・じつ】 - holiday, day off
18. この - this　(abbr. of これの)
19. 関係　【かん・けい】 - relation, relationship

We learned in the lesson about formal grammar that 「ではない」 was the negative of 「である」. So how would we say something like 「であろう」 but for the negative? The answer is to use yet another type of volitional for negatives and i-adjectives used only in formal and literary contexts. You can think of this grammar as a very old-fashioned version for i-adjectives and negative 「い」 endings.

The conjugation rule is simple: remove the last 「い」 and attach 「かろう」. You can use it for negatives and i-adjectives just like the 「かった」 past conjugation form.

Using 「かろう」 to express volition for 「い」 endings

- Drop the last 「い」 and attach 「かろう」
  Examples
    1. ではない → ではなかろう
    2. 早い → 早かろう

Examples

1. どんな商品でもネットで販売するだけで売上が伸びるというものではなかろう。

It's not necessarily the case that sales go up just by selling any type of product on the net.

2. 運動を始めるのが<u>早かろう</u>が<u>遅かろう</u>が、健康にいいというのは変わりません。

Whether you start exercising early or late, the fact that it's good for your health doesn't change.

3. 休日で<u>あろう</u>が、<u>なかろう</u>が、この仕事では関係ないみたい。

Whether it's a holiday or not, it looks like it doesn't matter for this job.

Covered by something

This is a short lesson to cover several specialized expressions that describe the state of being covered by something. Mostly, we will focus on the differences between 「だらけ」、 「まみれ」 and 「ずくめ」.

Using 「だらけ」 when an object is riddled everywhere with something

Vocabulary

1. 間違い 【ま・ちが・い】 - mistake
2. ゴミ - garbage
3. 埃 【ほこり】 - dust
4. この - this (abbr. of これの)
5. ドキュメント - document
6. 全然 【ぜん・ぜん】 - not at all (when used with negative)
7. 役に立つ 【やく・に・たつ】 (u-verb) - to be useful
8. 携帯 【けい・たい】 - handheld (phone)
9. ～年 【～ねん】 - counter for year
10. 使う 【つか・う】 (u-verb) - to use

11. 傷 【き・ず】 - injury; scratch; scrape
12. なる (u-verb) - to become
13. テレビ - TV, television
14. ちゃんと - properly
15. 拭く 【ふ・く】 (u-verb) - to wipe; to dry
16. くれる (ru-verb) - to give

「だらけ」 is usually used when something is riddled everywhere. It generally carries a negative connotation. As a result, you'll often see 「だらけ」 used with expressions like 「間違いだらけ」, 「ゴミだらけ」, or 「埃だらけ」. There is no conjugation rule to cover here, all you need to do is attach 「だらけ」 to the noun that is just all over the place. You should treat the result just like you would a regular noun.

Using 「だらけ」 to describe the state of being riddled everywhere by something

- Attach 「だらけ」 to the noun that is covering the object or place
  Examples
    1. 間違い → 間違いだらけ (riddled with mistakes)
    2. 埃 → 埃だらけ (riddled with dust)

Examples

1. このドキュメントは間違いだらけで、全然役に立たない。
   This document is just riddled with mistakes and is not useful at all.

2. 携帯を２年間使ってたら、傷だらけになった。
After using cell phone for 2 years, it became covered with scratches.

※Notice how the 「の」 particle is used to modify since 「だらけ」 functions like a noun.

1. この埃だらけのテレビをちゃんと拭いてくれない？
Can you properly dust this TV completely covered in dust?

Using 「まみれ」 to describe a covering

Vocabulary

1. 間違い 【ま・ちが・い】 - mistake
2. 血 【ち】 - blood
3. 油 【あぶら】 - oil
4. ゴミ - garbage
5. 彼 【かれ】 - he; boyfriend
6. なる (u-verb) - to become
7. 車 【くるま】 - car
8. 修理 【しゅう・り】 - repair
9. 頑張る 【がん・ば・る】 (u-verb) - to try one's best
10. たった - only, merely
11. キロ - kilo
12. 走る 【はし・る】 (u-verb) - to run
13. 汗 【あせ】 - sweat
14. 情けない 【なさ・けない】 (i-adj) - shameful; deplorable

「まみれ」 may seem very similar to 「だらけ」 but there are some very important subtle differences. First, it's only used for actually physical objects so you can't say things like 「間違いまみれ」 like you can with 「だらけ」. Plus, you can only use it for things that literally cover the object. In other words, you can't use it to mean "littered" or "riddled" like we have done with 「だらけ」 So you can use it for things like liquids and dust, but you can't use it for things like scratches and garbage.

The grammatical rules are the same as 「だらけ」.

Using 「まみれ」 to describe a covering by sticking

- Like 「だらけ」, you attach 「まみれ」 to the noun that is doing covering.
  Examples
  1. 血 → 血まみれ (covered in blood)
  2. 油 → 油まみれ (covered in oil)
- You can only use 「まみれ」 for physical objects that literally covers the object.
  Examples
  1. 間違いまみれ (not a physical object)
  2. ゴミまみれ (doesn't actually cover anything)

Examples

1. 彼は油まみれになりながら、車の修理に頑張りました。
   While becoming covered in oil, he worked hard at fixing the car.
2. たった１キロを走っただけで、汗まみれになるのは情けない。
   It's pitiful that one gets covered in sweat from running just 1 kilometer.

「ずくめ」 to express entirety

Vocabulary

1. 黒 【くろ】 - black
2. 白 【しろ】 - white
3. いい (i-adj) - good
4. こと - event, matter
5. 団体 【だん・たい】 - group
6. 去年 【きょ・ねん】 - last year
7. ニュース - news
8. なる (u-verb) - to become
9. この - this   (abbr. of これの)
10. シェーク - shake
11. おいしい (i-adj) - tasty
12. 栄養 【えい・よう】 - nutrition
13. たっぷり - filled with
14. 体 【からだ】 - body

The 「大辞林」 dictionary describes exactly what 「ずくめ」 means very well.

名詞およびそれに準ずる語句に付いて、何から何まで、そればかりであることを表す。すべて...である。

「うそ—の言いわけ」「いいこと—」「黒—の服装」「結構—」

In other words, 「ずくめ」 describes something that applies to the whole thing. For instance, if we were talking about the human body, the expression "is [X] from head to toe" might be close to what 「ずくめ」 means.

In actuality, 「ずくめ」 is an expression that is rarely used and usually with a color to describe people completely dressed in that color. For example, you can see what 「黒ずくめ」 looks like via Google Images.

Grammatically, 「ずくめ」 works in exactly the same ways as 「だらけ」 and 「まみれ」.

Using 「ずくめ」 to describe something that applies to the whole thing

- Attach 「ずくめ」 to the noun that applies to the whole thing.
  Examples
  1. 白 → 白ずくめ
  2. いいこと → いいことずくめ

Examples

1. 白ずくめ団体は去年ニュースになっていた。
   The organization dressed all in white was on the news last year.
2. このシェークは、おいしいし、栄養たっぷりで体にいいですから、いいことずくめですよ。
   This shake is tasty and filled with nutrients, it's good for (your) body so it's entirely good things.

Immediate Events

In this section, we will be covering some advanced grammar that describe an action that takes place right after something else has occurred. I suggest you look over this section if you are really serious about completely mastering Japanese, or if you plan to take the level 1 JLPT exam, or if you enjoy reading a lot of Japanese literature.

Using 「が早いか」 to describe the instant something occurred

Vocabulary

1. 早い 【はや・い】 (i-adj) - fast; early
2. 言う 【い・う】 (u-verb) - to say
3. 彼女 【かの・じょ】 - she; girlfriend
4. 教授 【きょう・じゅ】 - professor
5. 姿 【すがた】 - figure
6. 見る 【み・る】 (ru-verb) - to see
7. 教室 【きょう・しつ】 - classroom
8. 逃げ出す 【に・げ・だ・す】 (u-verb) - to run away
9. 食べる 【た・べる】 (ru-verb) - to eat
10. 口 【くち】 - mouth
11. 中 【なか】 - inside
12. 放り込む 【ほう・り・こ・む】 (u-verb) - to throw into

The phrase 「が早いか」 is used to describe something that happened the instant something else occurred. While very similar to the 「とたんに」 grammar, it has a strong emphasis on how soon one thing occurred after another as if it's almost simultaneous. This grammar is rarely used outside of Japanese language tests. To use this grammar, you attach 「が早いか」 to the first verb, then you describe the event that happened the next instant. While it's conventional to use the non-past tense (dictionary form) for the first verb, you can also use the past tense. For example, you can say either 「言うが早いか」 or 「言ったが早いか」. The curious thing about this grammar is that the 「が」 particle comes right after the

444

verb. Remember, you can do this *only* with this specific grammatical phrase.

Using 「が早いか」 to describe what happened the instant something occurred

- Attach 「が早いか」 to the non-past or past tense of the verb that just occurred Examples
    1. 言う → 言うが早いか
    2. 言う → 言った → 言ったが早いか
- You can only use this grammar only for events that are directly related.
- You can only use this grammar only for events that actually happened (past tense).

Examples

1. 彼女は、教授の姿を見るが早いか、教室から逃げ出した。 The instant (she) saw the professor's figure, (she) ran away from the classroom.
2. 「食べてみよう」と言うが早いか、口の中に放り込んだ。 The instant (he) said "let's try eating it", he threw (it) into his mouth.
3. 「食べてみよう」と言ったが早いか、口の中に放り込んだ。 The instant (he) said "let's try eating it", he threw (it) into his mouth.

Using 「や／や否や」 to describe what happened right after

Vocabulary

1. 早い 【はや・い】 (i-adj) - fast; early
2. 否定 【ひ・てい】 - denial
3. 見る 【み・る】 (ru-verb) - to see
4. 私 【わたし】 - me, myself, I
5. 顔 【かお】 - face
6. 何 【なに／なん】 - what
7. 言う 【い・う】 (u-verb) - to say
8. する (exception) - to do
9. 搭乗 【とう・じょう】 - boarding
10. アナウンス - announcement
11. 聞こえる 【き・こえる】 (ru-verb) - to be audible
12. 皆 【みんな】 - everybody
13. ゲート - gate
14. 方 【ほう】 - direction, way
15. 走り出す 【はし・り・だ・す】 (u-verb) - to break into a run

The 「や」 or 「や否や」 （やいなや） phrase, when appended to a verb, is used to described something that happened right after that verb. Its meaning is essential the same as 「が早いか」. It is also another type of grammar that is not really used in regular conversational Japanese.

「否」 (read here as 「いな」) is a Kanji meaning "no" used in words like 「否定」. The literal meaning of this grammar is "whether the action was taken or not". In order words, the second action is taken before you even take the time to determine whether the first event really happened or not.

You can use this grammar by attaching 「や」 or 「や否や」 to the dictionary form of the first verb that occurred. Since this grammar is used for events that already have occurred, the second verb is usually in the past tense. However, you can use the dictionary tense to indicate that the events happen regularly.

Using 「や／や否や」 to describe what happened right after

- Attach 「や」 or 「や否や」 （やいなや） to the dictionary form of the first verb that occurred Examples
    1. 見る → 見るや
    2. 見る → 見るや否や
- This grammar is almost always used for events that actually happened (past tense).
- This grammar can be used with the present tense for regularly occurring events.

Examples

1. 私の顔を見るや、何か言おうとした。 (He) tried to say something as soon as he saw my face.
2. 搭乗のアナウンスが聞こえるや否や、みんながゲートの方へ走り出した。 As soon as the announcement to board was audible, everybody started running toward the gate.

Using 「そばから」 to describe an event that repeatedly occurs soon after

Vocabulary

1. 早い 【はや・い】 (i-adj) - fast; early
2. 読む 【よ・む】 (u-verb) - to read

3. する (exception) - to do
4. 子供 【こ・ども】 - child
5. 掃除 【そう・じ】 - cleaning
6. 散らかす 【ち・らかす】 (u-verb) - to scatter around; to leave untidy
7. もう - already
8. あきらめる (ru-verb) - to give up
9. なる (u-verb) - to become
10. 教科書 【きょう・か・しょ】 - textbook
11. 忘れる 【わす・れる】 (ru-verb) - to forget
12. 勉強 【べん・きょう】 - study
13. 出来る 【で・き・る】 (ru-verb) - to be able to do

「そばから」 is yet another grammar that describes an event that happens right after another. However, unlike the expressions we have covered so far, 「そばから」 implies that the events are a recurring pattern. For example, you would use this grammar to express the fact that you just clean and clean your room only for it to get dirty again soon after. Besides this difference, the rules for using this expression are exactly the same as 「が早いか」 and 「や否や」. Just attach 「そばから」 to the dictionary form of the first verb that occurred. The past tense, though rare, also appears to be acceptable. However, the event that immediately follows is usually expressed with the non-past dictionary form because this grammar is used for repeated events and not a specific event in the past.

Using 「そばから」 to describe an event that repeatedly occurs soon after

- Attach 「そばから」 to the dictionary form of the first verb that occurred Examples
    1. 読む → 読むそばから

Examples

1. 子供が掃除<u>するそばから</u>散らかすから、もうあきらめたくなった。 The child messes up (the room) [repeatedly] as soon as I clean so I already became wanting to give up.
2. 教科書を<u>読んだそばから</u>忘れてしまうので勉強ができない。 Forget [repeatedly] right after I read the textbook so I can't study.

Other Grammar

Hopefully, you've managed to get a good grasp of how grammar works in Japanese and how to use them to communicate your thoughts in the Japanese way. In this final section, we'll be covering some left-over grammar that I couldn't fit into a larger category.

Using 「思いきや」 to describe something unexpected

Vocabulary

1. 思う 【おも・う】 (u-verb) - to think
2. ある (u-verb) - to exist (inanimate)
3. 昼間 【ひる・ま】 - daytime
4. 絶対 【ぜっ・たい】 (na-adj) - absolutely, unconditionally
5. 込む 【こ・む】 (u-verb) - to become crowded
6. 一人 【ひとり】 - 1 person; alone

7. いる (ru-verb) - to exist (animate)
8. この - this   (abbr. of これの)
9. レストラン - restaurant
10. 安い 【やす・い】 (i-adj) - cheap
11. 会計 【かい・けい】 - accountant; bill
12. 千円 【せん・えん】 - 1,000 yen
13. 以上 【い・じょう】 - greater or equal

This is a grammar I learned out of a book and was surprised to actually hear it used in real life on a number of occasions. You use this grammar when you think one thing, but much to your astonishment, things actually turn out to be very different. You use it in the same way as you would express any thoughts, by using the quotation 「と」 and 「思う」. The only difference is that you use 「思いきや」 instead of 「思う」. There is no tense in 「思いきや」, or rather, since the results already went against your expectations, the original thought is implicitly understood to be past tense.

Using 「思いきや」 to describe something unforeseen or unexpected

- Attach 「思いきや」 to the thought using the quotation 「と」. Example: ある → あると → あると思いきや

Examples

1. 昼間だから絶対込んでいると思いきや、一人もいなかった。
Despite having thought that it must be crowded since it was afternoon, (surprisingly) not a single person was there.

2. このレストランは<u>安いと思いきや</u>、会計は5千円以上だった！
Thought this restaurant would be cheap but (surprisingly) the bill was over 5,000 yen!

Using 「〜がてら」 to do two things at one time

Vocabulary

1. 散歩 【さん・ぽ】 - walk, stroll
2. 作る 【つく・る】 (u-verb) - to make
3. タバコ - tobacco; cigarettes
4. 買う 【か・う】 (u-verb) - to buy
5. 行く 【い・く】 (u-verb) - to go
6. 博物館 【はく・ぶつ・かん】 - museum
7. 見る 【み・る】 (ru-verb) - to see
8. お土産 【お・みやげ】 - souvenir
9. つもり - intention, plan

This rather formal and seldom-used grammar is used to indicate that two actions were done at the same time. The nuance is a bit difference from 「ながら」 in that some or all of the time spent on doing one action was also used to do another action as an aside. Remember, 「ながら」 is used to describe two exactly concurrent actions. The interesting thing about this grammar is that no verb is required. You can just attach it a noun, and the verb "to do" is inferred. For instance, "while taking a stroll" can simply be expressed as 「散歩がてら」. In the case where you want to employ a different verb, you also have the option of attaching 「がてら」 to the stem similar to the 「ながら」 usage. In addition, the verb or noun that is accompanied by 「がてら」 is the main action while the following action is the one done on the side.

Examples

1. 散歩がてら、タバコを買いに行きました。 While taking a stroll, I also used that time to buy cigarettes.
2. 博物館を見がてらに、お土産を買うつもりです。 While seeing the museum, I plan to also use that time to buy souvenirs.

Using 「～あげく（挙句）」 to describe a bad result

Vocabulary

1. 挙句 【あげ・く】 - in the end (after a long process); at last
2. 喧嘩 【けん・か】 - quarrel
3. 考える 【かんが・える】 (ru-verb) - to think
4. 事情 【じ・じょう】 - circumstances
5. ～時間 【～じ・かん】 - counter for span of hours
6. 掛ける 【か・ける】 (ru-verb) - to hang; to take (time, money)
7. 説明 【せつ・めい】 - explanation
8. する (exception) - to do
9. 納得 【なっ・とく】 - understanding; agreement

452

10. もらう (u-verb) - to receive
11. 先生 【せん・せい】 - teacher
12. 相談 【そう・だん】 - consultation
13. 退学 【たい・がく】 - dropping out of school
14. こと - event, matter

「あげく」 is a grammar used to describe a result, usually negative, that came about after a great deal of effort. The rule for this grammar is very simple. You modify the verb or noun that was carried out with 「あげく」 and then describe the final result that came about from that verb or noun. Because this grammar is used to describe a result from an action already completed, it is used with the past tense of the verb. 「あげく」 is essentially treated the same as any noun. In other words, you would need the 「の」 particle to modify another noun. 「あげくの果て」 is another stronger version of this grammar.

Using 「～あげく」 to describe a final result

- Attach 「あげく」 to the verb or noun that created the end result （「の」 particle is required for nouns） Examples
  1. けんか → けんかのあげく
  2. 考えた → 考えたあげく

Examples

1. 事情を2時間かけて説明したあげく、納得してもらえなかった。 (After a great deal of) explaining the circumstances for 2 hours, (in the end), couldn't receive understanding.

2. 先生と相談のあげく、退学をしないことにした。 (After much) consulting with teacher, (in the end), decided on not dropping out of school.

Made in the USA
Columbia, SC
January 2025

51241151R00259